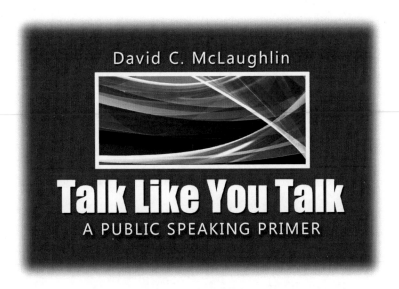

David C. McLaughlin

Talk Like You Talk
A PUBLIC SPEAKING PRIMER

Montana State University

Kendall Hunt
publishing company

www.kendallhunt.com

Send all inquiries to:
4050 Westmark Drive
Dubuque, IA 52004-1840

Copyright © 2009 by Kendall Hunt Publishing Company

ISBN 978-0-7575-9972-9

Printed in the United States of America
10 9 8 7 6 5 4

TO MY BROTHER JIM
1946–1975
MY FAVORITE TEACHER

Contents

CHAPTER 3

CHAPTER 4

CHAPTER 5

CHAPTER 6

CHAPTER 7

CHAPTER 8

CHAPTER 9

CHAPTER 10

CHAPTER 11

ACKNOWLEDGMENTS

I want to thank my editing/critique/support team: Catherine McLaughlin, wife, teacher, my cheerleader and life coach; Education major. Morgan Griffith, daughter, tutor/teacher, my best proofreader; Education major. Lindsay McLaughlin, daughter, swim instructor, my storyteller; Living Life major. Shannon McLaughlin, daughter, college student, my funny bone; English major. Rosemary McLaughlin, my mother, who loves every word I write; Nursing major. Brian McLaughlin, nephew, sports writer, my male conscience; Journalism major. Kelly McLaughlin, niece, insurance guru, my style checker; Communications major. Diane Donnelly, friend, neighbor, teacher, my "freshman" expert; English major. Lorraine Ekegren, friend, public speaking instructor, my topic expert; English major.

I also want to thank my new friends at Kendall/Hunt Publishing Company: Kimberly Elliott, Acquisitions Editor, Higher Education Division. Kimberly is the person who found me, somehow, and actually initiated this project. My right brain. Amanda Smith, Regional Project Coordinator, Higher Education Division. Amanda is the person who kept me on time and on target; the technical expert. My left brain. Craig White, Artist, who created many of the cartoons, and Jeni Fensterman created the book cover. My fun brain. For my second edition, I received wonderful support and advice from Clay Johnson, Managing Editor, and Beth Trowbridge, Senior Production Editor. They are both good brains!

Finally, I want to thank all my students. You keep me on my toes. You teach me as much as I teach you, and you inspire me every day.

INTRODUCTION

(See page 104, Five Steps of an Introduction)

ATTENTION STEP: (Play John Williams' Olympic theme song while slowly uncovering the artist's cartoon sketch of me.)

Hello. My name is David McLaughlin. I wrote this book. I did not draw this cartoon.

PURPOSE STATEMENT: (Overhead slide) The purpose of this book is to inform you about public speaking, in particular, and communication, in general.

MOTIVATION STEP: (PowerPoint slides, "Reasons to Read Book"; hold up book)

- Most people have some fear of public speaking; this book will reduce that fear.
- You cannot not communicate, so it behooves you to learn about communication.
- This book has theory and practical guidance, but it favors the practical side.
- Lessons in this book are ones I actually use in my speech classes, and in my life.
- My primary target audience is college freshmen taking a basic speech course.
- The book could supplement any course, any level, that has a speech component.
- It could be good airport reading if you want to refresh your speech knowledge.
- I am biased, but I also think it would help any teacher become more effective.
- Basically, this book gives you the tools to critique your own speaking or teaching skills, which you ultimately must learn to do if you really want to improve.
- I am optimistic enough to believe that good speeches = better knowledge and understanding, which = more motivation and compassion, which = world peace.

CREDIBILITY STEP: (Video montage of students giving speeches, animated, smiling.)

- I was born in 1950, so I'm old enough that people are starting to listen to me.
- I grew up in a family of five boys, so I had to speak up to get my share of food.
- I have three daughters, so I have to listen well, or they yell at me.

- B.S. in General Studies from the Air Force Academy, Colorado, 1972.
- M.A. in Human Relations from Webster University, St. Louis, 1977.
- Twenty-one years as an active duty Air Force officer (retired Lieutenant Colonel).
    - Ten years as a C-130 Hercules navigator, so I have a checklist mentality, and you'll find numerous checklists in this book. I taught and evaluated navigators.
    - Eleven years as an Air Force classroom instructor teaching history, national defense policy, leadership, and communications. I graded many speeches.
    - I have been in all fifty states and about fifty countries; I speak "world."
- I have been teaching public speaking at Montana State University since 1994.
- I bet I have graded more speeches than anyone else you will ever know.
- Above all, I'm credible to teach communications because I've been married to just one woman, starting in 1977. (Show photo of my family, get "Aaaaahs" from audience.)

PREVIEW: (Distribute handout of book's Table of Contents.)
- Scan the Table of Contents to see the main points of this book.
- The first six chapters are presented in the order you would build a speech.
- Appendix A, Summary Checklist for Summaries, is, actually, a great preview.
- I stress to use a variety of research, support, sensory aids, and delivery styles.
- I stress to keep it simple, keep it visual, and keep it energetic.
- Use proven organization: introduction, body, conclusion.
- People love effort; if you sincerely care about the topic and audience, you'll do well.
- Do not just "report" to us; show some critical thinking; bring the topic alive.
- Allow yourself to be human; smile some, and Talk Like You Talk!
- Above all, follow the Golden Rule.

CONTACT INFORMATION: (Go to blackboard to write out information.)
- If you want to communicate with me, please contact Kendall/Hunt Publishing, as shown on the copyright page.
- You can also try: David McLaughlin, University Studies, Montana State University, Bozeman, MT, 59717. Phone: 406/994-3532. E-Mail: dmclaugh@montana.edu.
- Mostly, I hope this book motivates you to get in better touch with yourself, so you'll know your public speaking strengths and weaknesses and strive to improve.

GOOD LUCK WITH YOUR NEXT SPEECH!

THEIR IS NO SUCH THING AS A PURFECT SPEACH.

Note: If you don't understand the humor in the above statement, please send me a copy of your SAT verbal score, and I'll try to get you some help.

"I Hate Giving Speeches!"
—You

Yeah, yeah. I've heard it a gadzillion times, as if you are the only one who hates public speaking. Students *love* to tell me how bad they are with speeches and how much it worries them. "I just can't do it," they say. "I get too scared!" Well, folks, let me tell you a secret: If you can talk about it, you can do it. People who are really afraid of public speaking don't even sign up for a speech class, and they certainly don't "brag" to me about their fear. They put off our Com 110 class here at Montana State University until the last possible moment, and then I see them in summer school after they have already marched in the May graduation ceremonies. They have all their requirements done, except. . . except for. . . speech. Amazing. I know public speaking can be scary, but you need to know that I have watched nervous people *excel* in my class since 1994. Afterwards, they announce to the world that the class wasn't that bad, and they wish they had taken it sooner in their student career. If you hate public speaking so much, why did you pick up this book? Seriously, if you have read this far, there is great hope for you.

GENERAL NERVES

It is VERY common to have some fear of public speaking. During my first lecture each semester (about 150 students), I ask people to raise their hands if they "get a little nervous" during a speech. Virtually every hand goes up, and I make them look around the room to see they are not alone. I have a Google page in front of me that says glossophobia affects 75 percent of us.

> **Glossophobia:** The fear of public speaking, from glossa, meaning tongue, and phobos, meaning fear or dread.

> **Agoraphobia** may also play a part: Fear of open spaces and crowds, as if you're on the open stage with a crowd (the audience) closing in on you and no place to hide.

More commonly, people call it "**stage fright**." My first thought is, if you have stage fright, get off the stage. Really, most of you who have a serious fear of speaking can simply avoid it, or at least postpone it until you are a bit older and more confident. Please consider, however, that very few of you have "serious" fear of speaking.

I've only had one student who went to a doctor to get a prescription to handle his nerves, and he was fifty years old, which is a nervous time, anyway. Jim did fine, until the day he overdosed. He was just talking along and started to get slower and slower until his eyes glazed over, and he stared at the floor and started to rock back and forth. We jumped up to keep him from falling, got him to sit down, and gave him some water. Then two people walked him over to the health center. He was okay. He went on to pass my course and save the world. The end. There are two very important lessons from this story:

1. If you are on medication of any kind, let someone know. A speech is more stressful than most activities, and it can cause some strange reactions. Jim had told me about his "nerve pills," so I knew what was going on.
2. Most important: **Public Speaking Will Not Kill You.**

When I was flying airplanes in the Air Force, we studied aviation accidents every year where people died. While teaching communications, I have never studied speech accidents where the speaker died. (Maybe the audience wanted to kill them, but that's illegal.) I like what Donald Trump said in his book, *Trump: How to Get Rich:*

> *Before you speak, remind yourself that it doesn't matter all that much. Don't feel that the weight of the world is on you. Most of the people in the room don't care how well or poorly you do. It's just not that important. It's merely a speech—not an earthquake or a war. You'll have a better time and be a better speaker if you keep it all in perspective.*

If you're thinking death, or just "failure" and total embarrassment, you are thinking that your nervousness is all negative. In truth, most of what you are feeling is really positive.

Eustress: Positive stress, from the Greek, *eu*, meaning well or good.

Eustress is a pleasant or curative stress. It keeps us excited about life. It is a healthy stress that gives us a competitive edge in performance related activities, such as:

• Downhill skiing at Bridger Bowl in Bozeman, MT, the best ski hill in the land.
• Cheering on North Carolina to another NCAA national championship. Go Heels!

- Getting this book written before the Kendall/Hunt deadline . . . please.
- Being successful in love (I guess this could be a noun or a verb).
- And finishing *your* next speech!!

Eustress is related to **adrenaline**, which can help you focus. It's the rush you get on a roller coaster or a mountain bike ride. You've heard stories of how someone lifted the bumper of a car to free a trapped friend, and when the incident was over, that savior couldn't budge the car one inch. Such strength comes from adrenaline, which helps us deal with "**fight or flight**" situations. I tell my students they can take flight and leave my class, but they'll most likely have to return someday if they want to get their degree. Therefore, most students choose to stay and "fight" their way through a few speeches.

Eustress is truly a constructive, motivating type of stress. It gives you fulfillment, that feeling of a "job well done!" If you believe that, then you can keep your eye on the end result, the goal, and the painful steps along the way won't feel so bad. I call it my **mountain climbing philosophy**, because it's like climbing a mountain; not easy, but the view from the top will make it worthwhile. Want to hear a true story? (I promise to never lie to you in this book.) I went on a hike one summer day with my wife, Catherine, and our three daughters, who were thirteen, eleven, and seven years old. Have you ever hiked with a seven-year old? It's like dragging a bag of wet cement. Shannon constantly kept stopping and complaining: "Oh, I'm tired. I'm hungry. I'm itchy and sweaty. I'm bored. I hate these bugs!" I kept pulling her by the arm: "Come on, come on. Keep moving. Don't stop. Let's go!" She kept complaining: "I hate this mountain. I hate this hike. I have to go to the bathroom. I hate you!" Finally, whew, finally we dragged her carcass to the very top. We sat to catch our breath, and she slowly stood up, looked around at the incredible view, spread her arms out wide, and started singing, "God Bless America." Even today when Shannon starts complaining about something being too hard, I remind her of our hike that day. "Remember the view from the top? Don't you want that feeling again?" So, how GOOD will *you* feel when you finish your speech? How GOOD will you feel when you finish this whole speech course? Climb one foot at a time, and keep the goal in mind. The journey is worthwhile and noble or you wouldn't be on it. Keep Smiling.

Image © nasirkhan, 2012. Used under license from Shutterstock, Inc.

The good road and the road of difficulties, You have made me cross, and where they cross, the place is holy.

—Black Elk, Lakota Holy Man (1863–1950)

Before I leave this topic of good stress, I'm reminded of a quote from Frank Sinatra, that famous singer who admitted that he used to get so nervous before performances that he would throw up. He said, **"It's good to be nervous; it shows you care."** Think about that for a moment. If you really did not care about anything, you would not be nervous. You wouldn't care if you failed, if you sounded stupid, if you upset the audience or wasted their time. You have those pre-speech jitters because you WANT to do well. I really believe that. I also believe two other critical axioms that I find in almost every expert speech text I've ever reviewed:

- **You cannot get rid of nervousness; you just have to learn to control it.**
- **You never *look* as nervous as you *feel*.**

Most texts talk about the butterflies in your stomach and how you can't get rid of them, so you have to train them to fly in formation. (There, now I've added that metaphor to my book. I do love aviation.) Hopefully, the rest of this book can guide you in such training. As for the second axiom above, most people don't believe me until they watch themselves on videotape giving a speech, a technique in which I believe strongly. When students critique themselves after watching their own tape, they commonly remark, "Wow, I really didn't look that nervous." Ask your friends. You look okay. Really.

I want to add a third axiom, which I only found in my brain:

You're never as good as you think you are (especially if you're the boss), but you're never as bad, either (especially if you're a freshman in college).

Since you can't get rid of nerves, you need to try to understand them better. You don't need to be an expert, and you certainly don't need to know all the theory behind the speech principles (unless you're a communications major). You'll be more relaxed, however, if you can comprehend and apply some basic hints to cope with nervousness. Let's start with some different factors in the academic world vs. the "real" world.

ACADEMIC WORLD NERVES

In the academic world, you must first know that **COLLEGE IS NOT JUNIOR HIGH!** Most of the hang-ups I see with students stem from a bad speech experience in junior high school (or middle school), those very awkward, awful days of puberty and hungering for peer acceptance. Dark, cruel days. Back in the day when I was giving a speech in Mrs. Dale's sixth-grade classroom at Eastover Elementary school in Charlotte, North Carolina. I was holding a paper with my notes, and I was nervous, and the paper was (gasp!) shakin' and rattlin' like Elvis on the *Ed Sullivan Show*. (Hey, it was 1961.) My friend (?) Mike started laughing and banging his desk. Mrs. Dale asked, "Why, Mike, whatever are y'all laughin' at?" (Hey, it was the South.) Evil Mike then said, "David's paper is REALLY shakin' and makin' a *lot* of noise! It's so funny!" Well, after I killed Mike and the police came, I learned a few lessons:

- Since my hands were shaking, I shouldn't have held a piece of paper. I could have put that paper on the table or a podium, or I could have used note cards. I could not have used an overhead projector or PowerPoint because, well, it was 1961. (Y'all are lucky.)
- I should move to Montana where no one knows me. My parents said no. So, instead, I took a speech course from a great teacher in the seventh grade and learned how to deal with my nervousness. I was motivated.
- Young people can simply be mean to each other. They will focus much more on clothes, hair, pimples, and "coolness" than on speech effort and content.

Welcome to College! You should find that these are the best audiences you ever met. Unless you're in a pure freshman seminar, there will be students of all ages (I regularly have students in their thirties and forties). People come from different states and very different walks of life. International students, in particular, lend an openness and awareness to the class that is refreshing. People are generally in college because they want to learn, not just because they have to be in school. I find that most people really want to help each other. They will be polite listeners because they want you to be polite when it's their turn to talk. Folks recognize "We're all in the same boat." I rarely have to ask someone to quit talking, put their cell phone away, or remove earphones. When you look out and see people really paying attention to you, it's a nice ego trip, not a nervous breakdown.

In most college speech classes, you will not know anyone else. People get to start out on a clean slate, without the baggage of preconceptions based upon some stupid event five years ago. If you make a mistake in a high school speech, it will be all over the hallways an hour later: "Hey, David gave a speech with his zipper down!" (This is a hypothetical example, of course.) And people never forget. You'll go to your twenty-year reunion, and some dude will approach you with a big beer grin on his face: "Hey, Zipperhead!" If you screw up in a college speech course, nothing happens, usually. People might tell the story to their roommate, but it's more about the event/lesson, NOT you personally. They probably don't know your name and probably won't see you again after that term. College audiences, trust me, are very understanding and forgiving about public speaking.

College Speeches Are NOT COMPETITION!

This is not "Speech and Debate" all over again. I find that some students with such experience actually have to *un*learn some things. Most people are more relaxed when they realize they are graded against some standards, not each other. Grades are normally given on a "bigger picture" scale than an exact checklist. These courses are usually designed to make you more comfortable, and the audience more comfortable, so that people can **"share meaning"**— which is **a basic**

definition of communication. They are not designed to put more trophies into the hallway case by the principal's office. You should be striving to become a more effective speaker, not a first-place winner. I do have students who sincerely want to be the best, and that's not a bad goal, but if you take it too seriously you will be an uptight speaker.

Go back to the first page of this chapter and look at that cartoon again. **There really is no such thing as a perfect speech.** You just can't please everyone 100 percent of the time. Flat out impossible. *Know* that. If you don't accept that early, you might be like the student I had one time who was about thirty seconds into her speech when she said, *uh*. She stopped cold and looked over at me with wide eyes and said, "Oh my Gawd, David, can I start over?!" I said, "Uh, why? What happened?" She cried, "I said *UH!*" I said, "Uh, that's OK. Really. Keep going. I'll only take off, uh, a thousand points."

I stress with my students that saying *uh* is really OK. You want to be human, not a robot, and *uhs* are pretty human. Having NO filler words or pause words is pretty mechanical, usually the result of someone trying too hard to have the perfect speech, which adds more stress. They end up memorizing or reading the speech, two very ineffective methods of delivery for most situations. (Chapter Six will elaborate on this point.) You will make mistakes. You have to laugh at them and press on. If you cannot laugh at yourself, you should not put yourself in a speaking situation very often.

Back to *uhs* for a minute. Early each term I ask my classes, "How many *uhs* are too many?" Every time, very quickly, someone says, "One." Then we discuss the story and philosophy I just described. I finish with this guidance: If you look out and see members of the audience making tick marks on paper for each *uh*, you have too many. *Uhs* certainly can be distracting and the person should be told so, but one *uh* is not a sin. In my experience, only one in fifty people have a serious *uh* problem.

> **NOTE:** The best cure for too many *uhs* is to practice the speech out loud once or twice so that your word choice is at the top of your brain, and it will come out quicker. Another outstanding technique is to film your speech and then count the number of *uhs* personally. You'll cut the *uhs* in half next time, I promise.

Academic Speeches Are Teacher Dependent

Your instructor might count each "uh" and take off a point. Some take off a point for every fifteen seconds you're over time. You need to learn the specific criteria your individual instructor will use. I personally think speech is 80 percent technique and 20 percent procedure, so I'm more of a "Big Picture" grader. I believe strongly that public speaking is more of an art than a science. Other teachers are more comfortable with a more structured approach and a more exacting grade sheet. People tend to grade speeches how they were graded, and they tend to start out with tighter controls and loosen up over time. I think the sample Peer Evaluation Sheet in the Appendix is a good tool to get you in the ballpark for most of the items that could be considered for grading your speeches. The more you understand the particular assignment and how it's being graded, the more relaxed you'll be. Ask questions!

Now I have some bad news and good news for you. The bad news is that these **academic speeches will be the hardest speeches you ever give in your life**. As I just said, they *will* be graded. Someone is sitting there, watching you intently, with a dadgum grade sheet! In addition to the teacher, other students will probably be critiquing you, and they will have been trained to look for structured parts of a speech, effective delivery techniques, credible support, and even a variety of visual aids. Somewhere out there will be, yes, a stopwatch! You won't hear the stopwatch, however. You'll just hear the beating of your heart. (Boom boom. Boom boom.) And then, when you think it's all over and the big rubber band around your waist is about to jerk you back into the safety of your seat, you'll have to stand up there and listen to an oral critique, done out loud by the instructor and your peers so the whole class can hear how you screwed up. Just you. (Can you hear the theme to "Jaws" in the background?) If you survive . . . the real world is easy.

The good news is that **most speech classes tend to accentuate the positive**. It's pretty common to use what I call the "Sandwich Technique" during critiques. Start and end with something positive; that becomes the two pieces of bread. In between, we offer constructive criticism (not destructive) for improvement. That's the "meat" of the sandwich. In a beginning speech class, I feel the philosophy should be to discuss "Things that went well" and "Things to improve"—not good and bad. Notice that my sample grade sheet in Appendix E has blocks across the top for letter grades, and then an "O" at the far right. The "O" is for omitted, which is a much kinder and gentler approach than the classic "F" for failure or the modern "S" for sucks. Most teachers know that a speech is much more sensitive for students than a paper or an exam, because it is performed in front of a jury of peers. If we stress the negative— what you did wrong—it makes you more nervous. If we stress the positive— what went well—and specific steps you can take to improve in a few areas, it makes you hopeful. Therefore, I find Public Speaking to be a more "touchyfeely" course than average. We often laugh; we've been known to hug.

Another thing that can be bad or good is **academic schedules**. If you are given a speech date and it conflicts with other coursework and your part-time job, that's bad. If you have several dates to choose from, then you can have more control and less stress. Keep in close touch with your instructor. He or she would prob-ably work with you so you don't have to have a speech and a big chemistry exam on the same day. Plan ahead. It is also true that some students are honestly sick on speech day and that "emergencies" happen. If you call your instructor as soon as you know, schedules can usually be rewritten, especially if you show the work you have already done, like outlines and visual aids. I also keep a book in my of-fice for the student with a terminal case of butterflies on speech day, or the per-son who gives a speech but it's really not as good as I know they can do. It's Judith Viorst's *Alexander and the Terrible, Horrible, No Good, Very Bad Day*. We all have days like that, even in Australia. Even in college, you might get a "do-over." Ask.

Before we leave the pleasant planet of Academia and travel over to the dark side of the real world, let me stress one important point about grades. Grades cause a lot of stress for many of you, so please know that **good students get good overall grades in public speaking courses**. You may be the 4.0 student who freaks out over a "B" on a speech, but I bet there are other aspects to the overall transcript grade. Good students always come to class, so they don't lose attendance points. They turn in better outlines with better research, they reflect more on self-evaluations, they display more knowledge of speech principles in class critiques, and they certainly do better on textbook exams. So, relax. You'll do fine, graduate, and get a great job . . . and give more speeches.

REAL-WORLD NERVES

The real world is not college, Dorothy, and you might have to leave Kansas and make a name for yourself. One of the best ways to get noticed early in the work-ing world is to have great communication skills—writing and speaking. You may not have to give a formal speech, per se, but the lessons in your speech course

will help you improve your **interpersonal communication** (two people, a dyad) and **group communication** (three or more people) inside and outside the office. Some of you, of course, could find public speaking to be a mainstay of your job, especially you teachers and preachers. If so, you should know there are some differences from the nervousness you felt in school.

Real-World Speeches Are Boss Dependent

You may get little or no real guidance about how to do a presentation because your boss may assume you learned how to give a speech in college. On the other hand, you may get too much direction if your boss likes to micromanage the workforce. Don't assume anything. Ask around to find out how previous presentations went, and get a good feel for what will make the boss happy. You may have less room to show "style" and creativity than you did in school. In other words, find out the criteria for a good grade; build your own critique sheet.

Don't Expect Much of a Critique

People don't generally give you much of a critique in the real world. You will rarely see the full touchy-feely approach used in college, and I've never seen a written critique of a speech. Oral critiques can be brutal and short, or nice and short. Mostly, they just say, "Good job." Time is money, and folks don't take time to give you strokes; you can improve on your own time. (One great way in the real world is Toastmasters. Google that name.) *That's why I tell my students to learn how to critique themselves.* The Appendix has some tools to help you get started on that road. Learn how to fight for feedback! If you ask specific questions of your friends about your speech, they will give you more specific, helpful feedback. But you gotta ask.

There is some good and bad news about public speaking in the real world, too. Good news is that people won't be writing on critique sheets as you talk, and you won't have to stand in front of class for an oral critique. It's also good that no one holds a stopwatch over your head. (If your boss asks for a ten-minute presentation, don't go twenty, but no one gets too upset if you go twelve or thirteen minutes, unless you're in the military.) It's also great that the topic will actually pertain to your job, and in most cases you will indeed be looked at as an expert. No more forced academic speeches on topics you hate. People will be there more for content, not so much for clever delivery (although that never hurts, you know.) It may be a topic you've done several times before, and the PowerPoint is already structured. You can get more audience interaction going because you usually have more time, and a question-answer period is more informal and creates less nervousness than an actual speech. You don't have to worry so much about covering all the material, because you can leave them with handouts or even a professional booklet. Many real-world speeches also come with lunch or dinner. I like food.

On the bad news side, you'll probably have to dress up. Professional suits and dresses are the norm in the real world. Buy a tie or some high heels, maybe both. There are no do-overs in the real world, and no one calls in sick on the day of a huge presentation that has been planned for months. You simply can't have a bad day. You can't cry and beg to start over when you screw up; you MUST laugh at yourself (on the inside) and correct the mistake, and then move on. You must plan all your own backup equipment. You'll probably have to plan the speech much earlier than you ever did in college because the bosses will want to see it so that *they* aren't so nervous at the last minute. Most importantly, you'll have a whole new list of reasons to be nervous that you never had in college: you might lose your reputation, a promotion, or even a paycheck. Just like in college, however, it is still against the law for your bosses to kill you.

Overall, I think people are less nervous for real-world speeches because it is part of their job, and they chose that job. If you truly hate public speaking, you can find a job that has little or no need for such a skill. This spring I had a rodeo bull rider in class. That's a good-paying job, and the talks with the bull only last eight seconds, on a good day.

Remember: *Very* few of us are guest speakers at a large banquet, graduation speakers at an Ivy League college, acceptance speakers at the Academy Awards, or keynote speakers at the Democratic National Convention. I don't have to be JFK or MLK . . . just DCM.

HINTS TO REDUCE NERVOUSNESS

(Hint: They also preview the whole book.)

If you comprehend basic speech mechanics and principles, you will be less nervous. Simple, right? So, read this whole book, and buy extra copies for your friends, or at least review my recommendations below for handling nerves:

PREPARE PROPERLY: I guess this step could actually include the next ten, but I want to stress the lessons found in **Chapters Two and Three.** Have a clear focus of your purpose and audience, and do some credible research. If you have interesting support data, you'll be more excited to share it. And plan EARLY! Most of the stress I see from students comes directly from gross procrastination. Leave time to actually practice your speech.

USE SENSORY AIDS: Sensory aids are the cure-all for everything evil in public speaking. See **Chapter Four.** They take the focus off of you and give you a chance to breathe or sip some water. If you use a variety of aids, it will be more interesting for your audience, so they will love you more and throw money. The single biggest stress item I see is electronic aids, especially PowerPoint. Check it out early; have backups.

HAVE A GOOD INTRODUCTION AND CONCLUSION: You should "almost memorize" your introduction and conclusion so you can deliver them with confidence and solid eye contact. Students have often told me that they worried most about how to start and stop a speech, so they were thankful for the guidelines you'll find in **Chapter Five.**

GET PHYSICAL! If you have stage fright, move down off the stage. Move left/right of the podium. Mingle with the audience. Movement and gestures help release some of that nervous tension, so find some reason to move, like using visual aids. Dress up for your speech; you'll feel better and stand up straighter and taller. Try minor stretching exercises. Do some deep breathing, like a Lamaze class. See **Chapter Six.**

TIME CONTROL: Use some sort of time control technique. The world needs more short speeches. You will be more nervous if your instructor or team cuts you off. See **Chapter Seven.**

KEEP IT SIMPLE: If it's too complicated, you'll be more nervous. See **Chapter Eight.**

THINK 'AUDIENCE FIRST': Try to focus on the audience rather than yourself. Consciously look for nonverbal signals and react accordingly. Try to get them involved, even if it's just a simple show of hands. Get a reaction early, and it will relax you. See **Chapter Nine.**

CRITIQUE YOURSELF: What do *you* want or need to work on? Know your weak areas and consider practical ways to improve. If you want extra instruction, ask for it. I often look over outlines and visual aids with students prior to speech day. See **Chapter Ten.**

USE YOUR IMAGINATION! Some books tell you to imagine your audience is naked, but that would scare me too much. DO imagine you'll be successful. On a practical note, use your imagination to put some creativity or humor into your speech. Tell a story. If you have a talent of any kind, find a way to use it. Make yourself smile. See **Chapter Eleven.**

USE DRUGS WITH CAUTION: It's common for people to take aspirin (head-aches) or ibuprofen (muscle tension) prior to a speech. Some people with asthma, like my daughters, take a hit off their inhaler.

As I mentioned earlier, you might even get a stronger prescription for anxiety from your doctor. The most common "drug" I hear about from students is alcohol; some people say a shot of whiskey helps them calm their nerves. (Remember, you heard that from students, not from me.) It seems two or three shots of whiskey would do more harm than good, and I have had five students in my career throw up during talks—all from alcohol/hangovers, not nerves. One last drug caution I must give you concerns marijuana. Some students think it's fun to smoke dope prior to a speech; some do it to relax. You should NOT use marijuana prior to a speech for any reason, because it will make you smile way too much and talk wayyyy too long. Really. Besides, to "play with your audience" would not be ethical. See **Chapter Nine.**

DON'T TAKE YOURSELF TOO SERIOUSLY: Don't take yourself too seriously. See **Chapter One.**

Here's a cute idea used in a 1997 speech, from a nervous student.

Image © Michael Onisiforou, 2012. Used under license from Shutterstock, Inc.

Anti-Stress Kit
Directions: Place on firm surface, follow directions in circle, repeat until anti-stressed or unconscious.

SUMMARY CHECKLIST FOR NERVES

Before Speech

❏   Know exact purpose of talk/assignment

❏   Do some audience analysis

❏   Pick a topic you're sincerely excited about

❏   Do your research early

❏   Plan a variety of sensory aids; let a friend check them

❏   "Almost memorize" introduction and conclusion

❏   Put key support from body of speech on outline *and* vis aid

❏   Plan some type of time control

❏   Actually practice out loud, once or twice (not ten times)

❏   Check out room and equipment early; bring backups

❏   Dress for success, and imagine it

❏   Do some deep breathing; have water available

❏   Serious talk with yourself: What exactly is causing nerves?

During Speech

❏   VisualAidsVisualAidsVisualAidsVisualAids

❏   Move!

❏   Tell a story

❏   Use some humor

❏   Look at audience and feed off their nonverbals

After Speech

❏   Fight for feedback, especially from friends

❏   Videotape yourself, if possible, and watch the tape

❏   Critique yourself soon afterward, using a structured checklist

❏   Seek out more speaking opportunities

That last line is important, because nothing helps nerves like experience. **It never gets perfect, but it will feel better.** No one goes backward in my class; I easily see improvement with each speech. I have seen literally hundreds of students grow more effective in public speaking just by following the basic guidelines in this book and actually doing three credible speeches. Try to remember this old Chinese proverb:

> *I hear, and I forget. (That would be my speech lectures...)*
> *I see, and I remember. (That's the many good peer speeches you'll watch)*
> *I do, and I understand. (And that's your own speeches, the best part)*

An old American once told me, "Speaking can be sorta fun, kinda." Let's get started.

Chapter 2
GETTING STARTED

I KNOW SO MUCH, I DON'T KNOW WHERE TO BEGIN.

Note: I saw a cartoon like this years ago in the *New Yorker*, and it caught my attention because I've actually heard people say this in speeches.

Whenever you're faced with a project, you need to start with some questions. I have learned to call these questions the **"Five W's"**: WHY, WHO, WHAT, WHERE, and WHEN. You need to start with "WHY" because it is the most important.

WHY GIVE THE SPEECH?

"Why me?" might be your first, knee-jerk reaction. In the academic world, it's because you have to get credit for a speech requirement so you can move into the real world where the answer will be because it's your job, and it's your job because you sincerely like it or you sincerely need the money, either of which is a good motivator. Sometimes it's you because you truly are an expert and people truly want to hear your thoughts. Sometimes.

"Why do we hafta give speeches, anyways?" you might also ask. In a democracy, speeches help to "clean our house." They are like a good speech critique: they praise what is good and reinforce it, so it will continue, and they mention what can be improved so we can make it better. The best speeches also recommend *how* to make it better and convince us that we should do so. In a democracy, we don't just have the right to speak; we see it as our *duty* to speak. Bishop Desmond Tutu, the cleric/activist once called "South Africa's moral conscience," said, "If you are neutral in situations of injustice, you have chosen the side of the oppressor." Freedom of speech is not kept alive unless we exercise that freedom. We need to hear conflicting opinions so we can choose the best course of action. It is the basis of our democracy, I think, that we hear those opinions. Evelyn Beatrice Hall, in a paraphrase of Voltaire's writings, said:

> *I disapprove of what you say, but I will defend to the death your right to say it.*

Public speaking is a very unique medium for communication because it is usually one person, standing up on a pedestal all alone, facing a judgmental crowd. That is *hard*, and we know it, so we listen harder. Therefore, speeches can have a unique impact on our culture. We need them to inspire us to fly to the moon, and we need them to heal our wounds after 9/11. They need to be effective, and effectiveness best comes from practice, and *that*, ladies and gentlemen, is why you hafta give speeches in school. Amen.

Once you're over the philosophical hump of speech purpose, you need to look at the practical reason for WHY you're giving this particular speech. My advice is to **Hit Me With a Board** (smack!), right between the eyes. In other words, "Tell me *exactly* what you want me to do or think when you are done with your speech." If that purpose is not crystal clear in your mind (clear enough to put concisely on a visual aid for me), then you're not ready to speak. Let's say you want to give a speech about seatbelts. Which purpose statement below would best reflect the reason WHY you want to give that talk?

- I want to inform you about seatbelts.
- I want to demonstrate the proper way to wear a seatbelt.
- I want to convince you that seatbelts save lives.
- I want to persuade *every* passenger in *every* vehicle to buckle up *every* time that vehicle is put into motion.

See the difference? (Say yes.) Sometimes after a speech, I'll ask the class what they thought the purpose was. Sometimes I get many different answers. If you want everyone to walk away with the same message, you MUST clarify your purpose.

In academia, your purpose might be given to you by your instructor, or you might pick it yourself. The class audience usually doesn't care. In the real world, however, the purpose would most likely be dictated by the needs of your audience. In either case, the specific purpose will evolve as you do research, so don't sweat the exact wording yet.

WHO IS YOUR AUDIENCE?

Look back at the photograph on the chapter opener. There are two words that are very wrong in that speaker's statement: "I" and "I." In audience analysis, "The 'I' doesn't have it." Instead of thinking so much about what "I know, I like, and I want," we really need to think about what the *audience* knows and *needs* to know. The speaker should have thought before her speech, "How much does my audience know, and where would *they* want me to begin?" Throughout the planning stages of a speech, you need to constantly think about your audience. What examples would make the best sense? What vocabulary might I use? What humor is appropriate? Which sensory aids would have the most impact? Effectiveness is defined by your audience, not you.

What is an audience? They are the *reason* you are giving the speech. You want to influence the way they think or act about your topic. I honestly believe that most audiences want to cheer on the speaker; they want you to be good. They are waiting for you to do the slightest thing funny, so they can laugh; the slightest thing thought provoking, so they can think. They truly want to stay awake and have a good time and learn something. It is downright painful to fight to stay awake during an awful speech; it physically hurts your neck and arms and eyeballs. You know the feeling. Listen to a boring speaker and see how fast and hard the audience will laugh at the tiniest bit of humor—because they have been waiting so long for it! Someone once told me that an audience is a group of people waiting to be bored, and that scared me for a while. Then I decided to reverse that: an audience is a group of people begging and pleading and dying NOT to be bored. That makes them an easy target, and the bigger the audience, the easier the target. If only one person laughs, it can set off a chain reaction. Imagine if ten or twenty people laugh. Really, audiences are your friend, NOT your enemy, mostly.

> *Public speaking is a lot like a box of chocolates:*
> *You never know what kind of audience yur gonna git,*
> *and sometimes it's messy.*
>
> **—Forrest Gump**

Remember when Forrest said that in the movie? (I may have made that up.) It's like something I have been teaching for years: There is no such thing as a perfect speech, because **there is no such thing as perfect audience analysis.** No matter what you do, someone out there won't like you. In truth, some people love to dislike you. They are only happy if they argue with you or get mad at certain words or photos, because, well, let's face it . . . some people just like to be unhappy, or angry. Some people will agree with you, some will disagree, and some will be neutral. The best you can do is aim for the middle and hope you don't upset too many people on the extremes.

> *All your hand's fingers are not equal.*
>
> **—Arabic proverb**

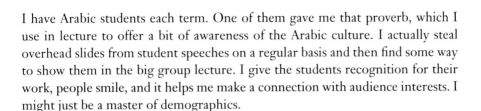

I have Arabic students each term. One of them gave me that proverb, which I use in lecture to offer a bit of awareness of the Arabic culture. I actually steal overhead slides from student speeches on a regular basis and then find some way to show them in the big group lecture. I give the students recognition for their work, people smile, and it helps me make a connection with audience interests. I might just be a master of demographics.

Demographics

Demographics are the various characteristics of your audience. Unlike attitudes and beliefs, they can actually be measured, given enough time and the right survey tools. In most cases, you can find out the general demographic makeup of your audience from the person who invites you to speak, or you could even ask audience members for a show of hands as a certain demographic concern arises. You want to get a feel for the demographics so you can get a feel for what you can get away with. You're a spy!

AGE

How old is the average audience member? This helps you better select examples they understand. I get excited giving speeches, just like that feeling I had watching Neil Armstrong touch the moon, with "one small step for a man, one giant leap for mankind." Remember? Probably not. Very few of my students were alive in 1969. I should use more current examples of excitement, like Jimmy Fallon having his own TV show! Generation gaps are now closer to ten years than twenty, so you can get "out of touch" with younger audiences in a hurry. I no longer mention Douglas MacArthur or Perry Como in my lectures, but when I give talks to folks my age, I even play some of Perry's music. Hot Diggity! And you kids can still learn from old folks. Just look at John McCain.

GENDER

Is your audience mostly men or women? This helps you be sensitive to issues that have more of gender concern, such as abortion for women or draft registration for men. You should also be aware of gender language and use both masculine and feminine terms. When I was a cadet at the Air Force Academy from 1968–1972, there were no female cadets, as there are now. Some instructors used photos of naked women to keep us awake in class. I'm guessing such techniques are not effective today. I had a male student at MSU give a talk that was laced with the word "chick" whenever he talked about girls. I wish I had videotaped the oral critique he got from the female students. We have come a long way since 1968 for gender equality. Just look at Hillary Clinton.

ETHNICITY

What ethnic groups are represented in your audience? This helps you avoid stereotypes that could get you into trouble. Just because two people are of the same color and ethnicity, they by no means have the same background, education, interests, or skills. I grew up in the South, so suffice it to say that I know we have come a long way since the '60s for ethnic equality, but we can go further. Just look at Barack Obama.

EDUCATION

What is the educational level of your audience? This helps you better select the vocabulary you might use. If they know a lot about your topic, you can use more technical language; if not, keep it more general. When I talk with pilots and navigators, I use more aviation terms and examples than I do with communication students. We've come a long way with education in America. Look at George W. Bush.

ECONOMIC STATUS

My main audience, students, is generally poor as dirt, so I don't analyze this demographic much. I do know an audience applauds more if you pay them.

JOB STATUS

What types of jobs do they have? Maybe they all have the same job, like the seminar I ran for all the Mayors in Montana. I related all my support to Mayoring.

RELIGION

I was always taught to avoid religion in a speech and on a first date. This topic can be sensitive and can upset people easily. Analyzing your audience's religious stance, however, does not mean you have to talk about it, just understand it. I have given speeches several times to groups who were all Muslim, both in Saudi Arabia and Morocco. It certainly helped for me to study that religion beforehand and to talk with my hosts about some differences in public speaking protocol between their culture and mine. I was told not to move around much, not to use so many gestures, not to use examples or photos of women, and absolutely avoid all profanity. Any guidelines like that are easy to follow, but you have to research properly to learn them.

INTERCULTURAL GROUPS

Every year, I notice more people from other countries in our audiences. As with all other demographics, we just need to avoid stereotyping. Because of the language barrier, speakers also need to slow down on key points, probably use more visual aids, and be particularly aware of idioms. **Idioms** are basically words that already have one meaning, but now take on new meaning. For example, I might say, "Don't worry about grades; just burn some midnight oil and your ship will come in." Americans will think, "Okay, I'll work hard and earn my reward." International guests will be wondering what oil and ships have to do with grades. Try to explain your idioms.

GROUP MEMBERSHIP

This demographic can cover many types of groups, such as politics, athletics, honor societies, and the Air Force Association. They may be organized with officers and publications, or they may just be informal groups to promote a hobby. Whatever the purpose, group membership gives you a feeling about an audience's interests and values and can help you decide on some great quotes and examples to use. For example, if I'm talking to football players, I'm quoting Vince Lombardi, for sure.

PEOPLE WITH SPECIAL NEEDS

This is a demographic I have not seen addressed in any other speech text, and it's overdue. Kids today often use the term "retard" to refer to a friend who is doing something stupid. That term can be quite offensive to families with a child who has special needs. The audience probably also has connections with people who are blind, deaf, or in wheelchairs. Other special problems that are being discussed more and more today are dyslexia, attention-deficit-disorder, clinical depression, and bipolarity. Such people are not technically "special needs," but they may need special attention from you. Just be aware. The Special Olympics Oath should be used by all of us:

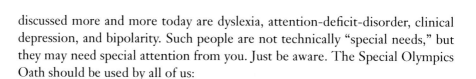

Overall, you should analyze demographics to see what audience members, and you, have in common with each other, and then use those connections. Never forget that people of each demographic want one main thing from a speaker: Treat Me Fairly.

Psychographics

Psychographics are much harder to measure accurately than demographics, because they are more mental than physical, harder to observe, and they can change over time. We're talking about attitudes, beliefs, and values. If you can "psyche-out" your audience, you're more apt to touch their bottom-line value system, and that's how you can get them to think or act differently. If you have time, you could run a survey and ask questions:

- Do you believe in the death penalty?
- What given political candidate would you vote for?
- Should illegal aliens be given free medical care?

The purpose of using psychographics is to see what motivates your audience, what upsets them, and thus better understand their needs. Try to be that market analyst who develops a product that the people *need*. Many of you have studied "Maslow's Hierarchy of Needs." (Worth a Google now.) If your speech fulfills a need, you will be more effective.

Mixographics

Mixographics is not a word you should google, because I just made it up. To me, it's all the other little odd things you might consider about your audience:

- How *big* is the audience? The larger the size, the less you have interaction, and the harder it is to analyze for demographics and psychographics.
- Are they *volunteers* to hear your talk, or is it mandatory training for them? Voluntary groups are usually easier on the speaker.
- How much do they know about your topic, and what do they *need* to know? Sometimes I've been the "supplemental" instructor, and been given a lesson plan.
- If you have a controversial topic, you should know if they *agree or disagree* with you. With a "hostile" audience, you must be more objective and less emotional.
- Anything else *you* can think of? After all, you are part of the audience, too.

Professographics

Professographics could also be called **Bossographics,** if either were a real word. In other words, don't forget that your academic instructor or your real-world boss will also be part of your audience. (Your boss may not be there physically, but he or she *will* get feedback on your performance.) If they have special guidelines for you, follow them. Instructors will usually build a "box" for you to work within: How long you will talk, required number of sources or visual aids, specific format for outlines, whatever. You must know the criteria by which you'll be graded or judged.

Your audience analysis will continue *during the speech*. You need to be watching for nonverbal feedback. Do they seem restless, tired, bored? Getting some applause? Have you lost their eye contact? Do they look confused, or angry? Giving you a "thumbs up," or maybe some other gesture? Straining to hear you? Daydreaming? Playing with cell phones? Probably smiling and laughing, right? Such physical reactions are important clues that you are doing well or you need to adjust something, like move more, get louder, or clarify a visual aid. *After the speech*, you could also get audience feedback through questions or surveys. Did you meet their needs? **Audience analysis never really stops.**

WHAT TYPE OF SPEECH?

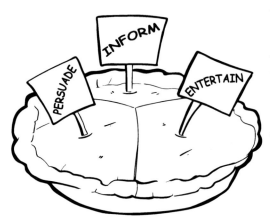

This question is closely related to the purpose of your speech. Your instructor or boss may just dictate the type of speech, or you may have a choice, based upon the needs of the audience. Your three choices are "**Easy as PIE**" to remember: **Persuade, Inform,** or **Entertain.** No matter what planet or parallel universe you're in, no matter what century, and no matter the audience, human or robotic, these are your only choices. Every speech I can possibly think of falls into one of these categories. Pick ONE, the one that best matches the goal of your speech. There is much overlap between the three, but don't confuse your audience by saying, "I want to inform you about the dangers of drugs and persuade you not to use them and hopefully entertain you with scary stories and examples." Just say, "I want to persuade you not to use drugs." Keep it simple.

Persuade
Inform
Entertain

Persuasion Speeches

These are the reason you're taking a speech course. Really, all the speech lessons are aimed at making you a more effective persuasive speaker. They are hard speeches because you are basically trying to get people to change how they think or act about something, and people tend to resist change. Therefore, you have to prove you have stronger credibility, use more convincing support, and evoke more audience emotion than is required for informative talks. This mix is a very old, very proven combination, perhaps labeled best by Aristotle in *The Rhetoric:*

- **Ethos:** Credibility of the speaker, based upon character and reputation
- **Logos:** Logical appeal, based upon form and substance of an argument
- **Pathos:** Emotional appeal, based upon values and feelings of the audience

Those exact definitions came from *Mastering Public Speaking,* by George L. Grice and John F. Skinner. Variations exist in virtually every communications text I've read because the concept is just that basic to public speaking, especially persuasion. My variation is:

- **Ethos:** Tell the audience your credible research and personal connection with the topic
- **Logos:** Use a variety of clear, logical, organized support (See **Chapters Three** and **Five**)
- **Pathos:** Use a variety of emotive sensory aids and delivery (See **Chapters Four** and **Six**)

No matter the type of speech, if you can balance those three areas, you'll be more effective. There are some **persuasion subsets:**

- A speech *to convince:* Used to cause change; aimed at the audience which disagrees with you or is neutral. Controversial topics, like the Iraq war.
- A speech *to reinforce:* Used to strengthen a stand; aimed at the audience who agrees with you. Less controversial, like the need for alternative fuels.
- A speech *to actuate:* Used to get action; that action could be controversial (buy my product or join my group) or not so much (recycle; drink more water).
- A speech *to inspire:* Used to increase positive emotions; aimed at groups to make them feel better. Think pep talks, tributes, eulogies, graduation speeches.

Regardless of the type of persuasion speech you may choose, I think the **influence model** below will help you better appreciate your goals. (The basic concept for this model also came from Grice and Skinner.)

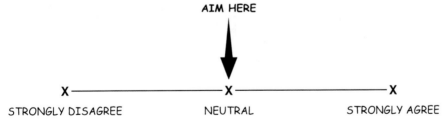

Your job in persuasion is NOT to take someone who strongly disagrees with you allllll the way across the spectrum to where they strongly agree with you. Consider that you are pro-life on the abortion issue. In one short speech (most academic speeches are less than ten minutes), is it realistic to think you'll get a strong pro-choice person to agree with you? No. Most experts will tell you not to even aim at the strong pro-choice folks. (Consider their opinion? Absolutely. But don't make it your goal to change them.) Instead, aim at the neutral parties, the people who really haven't studied the issue much and have no opinion, yet. It is very realistic to think that in ten minutes of credible ethos, logos, and pathos that you could "nudge" some people off the neutral bubble, moving them ever so slightly, barely, in your direction. *That*, honestly, is an effective talk.

You must understand that **persuasion happens in very, very, very small steps,** over a longgggggg period of time. Don't expect to change the world in one speech. Your talk will be just one tiny part of a huge machine that might make changes over time. Be comfortable with the thought that if you change just *one* person *one* tiny bit, you did a great job. After all, **persuasion is more about "influence" than "power,"** and influence takes time. What's the difference? Think about World War II: Franklin Roosevelt and Winston Churchill were influence, and Adolph Hitler was power. Influence lasts longer.

Academic note: When my students are done with persuasion speeches, I do not take a class vote to see how many people were "changed" by the talk. "Oh, I'm sorry, Fred. No one says you convinced them to save water by only flushing home toilets once a week. I guess you fail." What I look for is a comprehension of ethos, logos, and pathos.

Early in your persuasion talk, you should **acknowledge the opposition.** You will be more persuasive if you are objective. There *will* be another side to your argument, or you don't have a persuasive topic. (e.g., Michael Jordan should be in the basketball Hall of Fame. Would even one person disagree?) When you mention your purpose, and you **must take a stand,** someone should want to debate you immediately (e.g., the drinking age should be lowered to 19). In the military, I learned that "We must know our enemy," and the same is true in public speaking. Study the other side, and talk about it some. If they see that you can at least acknowledge their side, they will listen longer. Leave the door open a crack for them.

In that light, are you ready to hear the *four most important words in the English language?* Can you handle the truth? Drum roll, please . . . .

If you want to stay married more than six weeks, you should learn to say, "I might be wrong." (Didn't John Edwards learn anything from Bill Clinton?) If you want to persuade an audience, say it at least once in your speech. If you agree, then you would also follow this guidance: **avoid all absolutes** (AAA) . . . even this one. People who talk in absolute phrases tend to annoy their audience. "Everyone needs to learn a second language in every job in every country, all the time." If you speak absolutely, people will absolutely find one exception and quit listening, probably. It's better to use phrases like: "The trend is, There is a tendancy for, Most people seem to think, or Statistics generally show." Think of it as being firm, but polite.

Finally, and most importantly, you must constantly work toward answering the question "WHY?" Be an obnoxious two-year old.

MY EXAMPLE PERSUASION SPEECH

I grew up in North Carolina where they make most of the world's cigarettes, and I smoked myself for twenty years. I've read x-number expert articles on the subject

Informative speeches answer the questions Who, What, Where, When, and How. Persuasion speeches answer the questions Why and How Much.

and interviewed doctors and morticians (**ethos;** credibility). I know it's fun to smoke and rebel against your parents and be wild and crazy and cool, and it can be physically relaxing, and I know that cigarettes are great for the economy in North Carolina (acknowledge the **opposition;** tell both sides). I might be wrong, but I want you to avoid smoking (clear, concise **purpose**). I then show the gross ingredients in cigarettes, show graphs of smoker death rates, compare life insurance costs with non-smokers, and tell a personal story of how much money I spent on cigarettes, which was about $18,000 (**logos;** logical support). Finally, I show photos of a smoker's lungs, a video of some guy talking with half his face removed from mouth cancer, and then tell the story of my mother-in-law, Mary, who died from throat cancer and couldn't even talk on the phone with her grandchildren. I might cry a little bit (**pathos;** emotional photos, stories, and delivery). This is **WHY** you should quit smoking. The end.

P.S. I could give my children this speech, and tell them if I ever see them with a cigarette, I will take away their cars and cell phones (**power**), but they would only learn to smoke behind my back. It's best that I quit smoking myself (credibility) and live a life cigarette-free, day-by-day, for a long time (**influence**). I did quit smoking December 16, 1991 (applause).

Informative Speeches

These are much easier than persuasive speeches. They are the talks you've given since grade school. You just give us the information, and we do what we want with it. (In persuasion, you give us the information, and then tell us what to do with it and why it's important that we do so.) There are three main types:

- **Share knowledge:** Topics such as people, animals, places, things, events
- **Clarify knowledge** (understanding): Topics on a process (ACL surgery), concept (integrity), condition (poverty), or an issue (immigration)
- **Application of knowledge:** Demonstration-type talks to show "How To"

Sometimes people slip into a persuasive area during an informative talk, and I don't think it's a crime. For example, students often give informative speeches on great places to visit, such as Cancun, Mexico. They might say, "You should go there for Spring Break," which is persuasive. Most of the speech, however, would be clearly informative, just relating some main points like location, cost, and activities. They might talk about beer.

Some real-world, special occasion talks that basically give information are introducing a guest speaker, presenting an award, or accepting an award.

Entertainment Speeches

These are the hardest speeches to give, but most people never give one. Some audiences don't want to think much, especially after a big banquet dinner or an awards event. They don't want a lot of information, and they most certainly don't want to be persuaded. They just want to be "entertained," and it's more than just a comedy act. It is still an organized speech with a theme, but it's lighthearted and definitely creative. I have never heard of a college syllabus that mandated such a speech for students. In real life, you would only do this if you were already an accomplished speaker, so it warrants little attention here.

Let me stress, however, that just because your main purpose may not be to entertain, that doesn't mean the audience wouldn't like you to be "entertaining." And that does NOT mean you have to be Jerry Seinfeld. People are quick to think that entertainment means humor, or acting, or singing and dancing. Instead of thinking "entertaining," think about being "interesting." Fun facts, startling statistics, and vivid photographs can be very interesting, along with exciting movie clips and colorful posters and your personal story of skydiving. I like to define entertainment as anything that keeps your audience awake, which is every speaker's job. I hope you'll entertain that thought.

WHERE WILL IT HAPPEN?

When you are invited to speak, don't forget to ask about the setting and equipment:

- What is the size and shape of the room? (I want to move around)
- Good lighting and acoustics?
- Sound system? Will I need a microphone? (They MUST hear me)
- Podium? Tables to set my junk on?
- Raised stage, or on same level with audience? (I MUST have eye contact)
- What kind of seating for audience? Can it be moved around?
- Electronic Equipment: Computer with LCD projector; overhead projector? I still like to use TVs with DVD or VCR, and boom boxes. (I'm old) Ask for their equipment, but bring mine, too. Also bring extension cords.
- Screen? Maybe two screens? Could I project on the wall?
- Copy machine available? (maybe to make overheads or handouts)
- Blackboard/Whiteboard? Got chalk or markers?
- Tri-pod for posters or flip charts?
- And then I always ask if there will be coffee and water (maybe M&Ms?)

Do not ever assume that the room will be what you want. **Go early and check it out!** When I go out of town, I try to go the night before and check out the conference room where I will speak. Try to practice in the actual location. Know where to find the sound and light controls. Definitely run through your PowerPoint presentation, and be sure to have "backups for your backups" when it comes to computers. If any of the items listed is not what you prefer, you have to adapt, so it's better to find out early.

Academic Note: Students, you normally will know your setting, but you might be able to move chairs around or obtain extra equipment. Want to get into the room early? Ask.

WHEN WILL IT HAPPEN?

Your last "W" is for all the *time factors* you might consider:

- When is the big event? How much time do you have to prepare? You may want to build a timeline for yourself.
- What time of Day? Do you have control over it? Mid-morning and right after lunch are best for audience involvement.
- How much time is allowed for the talk? Short is better; under twenty minutes is actually very good in real life. Many conference blocks are fifty minutes, so it's more like a class/lecture than a speech; more relaxed. I have often had the coordinator say, "Talk as long as you want." Then I give them a time, so the audience can know what to expect before I begin.
- Do NOT go overtime, especially if you're part of a series of speakers.
- Does the date have any significance? Maybe it's a key date in history, a key date for the organization, or even the birthday of an audience member. If so, work that information into your talk to help audience bonding.

Academic Note: My students tell me that our eight-minute informative speeches take about four hours of preparation; the ten-minute persuasion talks take about six hours to prepare.

For all speakers, remember the advice of Mark Twain:

IT USUALLY TAKES MORE THAN THREE WEEKS TO PREPARE A GOOD IMPROMPTU SPEECH

SUMMARY CHECKLIST FOR GETTING STARTED

- ❑ **WHY** am I giving this speech? What's my purpose?
- ❑ **WHO** is my audience? What demographics and psychographics are there to consider?
- ❑ **WHAT** type of speech should it be? Persuasive, informative, or entertaining?
- ❑ **WHERE** will it be? Will the setting and equipment work for the audience and for me?
- ❑ **WHEN** will it be? Do I have time to prepare properly?

Once those questions have been answered, it's time to start some research.

Image © nasirkhan, 2012. Used under license from Shutterstock, Inc.

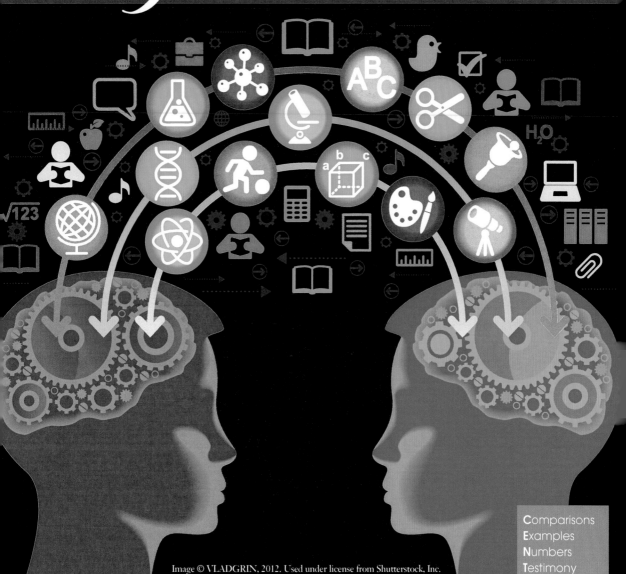

Image © VLADGRIN, 2012. Used under license from Shutterstock, Inc.

Comparisons
Examples
Numbers
Testimony
Stories

IT MAKES GOOD CENTS TO USE A VARIETY OF SUPPORT

Note: I thought it made sense to create an acronym to remember the varied types of support that make the ingredients for a good speech, CENTS: Comparisons, Examples, Numbers, Testimonies, and Stories. Let your mind "explode" with the possibilities!

In 1984, I crossed through Checkpoint Charlie in the Berlin wall, into the sterile world of East Berlin, Germany. I thought going from West to East Berlin was like going from Disney World into a no-name, empty prison yard. Our guide showed us a square where Hitler had ordered all of the books in Berlin to be piled together and burned. Burning books, like burning knowledge. (Remind you of Ray Bradbury's book, *Fahrenheit 451?* Except this was not fiction.) When Hitler took control during WWII, he did not want people to do any critical thinking, and he did not want Germans to question his authority, so he removed their ability to do research. No research, no analysis, no debates, no growth, no humanity. By 1984, the Nazis were long gone, but Communist Russia had maintained the tension in the Cold War–divided city, a city where people still weren't totally free to think for themselves. We are SO lucky to live in a time and place where research and communication are not only allowed, but expected, so that we can improve our lives. We must never take such freedom of thought for granted.

TOPIC CHOICE

After getting started (Chapter Two), you already know your audience and the type of speech (easy as PIE to remember), which provides a general purpose for your talk. Now you have to come up with a general topic. Once again, there are some subtle differences between choosing topics that are academic vs those that are real world.

Academic topics are more governed by the instructor, so you must be sure you understand your teacher's particular guidelines. Ask for help. Some instructors provide a list, and each student picks a topic from the list. Some give you a general area and let you pick the specific topic. Air Force cadets, for example, might be told to report on an airplane or a military leader, but they get to pick which particular aircraft or person they want to research. In a history class, you would most likely need a topic that dealt with some famous person or happening in history, and that topic itself, with its history lesson, would be more important to the instructor and the course goals than the actual speech, per se. In a speech class, however, it is the *process* of speechmaking that is always more important than the topic. We speech instructors want to see that you comprehend the principles of speech, and the exact topic is just a tool by which you show that comprehension. Therefore, in academia, I stress that you should not spend two weeks sweating over a topic. Follow some of the *general guidelines* below and get started sooner:

- Most important: Don't look online for a topic, LOOK IN YOUR HEART!
- Look at extremes; what makes you really happy or angry?
- What's your major? Can you find a topic that relates to future courses you'll take?
- What other courses are you taking now? Maybe you can kill two birds with one stone and do research for this speech that can also be partially applied in another class.
- What are your hobbies/jobs/talents? I hear many speeches based on this question. (If you pick a topic related to your major/job/hobby, you'll have more credibility.)
- What are your family's concerns and interests? They could help you.
- What are your friends excited about? They could also help you.
- What are the current hot topics in the media? You could find a lot of information, fast.
- What are the current hot topics on campus? Audiences love local topics.
- What professionals could you interview? They can help you narrow the topic.
- Which topic might be better for visual aids? You'll have to make some.
- Can you handle the topic emotionally? Some topics do hit close to home.
- Do you have immediate research ideas for this topic, or are you drawing a blank?
- What just sounds like fun? If you have fun, your audience will have fun.
- Is it a "college level" topic? I know that you know what this means.
- What was your <u>first</u> thought? You had that thought for a reason, right?

Real-world topics are more governed by your boss and the needs of the audience. In most cases, however, you will probably still have much freedom to choose the specific content and style of your speech, if not the specific purpose. I think most of the guidelines listed are also useful in the real world, and I would stress a few others:

- Most Important: What does the audience *need?* You could survey them.
- What do the bosses want? They should have a grip on audience needs themselves.
- What similar presentations have been given? Lessons learned from them?
- Don't try to save the world with your one speech. Keep the topic simple.

With these guidelines in mind, it's time to brainstorm some specific topics.

"Brainstorming" is a term that is often used and often abused. The term has been around since the late 1930s when Alex Osborn wrote a book called *Applied Imagination.* Basically, brainstorming is a technique to gather ideas quickly. It was mostly designed for groups, but also works well for individuals. There are four main **brainstorm rules:**

- Quantity vs Quality: Lots and lots of ideas give you a better chance for a good one
- No Criticism: If you evaluate ideas when you hear them, you get less ideas
- Be Crazy: Be wild and crazy and have fun; weird ideas are sometimes best
- Hitchhike off ideas: Let one idea spark another, even if it sounds similar

Brainstorming is just to get the ideas, *then* you can sit down and take your time and debate the quality or usefulness of the idea. But you have to get the ideas first! I find that individuals violate the rules often. As soon as they get an idea, they critique it: "Oh, that topic would be too hard, take too long, and be boring. Besides, the instructor would never let me do that." Do not criticize yourself while you are gathering ideas! You'll have plenty of time for that *after* you get the idea. These brainstorm rules can also come in handy in other areas of your speech preparation, such as main points, types of support, sensory aids, and how to research, including who to interview. Anything.

I think the best way to brainstorm is to *do it fast*, sixty to ninety seconds. That's all. If you do it right, it can be exhausting. You're trying to let a storm sweep through your pea brain and clean out any idea whatsoever you might possibly have and dump it down on paper. For example, I just spent sixty seconds (honest) and brainstormed the following list of topics:

Marijuana laws	Drinking age	Suicide	War in Iraq
Smoking bans	Alternative energy	Cloning	Media influence
Censorship	Reality television	Abortion	Meth kills
Mark Twain	Auburn football	Terrorism	China Olympics

Okay, maybe Auburn football is not a college-level topic, but then again, it could be, and it is about college, right? (See, now that I have the idea, we can debate it.) Bounce the topic idea off yourself, then your friends/family, and then your instructor/boss. By the way, look in Appendix H for a longer list of speech topics I've actually heard.

Please remember that it's not your topic that makes or breaks your speech, it's you. I have learned that any topic can be great (or awful) depending upon your approach, as well as *your* balance of research (ethos), content (logos), delivery (pathos), and organization.

Some people are just better at balancing acts (speech) than others. I'm reminded of a story from *Yeager*, the 1985 autobiography by General Chuck Yeager and Leo Janos. Chuck Yeager is perhaps the most famous test pilot in U.S. history, especially since he was the first person to break the sound barrier: October 14, 1947 in the Bell X-1, Glamorous Glennis, named after his wife. (He went 1.07 Mach, or about 700 mph.) Later, in February 1954, he was participating in dog-fights with other test pilots to see which aircraft was better, the U.S. F-86 Sabre or the Russian-built MIG 15. Yeager won the dogfight when he was in the F-86 and also when he was in the MIG, and he maintained that the aircraft didn't matter that much; it was the pilot. "The pilot with the most experience is gonna whip your a_ _ no matter what you're flying, it's that simple." Yeah. So now I get my best slow, deliberate, Yeager drawl going and tell people that the speaker with the most experience and the best balance of research, content, organization, and delivery is gonna whip your a_ _, no matter what the topic is—it's that simple.

And it begins with research. So, academic or real world, my best advice for topic choice is to pick a topic that you 100 percent sincerely, really, truly *want* to research. If possible, pick a topic you know, but also a topic you *want* to learn more about. Even experts want to research what other experts say about their topic. If your primary reason for a topic is that it's easy, you will have a poor speech. Lazy researchers are lazy speakers, and you can't hide that fact. The worst topics I hear are the ones that a student has done several times already in other classes (they are bored with it themselves) or the ones they give on their jobs, like the guy who sells cell phones and now wants to give his pitch in class. It's a pitch developed by someone else, so the student is just repeating someone else's words, like plagiarism. (In the real world, we all love those "canned" presentations, don't we? You know, the ones with no personality or creativity whatsoever.) Pick a topic you want to work on, and then gosh darn it, *work* on it! Develop your own speech, with your own words, and you'll be more excited. And **if you work for your audience, they will work harder to listen to you.** It is decreed, so be it. I shall end my sermon and move on.

RESEARCH (SMILE)

Once you think you have a general idea of your topic, start your research. You don't have to know the exact, specific purpose until you finish planning your whole speech. I stress to **let your research narrow down your topic.** It's like going through school. You start out general in elementary school and get more specific as you move into high school and can pick some classes on your own. Then it gets more specific in college when you pick a major, and it can be down-right narrow as you complete graduate school. So decide on "music" as a topic. Brainstorm some main points—such as "types, training, uses, need"—and then start your research. If you find some great articles on how music study helps SAT scores, make that your specific topic. **Talk about what you find,** and don't waste days trying to find what you think you want to talk about . . . in most cases.

SMILE!
RESEARCH CAN
BE FUN

Way out here in Montany, we like to say that "Tossin' a rope before buildin' a loop don't catch the calf." I've never actually said that, but I read it in *Savvy Sayin's*, a collection of old-time Western wisdom by Ken Alstad. Research is like buildin' a loop to try to catch your audience, and I created an acronym to remember the various types of research that will lend credibility to your speech: **SMILE.** The letters stand for *Surveys, Media, Internet, Library,* and *Ex-pert Interviews.* The basic thought is that a varied approach to research not only gives you a better chance to improve your content, it also gives you more credibility. When you say, "Oh, I found this on the Internet," it just doesn't carry the same weight as, "Oh, I did a survey with some students, interviewed a professor, watched a CNN interview, and read some government documents in the library." I actually know students who only know how to research online, and they tend to freak out when the Internet is down.

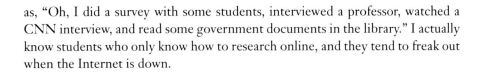

"Variety is the Spice of Life," and that axiom is true for visual aids, delivery, content, and, of course, research.

Surveys

- First of all, survey *yourself*. What do you already know on the topic? What previous research might apply to this project? Survey old bibliographies you may have kept and revisit those sites you liked before.
- Survey your favorite *coworkers* for their expertise/advice.
- *Networking* could be a type of survey (as well as a type of expert interview); check with folks you have met at conferences or who went to college with you.
- If possible, survey the *audience* to find their demographics, attitudes, and needs.
- Don't forget the *general public*, to get the layperson's views. Mark Twain said, "Its name is Public Opinion. It is held in reverence. It settles everything. Some think it is the voice of God."
- Surveys can be *formal or informal*. Formal surveys must follow some strict, legal guidelines if you hope to publish your research, so get help from a university graduate department or a professional publisher. Informal surveys are just a quick spot check on a group's attitudes. They don't carry the credibility weight of formal surveys, but audiences like them because they show you did some extra work and they are just fun, like "man in the street interviews" on late-night talk shows. I encourage students to run a five-question attitude survey by fifteen to twenty of their classmates.
- *Published surveys* are usually formal and credible. The results make great visual aids, since they can be easily formatted into pie charts, bar graphs, and tables.

Surveys
Media
Internet
Library
Experts

Media

- Watch *television*. There is actually a lot of good stuff on TV. News shows can give you all kinds of support for a speech; listen for statistics, examples, and quotes. The nature and history channels are full of material for informative speeches and could even help you decide on a topic. Expert interviews are on news channels and talk shows every night. I can't think of many topics that are not satirized on *South Park* or *The Simpsons.* A great benefit of TV is its variety.

- *Movies* can provide exciting clips for visual aids and examples of many cultural issues such as teen pregnancy, suicides, racial tensions, and *High School Musical.*
- *Music* is a very powerful medium with most audiences. Try to find some lyrics that represent your message, and show us the words while we listen to the beat.
- Bring in some *magazines* and show them to us. Holding up the source is always better than just saying, "I read this article on the Internet." We like to see objects.
- *Newspapers* can have the same credibility when you hold them up, and they tend to reflect more local news and attitudes. Local is good; touches home with audiences.
- When researching media, remember the old Yellow Pages jingle from years ago and "let your fingers do the walking." Call the TV station or video/music store before you waste time driving all over town looking for something.
- This media genre helps provide that "entertainment factor" that enhances speeches.

Internet

This is the most used and therefore most abused research source. Most of you know how to use the Internet better than I do, but if you don't (Mom, are you reading this?), ask for help from friends, instructors, and librarians. Longer, more credible communication texts have great sections on how to research on the Internet, but I want to stress some simple points you may not read elsewhere. Too many people see the Internet as their *only* source, and some educators (and employers) fear that today's students are not learning how to research; they just know how to google a word (i.e., if the Internet is not connected, neither is the mind). Traditional research methods are still valid, and still necessary, as long as the Internet remains "unfiltered." The Internet screening process is getting better all the time. (Education domains are good, along with those by the government, military, nonprofit organizations, business/commercial organizations, and networks. So look for .edu, .gov, .mil, .org, .com, and .net.) But there is still a lot of junk out there. A 2003 survey by the Center for Communication Policy at UCLA said that only 53 percent of users believe most of what they read online, down from 58 percent in 2002. Most of us are aware of the "urban rumor virus" which infects us with lies and

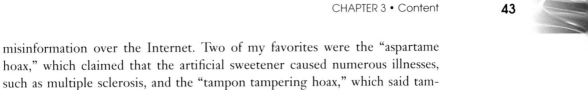

misinformation over the Internet. Two of my favorites were the "aspartame hoax," which claimed that the artificial sweetener caused numerous illnesses, such as multiple sclerosis, and the "tampon tampering hoax," which said tampons were contaminated with asbestos so that women would bleed more and buy more tampons. Both were completely refuted, but I still heard speeches on both topics in my Public Communication class. **You must know that just because something is on the Internet, it is not necessarily true.** If you cannot identify the source well enough to know the authors and/or the organizations and their credentials, you should not use it. (This same advice, of course, goes for every other research source you use.) The Internet is a very good source, overall, and it's getting closer to being true "one-stop shopping" where you can find surveys and books and magazines and interviews and media without ever leaving your seat . . . but it's not there yet. And the personal credibility you gain by "walking the beat" yourself is priceless. Instead of just reading the Internet, why not try to be the type of researcher who puts information *on* the Internet? **Definitely use the Internet, but use other sources as well.**

Library

I heard an urban myth the other day that it is still possible to find research material in the library. There are actually many sources . . . all in one place, sorta like the Internet. The key difference, however, is the librarian. He or she is like the key holder for the door into a parallel universe of knowledge. Please don't be afraid to ask librarians for help. They live to help you. They can be your surrogate parents on campus. When you have questions online, you're probably alone. When you have questions in the library, you have a friend. I strongly recommend new students ask the librarian for a tour of the campus library early during their first semester. (Show them this paragraph! It's a secret message that ensures your librarian will be nice to you.) Each library is a little different, so ask for a handout of key resources. Here's what to look for:

REFERENCE MATERIALS

This includes such things as dictionaries, encyclopedias, almanacs, atlases, and books of quotations. Dictionaries explain words, encyclopedias are a great start for general overview information, almanacs have facts/statistics that are usually updated annually, an atlas can orient you geographically with maps and provide demographic comparisons, and books of quotes can, well, give you a great quote:

> *What I remember the most from college is what I found myself, not what the professor gave me.*
>
> **—David McLaughlin, student of life**

I think every speech should have a few expert quotes, or a layperson quote at least. One **caution** on reference material: It is very good "filler" that can add spice and interest to a speech, but **it is not normally considered "college level research."** If your instructor asks for three references, make reference materials the fourth or fifth source in your bibliography, not one of the three main "counters." So remember . . . Wikipedia and fact sheets, maps, and lists of quotes that you find on the Internet are reference material, not "serious" research.

BOOKS

The books in the library are often ones you won't find in a bookstore. They can be older, even out-of-print, but still credible; more "academic." *Did you know we believe in books for research more than any other source?* A study from the UCLA Center for Communication Policy from a 2004 update said that among all mass media, both electronic and print, books were perceived most often as an "important source of information." Seventy-three percent of those surveyed listed books as important, compared to 69 percent for newspapers, 67 percent for the Internet, 53 percent for TV, 47 percent for radio, and 44 percent for magazines. (I think gossip from friends was about 2 percent, but I might be wrong.) I think people believe books more because they are screened and cross-checked so carefully by experts. They also touch our inner soul; our parents read to us from books as we sat in their laps. I promise you your audience will be impressed if you hold up a book and quote from it.

GOVERNMENT PUBLICATIONS

Try the Guide to U.S. Government Publications in print in the library, or online (*www.access.gpo.gov*). Did you know our government was the most prolific publisher in the country? You can find just about anything. You might want the librarian's help with this one the first time. Most of the information comes from

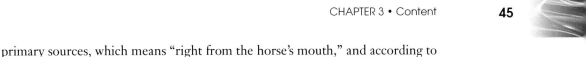

primary sources, which means "right from the horse's mouth," and according to *Savvy Sayin's,* "The good thing about talkin' to a horse is that he don't talk back."

JOURNALS

Check with the librarian to see what your library has and how to obtain other journals through full-text databases, like InfoTrac Online. If you name a topic, you can find a journal, and they are usually written by experts for other experts = "scholarly." My daughter, Morgan, said she used InfoTrac Online a lot in graduate school.

PERIODICALS

I believe an actual magazine carries more credibility than an online magazine, and the library usually has a great collection of credible magazines that you might never have seen. Professional organizations have their own magazines = "expert."

Expert Interviews

I strongly suggest that any speaker get a general idea for the topic, and then do an interview with an expert as soon as possible. Here's why:

- Experts will help you narrow down your topic and better define it, saving you time
- They can help you decide on main points and what order to present them
- They will give you more ideas for research, including other interviews
- Expert knowledge can be more current and local than anywhere else
- Their information might not be published, which means "not online" yet
- Often, they can give you research material, or you can quote their words
- Sometimes, they can give you visual aids and maybe a cup of coffee
- Always, **they will give you more credibility** with your audience

In other words, experts will save you time and give you a stronger product. Ta Dah! (Can you hear the emotive John Williams background music?) Really, why would you not want to do an interview? Mostly, students tell me they just think it's too hard and will take too long, or they say they're too shy. Interviews are not easy, but they are not that hard, either. A good length is about twenty minutes. Here are some **hints to conduct a good interview:**

- Plan ahead; interviews can take a week to schedule, so call early
- Research the person and topic a little bit and prepare some good questions
- Be professional: dress up, be on time, be polite, be brief, leave on time

If you go into an interview wearing a Coors t-shirt and put your feet on the person's desk and say, "Uh, yeah, like, what do you think I should know, dude?" the interviewee will find a quick way to nudge you out of the office. If you make an appointment and actually show up early, looking clean and neat, and you show that you know something about the person and his or her work, and you're polite, with a list of good, thoughtful questions, the expert might pull down a whole PhD thesis and just hand it to you. Experts love to talk with people, especially students, who seem to really care about their world.

Malcolm Kushner wrote a book called *Successful Presentations for Dummies*, which has much more detailed advice for speakers than I can offer in this short book. It is full of funny and truly practical wisdom. This is what he says about interviews:

> *One of the best, and most neglected, sources of primary material is other people. They have stories. They have experiences. They have insights. You just have to interview people to get ahold of this vast source of information. Writers and journalists do it. Police do it. Even game show hosts do it. Speakers, however, tend to ignore interviews as a source of information, and that's a mistake.*

On a campus, you can probably find someone to interview for most topics. If not, experts off campus really like to talk with students. It breaks up their day and gives them the feeling that they have a thumb on the pulse of America's future. Honest. For you poor working souls, interviews can be a great way to get to know key personnel better and find out more about your organization. Interviews create better networking. If you can't find time to do the interview in person, at least talk on the phone or swap some e-mails. When you make the extra effort to contact an expert yourself, your audience will note it.

Image © Login, 2012. Used under license from Shutterstock, Inc.

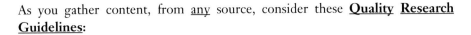

As you gather content, from <u>any</u> source, consider these **Quality Research Guidelines:**

* Start your research early! Make sure you have enough research, and then you can procrastinate and put it all together at the last moment . . . but get it first.
* Research about four times the amount you think you'll need; quantity leads to quality.
* Track your notes carefully so you can remember the source and cite it correctly.
* Look for material from true experts or laypeople with true connections to the topic; if you can't identify the author/organization as credible, be very suspect.
* Try to define the length/depth/breadth of a study; bigger studies tend to mean more.
* Try to use current data; older material serves a purpose as a spot-check in time or as a comparison to today, but recent material is usually more pertinent to listeners.
* Try to use local information vs global, if possible, to better relate to your audience.

I believe college and real life are less about knowledge and more about the *process* of gaining knowledge. Long after you've forgotten the facts, knowing HOW to research will be the key to learning new facts and therefore maintaining your independence. Remember, the Nazis knew this simple truth . . . and that's why they burned all the books.

SUPPORT VARIETY (CENTS)

Comparisons
Examples
Numbers
Testimony
Stories

The quote on the next page is famous in the public speaking world. It is quite time-tested, from the first century A.D., spoken by Saint Dionysius the Areopagite, First Bishop of Athens. I think it applies to all facets of preparing a speech, but it might apply best to research and support. If you don't do some good research and reflection to find some good support, do you really have anything worth sharing? Research is not just copying forty pages straight off the Internet. (What a waste of time and money!) Before you copy a whole article, use some critical thinking and scan the article for good support, and just take notes on what you think you might use. In other words, look for information that makes **"CENTS"** (*Comparisons, Examples, Numbers, Testimony, Stories*). You want a variety of such support because it is more interesting/meaningful. Would

you like to listen to a five-minute speech with forty-four numbers, and nothing else, or maybe a talk with just thirty-five quotations? No, so don't do that when you're the speaker. CENTS is my checklist to gain variety.

Comparisons and Contrasts

- *Literal* comparisons compare things that are similar: Let's look at the mistakes we made in Vietnam and see if we are making the same mistakes in Iraq.
- *Figurative* comparisons associate items not similar: Sky diving gives me the same rush as getting an "A" on my speech . . . but not quite as strong.
- *Similes* use the words "like" or "as": When CBS analyst David Feherty described the crazy, wild swing of golfer Jim Furyk, he said, "It looks like an octopus falling out of a tree, or a man trying to kill a snake in a telephone booth."
- *Metaphors* are implied comparisons of two things, without saying like or as: Peyton Manning never threw a boring, old football, because sports commentators know to spice it up, so "He threw a missile! He threw a bomb! He threw a wounded duck!"

- *Contrasts* can also be literal (real) or figurative (creative), showing differences between two things: In Bozeman, Montana, I drive three miles and go through one stoplight to get to work, not at all like my relatives who drive the Washington, D.C. beltway (real). I think Bozeman vs. D.C. is like the Flintstones vs the Jetsons (creative).

With comparison/contrasts (also called analogies), it's best if you can compare something the audience is familiar with to the new thing you're presenting. When we moved from Alabama to Montana, my kids wanted to know how big Montana was, so I pulled out an atlas and showed them how Montana would cover up all of Georgia, Alabama, and most of Mississippi. They could relate to that comparison since we had driven all around those states, and they knew they were longgggggg drives. Another great hint for comparisons is to use a visual aid. Bar graphs, pie charts, and line graphs display statistical comparisons much better than you could with just words.

Examples and Explanations

- Examples are the most common type of support
- Each main point should have at least one example
- *Personal* examples are generally better than third person
- *True* examples are generally better than hypothetical
- *Hypothetical* can touch a fun, entertaining nerve better
- Examples are best if the audience can relate to them
- Examples should be short (fifteen seconds) and to the point
- Visual examples are, so I've heard once or twice, worth 1000 words
- When in doubt if the audience understands . . . give an example

For example, I'm not sure if you understand examples, so it's time for one of my favorite times in teaching—when I get to give an example of an example. Let's say I'm talking about the evils of drinking and driving, so I need to give an example of an evil. I might say you'll injure someone, and give a hypothetical example of *Law and Order*, a popular TV show that hopefully the audience saw, of a drunk guy who ran over a child. It's better if I offered a personal and true example of my cousin, Mary, who was run over by a drunk driver and almost died, losing 90 percent of her eyesight. The audience wouldn't know Mary, however, and it was not a recent accident, so it would be best if I could find a current, local example of a drinking and driving evil that included a driver who matched the demographics of my audience, and maybe some people even knew.

When giving examples, like all other types of support, it is best to BE SPECIFIC. As a great example of non-specific words (and the culture of a small town), I want to share an actual, local, current police report from the July 12, 2008, *Bozeman Daily Chronicle:*

> *A caller from Hidden Valley Road in Bozeman called around 2 a.m. to report that two teenagers 'threw something at something' and made a loud noise and then ran off. A deputy was unable to locate something damaged by anything.*

You can see why the police reports are my wife's favorite part of our local newspaper.

Besides being specific, examples should also make an idea clear or understandable. To do that, you may have to elaborate a bit more, in which case the example may become a type of **explanation,** which is usually "explained" in four forms: *D*efinition, *E*xposition, *A*nalysis, and *D*escription. Yeah, it's boring, so I call it the "DEAD Zone."

DEFINITIONS

Definitions are often used in speeches, and they should be. Do not use a new word or acronym without first explaining it. Technical/scientific words might make you feel smarter, but overuse can really make you appear pompous. Use synonyms so you don't have to use the same word multiple times, and explain the meaning of new words, especially idioms. I quickly mentioned **idioms** in Chapter Two (page 23), but here's more:

DEFINED BY DICTIONARY: Idiom is an expression whose understood meaning is not expressed by the exact meanings of the individual words. Huh?

DEFINED BY EXAMPLE (BETTER THAN THE DICTIONARY): When Ann Richards, the Texas governor, gave her famous address to the 1988 Democratic convention, she said, "Tonight, we're going to tell how the cow ate the cabbage." If you look at each word, you might think the speech is about animals and vegetables, but the cultural meaning of that phrase is, "We're going to be honest." Well, at least in Texas.

We all must become more aware of idioms as our American audiences become more and more inclusive of non-American guests. An international friend might be lost with phrases we accept as common, like, "I hit the ceiling when Calvin asked for money. I am not betting on an inside straight and dig myself a grave. I told him to go fly a kite and find a new sugar daddy." Too many idioms = idiot. Do I have to define that word?

I wish you athletes could hear yourselves when you give talks about your sports, throwing around terms only other athletes in your sport would know. Nursing students sometimes think we're all in the medical profession, photography majors think we all look at the world through the same lens, and don't even get me started about lawyers and all their legaleze mumbo-jumbo. You know what I mean—think about your audience and how well they can follow your jargon, your special business talk.

Too many acronyms and abbreviations can also be totally confusing to your audience. During my first lecture each term I like to "explain" my military background. I say stuff like, "I got out of USAFA and went to UNT in ATC, then to Pope in the C-130 with MAC, where I was an IN and a SEFE, then to ROTC at RPI as the COC, but I had to go back to the C-130, so I went to Rhein Main, where I did tactics and HALO, followed by ACSC at AU as an FI and IOC, and finally MSU in AFROTC as the PAS. Are there any questions about my background?" Some folks still looked stunned at this point, but most are laughing with me because they see the lesson. I then put up a slide that says *Always Avoid Acronyms* and welcome them to join that international Triple-A group with me. You don't really have to avoid acronyms, but explain them during the first use, hopefully with a visual aid, maybe even a handout with other new terms you may use.

EXPOSITION

Exposition talks are sometimes called demonstration speeches. "How To" explanations can also be one of the main points of a speech. If you can tell us where to fly fish, explain the required equipment, and then show us "how to" use the rod, you have created better understanding of your topic than just telling us about the sport. Go fish!

ANALYSIS

Basically, you use analysis to explain how something works. I had a student this week explain how a bio-diesel engine worked during her talk on alternative fuels. The critique, or review, of her speech was actually an analysis of how a good speech works and how well her talk matched up against some proven standards. She got an "A."

DESCRIPTION

Description makes more conscious effort to appeal to the five human senses of sight, hearing, touch, taste, and smell. You can use verbal sensory images (see Chapter Eleven) and/or use sensory aids (see Chapter Four). If you were describing a good red wine, you might show us the rich color, let us hear the wine being poured into a glass, let us rub some wine between our fingers, and have us smell and taste the wine. This is obviously a real-world speech, since most schools would never allow real wine in class, of course. Never. Or could this be the seduction scene in *The Thomas Crown Affair?*

Numbers

- I would include FACTS here (It's a fact they must go somewhere).
- I also include DATES here; if you use a lot of dates, use a timeline aid.
- Limit your use of numbers. Every main point could have a number, or two or three, but do not group them all together and call one of your main points "statistics." That would be overload, and your audience would quit listening.
- We rarely remember the actual number; more often, we remember the comparison, example, or story that helped explain the meaning of the number.
- Keep it simple. **Round off your numbers!** Instead of 68.7345 percent, say 70 percent.
- Make it visual; your most important numbers should be on a visual aid.
- Numbers in comparison are very strong, so use graphs and charts if at all possible.

- Use American units of measurement (in America, of course); if your research is about imperial gallons or the value of oil in euros, do the conversions for us.
- Use current numbers, within the last ten years, wherever possible.
- Always pay your guest speakers a good number of dollars and compliments.

There's a number of other things I want to say.

Remember, you don't have to just find numbers in your research. For you graduate students and real-world speakers in particular, you can generate your own numbers with professional surveys and experiments. To me, those are the most interesting numbers.

Think about the impact of large numbers. We talk about so many millions and billions and gadzillions that large numbers can actually lose their impact. Relate such figures to something we know so it means more. Perhaps you have seen the following comparison:

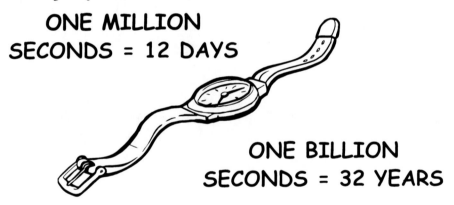

ONE MILLION SECONDS = 12 DAYS

ONE BILLION SECONDS = 32 YEARS

There is a *gigantic* difference (Wow!!) between a million and a billion, but we throw those numbers around like they are all about the same. Slow down and draw such distinctions for your audience the next time you give a talk on the national debt.

The *Wall Street Journal* posted a story in 2002 that grabbed my attention due to its vivid comparison with numbers. It said Bill Gate's net worth at the time was $37 billion. Such a number is beyond my comprehension, but I could relate to the comparison that if Bill Gates were to buy a $250,000 Lamborghini (I think that's a car, kinda like my Dodge mini-van), that would be like you and me (Joe the Plumber) spending 63 cents. Gosh, I think I would be patriotic and buy a red, a white, and a blue Lamborghini.

Another comparison I love to share came from Dr. William F. Harrison in an article entitled "Smoking is Harmful to Human Health." As a former smoker–fool, I noted that "Smoking kills an average of 450,000 people a year." That's another huge number that can lose its impact, but what if you knew those deaths were equivalent to "eighteen jumbo jet 747s crashing each week for a year!?" I heard that three years ago; I still remember it.

Numbers should help answer questions from your audience, so be careful not to create unanswered questions. Remember how big Montana is? Well, if you want to give a mechanical answer that creates no mental picture, you would say 147,138 square miles. Ugh. I will forget that number about the time it leaves your lips, and it creates the question, "How big is a square mile?" You could relate that to something we know, like the size of the MSU campus, roughly, but 147,000 (round off) MSU campuses is too hard to think about. It would be better to say Montana is the fourth largest state in the union, but then that creates the question, "What are the three bigger states?" So you, as the speaker who can get into your audience's heads, must tell them before they ask: Alaska, Texas, and California. People will think you can read their minds! Wad-ja-think of that?

As a transition from statistics into quotations, I thought I'd use a quote:

> *Information's pretty thin stuff, unless mixed with experience.*
>
> **—Clarence Day, *The Crow's Nest* (1921)**

Testimony (Quotations)

Testimony is a way to mix experience with the numbers. Find people who have experience with your topic, and borrow their words to say what you want to say. It's like being part of a group speech where the audience gets to hear several different people talk, except those other people just have to borrow your voice. Even experts quote other experts to aid credibility. Here are some hints I've learned about testimony:

- Testimony can be expert or layperson; I think expert is better for logos (logic) and a layperson can be better for pathos (emotion). For drug topics, quote a doctor on physiological effects of drugs and a drug user's spouse on financial/social impact.

- I define an "expert" as someone whose research or job deals with your topic, and a layperson as someone who has some practical, human experience with the issue.
- Testimony can be third person or personal; don't forget that your experience and research with a topic should always be explained as part of your own credibility.
- Part of the power of quotes is that they can include other types of support. I quote Chris Rock and also get a simile/comparison: "Women are like the police. They could have all the evidence in the world, but they still want the confession."
- Short quotes are better than long quotes.
- Most quotes should be shown on a visual aid.
- Do NOT over quote one source. Use one Bible quote, not ten.
- If you did an interview, definitely fit in a quote or two from that person.
- Try a "surprise" quote that people don't expect. President Ronald Reagan, "The Great Communicator" and a Republican, often quoted Democratic presidents.
- Be careful with President George W. Bush quotes, like this one, heard in Rome on July 22, 2001: "I know what I believe. I will continue to articulate what I believe and what I believe—I believe what I believe is right." Thesaurus, anyone?

I believe in books of quotations. I usually fit one or two such "category" quotes into each of my speeches or papers. (They can be good for attention steps and closure statements, to be discussed in Chapter Five.) For example, I wanted a quote on good public speaking, so I looked under "Speaking" in my book of quotations and found this:

"THE TONGUE IS MORE TO BE FEARED THAN THE SWORD"
–JAPANESE PROVERB

Mouth image © lineartestpilot, 2012.
Used under license from Shutterstock, Inc.

We like to hear **proverbs** because they represent a universal lesson born of long, noble experience. All cultures, especially the Chinese, seem to have their own proverbs, except Americans. Why don't we ever see great advice listed as an American proverb? We actually do have such cultural wisdom; we label it Abraham Lincoln or Mark Twain.

Stories

- A story is also called narration, parable, anecdote, fable, legend, or lie
- Personal stories are usually better than third-person, but any story with people is good
- True stories are usually better than fictional stories, like parables
- Parables can highlight moral lessons without sounding like a preacher
- Stories of success are generally better than stories of failure
- Short stories are better than long ones (sixty to ninety seconds is good)

I stress that *every speech should have a story!* Why?

- We remember stories longer than any other type of CENTS.
- Facts and figures (logos) make us think; stories (pathos) make us act.
- Stories "put a face" on the numbers so that the lesson is clearer. If I tell you many statistics about the dangers of smoking, you would forget them soon. Remember my mother-in-law who died of throat cancer from a lifetime of smoking? If I vividly described her pain, with photos, you would remember much longer.
- To use an idiom, stories "put your heart on your sleeve" for us to see, and if we don't see a little heart from a speaker, we don't listen very long.
- When you tell a story, you have more natural delivery and show more emotion than when you explain a bar graph; I see this every day and it's very cool.
- Stories "bring out the child" in us, and we love childhood memories. It reminds us of sitting on our grandfather's lap and hearing about the "good ol' days."

> *The story, from "Rumplestiltskin" to War and Peace, is one of the basic tools invented by the human mind, for the purpose of gaining understanding. There have been great societies that did not use the wheel, but there have been no societies that did not tell stories.*
>
> **—Ursula K. Le Guin, prolific American writer, 1979**

- Stories allow you to have a little fun, to use some **hyperbole:** deliberate exaggeration used for effect; not intended to be believed by the audience. My good storytelling friend from Maine, Rob Suminsby, was the first one to teach me that "You should never let the truth get in the way of a good story."

I was watching *American Idol* in 2006 (yeah, I admit it) when Barry Manilow (*Oh, Mandy!*) gave some great advice to the contestants: "A singer's job is to tell a story." Motivated, I sat right down and wrote the following advice for my students:

If all you give us is a bunch of facts and numbers . . .
just give us a fact sheet and let us go home early.

If all you do is read to us . . .
just give us a paper and let us go home early.

YOUR JOB as a speaker is to:
- *"Put a Face" on the numbers!*
- *Bring it Alive!*
- *Take us on a trip!*
- *Be a *!#! STORYTELLER!!*

SUMMARY CHECKLIST FOR CONTENT

Pick a Topic

❑ Look in your heart before you look online; strongly consider your first thought
❑ What's aligned with your interests/talents and the audience needs?
❑ What gives you the most ideas for research and visual aids?
❑ Just grab a general topic and start your research to narrow it down

Research (SMILE)

❑ Surveys: yourself, public, or experts; formal or informal
❑ Media: TV, movies, music, magazines, and newspapers
❑ Internet: Be sure it's a credible site; don't use the Internet exclusively
❑ Library: the librarian, reference material, books, government pubs, journals
❑ Expert Interview: Recommended to do first to help you with other sources; gives you more credibility.
❑ Do research early, then you can procrastinate and put it all together later
❑ Look for material that is current, relevant, accurate, expert, unbiased, and specific
❑ Oh, yeah, try to find some humor; don't forget to SMILE!

Content (CENTS)

❑ Comparison/Contrast: Literal (real) or figurative (creative)
❑ Examples/Explanations: True or hypothetical; includes definitions/descriptions
❑ Numbers: Logical; best done with comparisons, examples, and visual aids
❑ Testimony (Quotes): Expert or layperson; comes from research or experience; every speech needs a quote.
❑ Stories: Most memorable part of CENTS; every speech needs a story

Overall Advice for Research and Content

- Real is better than fiction
- Short is better than long
- Personal is better than third person
- Variety is the spice of life!

- Visual is better than words
- Specific is better than general
- Best if audience can relate
- Balance ethos, logos, pathos

Try to remember the great advice (universal wisdom) from the following quote (proverb), from Mark Twain, probably paraphrasing Abe Lincoln, who probably used Dionysius:

IT IS BETTER TO REMAIN SILENT AND BE THOUGHT A FOOL, THAN TO SPEAK OUT AND REMOVE ALL DOUBT

Remember to SMILE and use good CENTS, and ye, good soul, shall never play the fool.

Chapter 4
SENSORY AIDS

DON'T BECOT WITHOUT SENSORY AIDS!

Image © Digital Genetics, 2012. Used under license from Shutterstock, Inc.

Note: I didn't want to "be caught" without an acronym for this critical component of public speaking.
BECOT: **B**lackboard, **E**lectronics, **C**ostuming, **O**bjects, and **T**ransparencies.

Blackboard
Electronics
Costuming
Objects
Transparencies

Once upon a time way back in 1998, I had a student who was so afraid of public speaking that she had dropped our course five times. It was summer school and she was trying again because it was now the last course standing between her and graduation. After two weeks, she predictably came to me to disengage with the enemy for a sixth time, saying she was simply too nervous to give a speech. I said, "Dawn, if you use lots of visual aids, you can take the attention off you for a while and sip some water and even breathe again." Sure enough, she came in with a stuffed animal, pictures, lists, a map, and, no kidding, a live baby bear! She not only finished a good speech, she had fun, and she definitely made a memory for all of us. Then she graduated, went on to veterinarian school, and is now the savior of all the bears in all of North America, I'm sure. The end.

Some public speaking textbooks list visual aids under "Support" (Chapter Three) and some others under "Delivery" (Chapter Six). The sharper textbooks (cough, clear throat) have a separate chapter because the topic is just that important. Good support certainly can make a memory, but sensory aids make a longer-lasting memory for your audience, especially if they are members of the TV generation. Most of my students grew up on 123 Sesame Street with big birds and cookie monsters. Their teachers incorporated TVs and videos in the classroom on a regular basis, and the explosion of cable TV in their homes enhanced their visual/auditory learning senses. In short, we deal with more visual learners today than yesterday, and we speakers must adapt.

Image © Helga Esteb, 2012. Used under license from Shutterstock, Inc.

> *I feel strongly that the visual arts are of vast importance.*
> *Of course, I could be prejudiced. I am a visual art.*
>
> **—Kermit the Frog**

To emphasize the value of visual arts in public speaking, I submit to you members of the jury that graduation speeches are dull. Do you look forward to them? Garry Trudeau, the author of the "Doonesbury" comic strip, said, "Graduation speeches were invented largely in the belief that college students should never be released into the world until they have been properly sedated." Some graduation speakers don't have the skill or the desire to paint pictures with their words, so they could really use some visual aid help, yet sometimes they just stand behind a podium and read from a dry script, and we parents daydream about empty nests and beer. (Sorry, I think I had a flashback there for a moment.) It doesn't have to be that way. On May 15, 2004, we attended my daughter Morgan's graduation from the University of North Dakota. The speaker, NASA administrator Sean O'Keefe, linked up with the International Space Station and astronaut Mike Finche talked to us live, on a huge video screen, from space! It was, as you kids say, "totally awesome." Sensory aids work because of very tried and true principles.

PRINCIPLES (THEORY)

Military people talk about the "Fog and Friction" of war, the confusion that arises in combat from an unexpected chain of events. Well, I think there is a certain fog and friction of public speaking, too. You cannot anticipate everything (remember, there is no perfect speech), but good planning certainly helps you win the battle. I stress that solid planning with **sensory aids can be the cure-all for all the ills of public speaking.** Let's review some common **fears of speakers**:

- Boring: Sensory aids make your presentation (and you!) more interesting.
- Eye Contact: Your eyes won't be buried in your notes as much.
- Movement: You can set up your aids to create natural movement.
- Monotone Voice: Your voice naturally fluctuates while you're moving.
- Confusion: Your audience understands information better with aids.
- Time Control: You can cover more material in less time, and do it better.
- Forget What to Say: Aids become another way to remember key points.
- Nervousness: Aids take audience eyes off you for a moment; whew!
- Credibility: Aids indicate more caring for the topic and the audience.

And let's review some **fears of the audience**:

- Lazy Speaker: Aids show a willingness to work for the audience.
- Pompous Speaker: Aids can show a "human" side to a stiff speaker.
- Complex Data: Graphs, charts, and tables simplify difficult information.
- Boring Data: Videos, pictures, cartoons, and music enliven dry material.
- Believability: Visual citations on an aid show expert research.
- Falling Asleep: Aids = movement = eye shifts = thinking = brain awake.
- Too Much Business: Aids bring out the fun side, the "child" in us.
- Forget What Was Said: Aids help us retain information much longer.
- I'll have to use the bathroom during the talk: Aids will not help this fear.

Sensory aids are so powerful because they appeal to both the left and right side of our brains. The left side (more logic, logos) just loves facts and figures which

MAKE ME A
MEMORY

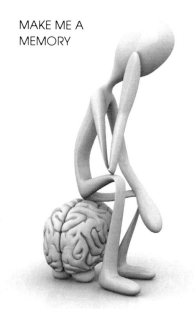

"come alive" in graphs and charts—MUCH more effectively than just telling us the numbers. The right side (more emotion, pathos) just loves the human/feeling element of pictures, videos, and cartoons. Aids also enhance the credibility (ethos) of a speaker because the audience can better see the comprehension the speaker has for both the topic and the audience. Overall, aids do much better in making a memory, something an audience really desires.

Visual aids can create a much better memory than just a big ol' pile of verbal dung. Why would you want to give a speech if you knew the audience would forget most of it right away? What a waste of your time and theirs. Numerous studies support the following claim of David Peoples, the popular author of *Presentations Plus:* "Words and pictures used together are six times more effective than words alone." He also has a great line that struck a loud gong in my head: "People often say, 'Oh, I get the picture!' Have you ever heard anyone say, 'Oh, I get the words?'" Sensory aids help me make a memory when they are short & simple, credible & current, local & lively, personal & professional, and vivid & visual—and the most important word in that list is "visual."

> *Things seen are mightier than things heard.*
>
> **—Alfred Lord Tennyson, "Enoch Arden" (1864)**

I always loved Tennyson's epic poem, "Charge of the Light Brigade," because it touched so many of my senses, especially since it commemorated an actual deadly cavalry charge in the Crimean War. Here are a few of Tennyson's key phrases: "Valley of death, someone had blundered, theirs but to do or die, into the mouth of Hell, flashed sabres bare, cannon volleyed and thundered, horse and hero fell, noble six hundred!" The words alone tear me apart; can I even imagine what the video would be like? I should have been an English teacher. (Sorry, I digress.) I feel like Spiderman; my senses are tingling. What are those **five primary senses?**

- *Taste* (tongue): Just this week Katie gave a speech on Rome, and she gave us all bread with balsamic vinegar so we could share her favorite taste from Italy.
- *Touch* (fingers): If Jackie gave a speech on elephants, I would expect her to pass around some of her elephant figurines. Remember the bear cub that Dawn brought to class? I'll never forget how coarse his fur was and how strong and taut his muscles felt. Whoa!
- *Smell* (nose): The bear cub also defined "pungent" smell! I'll never forget three "smelly" speeches; poop (organic farming), blood (pro-life), and bacon cooking (bacon). During a speech on vinegaroons, white scorpions that emit a vinegarlike odor, a speaker used a spray bottle to squirt vinegar around the room. Strong stuff!
- *Hearing* (ears): If Mike and Laurie gave a speech on John Denver, I would expect to hear *Rocky Mountain High* somewhere in that speech. That's just a hint. If you don't know who John Denver was, I would expect you to be a communist.
- *Sight* (eyes): If Tom tells me Magic Johnson was a great point guard, it doesn't mean as much as if he shows me video clips from the Olympic Dream Team, the real one, from Barcelona, 1992. Wouldn't *you* expect to see such a clip?

I try to say "sensory aids" because I challenge people to appeal to all our senses during a speech, but realistically, I usually say "visual aids" because most aids are visual, and because sight is our strongest sense, by far. The TV shows *CSI* and *Law and Order* taught me that any judge prefers an eyewitness over a witness who just heard the gunshot (an earwitness?). In *Presentations Plus*, David Peoples taught me that "of the total inventory of information you have in your head, **75%** came to you **visually,** 13% through hearing, and a total of 12% through smell, touch, and taste." The eyes have it!!

I personally overemphasize the use of sensory aids in school speeches, so that in real life, people might actually use a few more aids than normal. I like students to use at least one type of sensory aid that they haven't seen yet in peer talks. There are so many types that I could not possibly cover them all in one class or one book. It's fun and interesting when a group slowly begins to teach each other about what works and does not work in a speech, especially with sensory aids. So I say, "Have so many aids that I beg you to stop using them," and so far, I have never begged. I understand that some experts say it is possible to use too many aids; in real life, I have never seen this phenomenon. If used incorrectly, one aid could be too many. If used properly, to enhance a presentation and not take it over, sensory aids might know no boundaries. The key? VARIETY!

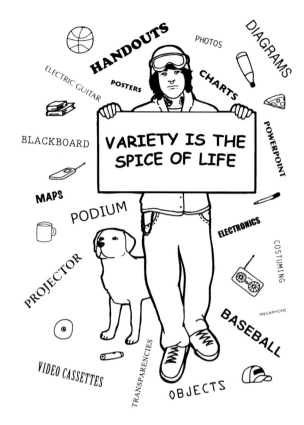

Blackboard
Electronics
Costuming
Objects
Transparencies

VARIETY OF AIDS (BECOT)

In the use of sensory aids, you are only limited by your imagination. Aids help reflect the enthusiasm and imagination you have about your topic, but more importantly, they also draw out imagination from your audience. I imagine that's a good thing.

Imagination is more important than knowledge, for knowledge is limited to all that we now know and understand, while imagination embraces the entire world, and all there ever will be to know and understand.

—Albert Einstein

If you want help "imagining" sensory aids or making them, start with friends. When they hear your topic, what aids would they expect to see? When a classmate/coworker uses an aid you like, ask them how they made it. You can also ask your instructor for help, really, and most campuses have a Media Services office you can contact. Those folks are like the librarians of sensory aids, and their advice is free. (They also have equipment you can usually use for free to make aids, and maybe some rental equipment such as video cameras for use off campus.) Some schools even have semester courses you can take to learn more about the vast world of sensory support. In the academic or real world, don't forget the many commercial sources available. Office supply stores and copy centers are gaining more expertise every day in this area, and they will often show you how to do the work yourself so that you can save some money. Some students complain that sensory aids cost a lot of money, but they don't have to cost a dime.

When students complain that they have no money to make aids, I tell them I have never met an instructor who charged students for using the blackboard (hint: free!). I often see people borrow someone's computer (hint: you gotta ask) to create some PowerPoint slides or download some photos. Anyone can "dress up nice" (hint: not just a t-shirt and shorts), and everyone can bring in some object (hint: research book/magazine) that they can hold up. Finally, they can probably borrow some overhead transparencies from someone (even the instructor?) and draw something on them by hand (hint: use your imagination). So—**you never have to BECOT without sensory aids!**

Blackboard

We all love simplicity (See Chapter Eight), and chalkboards/whiteboards are the simplest visual aid. (I just call them all blackboards, because I'm old, and I needed a "B" in my acronym.) They are always in the classroom and often in the real world, especially if you plan ahead and request one. All you have to do is plan what you will put on the board and ensure that you have the necessary chalk or markers. Why else are they good?

- They create movement: You have to get away from the podium.
- Chalkboards create noise: Some noise helps your audience stay awake.
- Whiteboards add color: Audiences prefer color to black and white.
- They show a human touch: We get tired of "professional" computer graphics.
- You can keep the lights on when you're using a blackboard.
- They are great to record ideas during short brainstorming sessions.

- Great for step-by-step teaching; we like to watch you build the aid.
- They are great for emphasis: If I make the statement in my speech that 63 percent of mature males are North Carolina basketball fans, I can emphasize my point by quickly and emphatically writing "63%" on the board, with a smiley face.

The big caution, of course, is *do not turn your back on the audience too long.* If you start talking into the blackboard, the audience starts to play with their cell phones. To avoid this problem, keep your words/drawings simple:

- Fast numbers, and round them off
- Use key words, not full sentences (except for direct quotes)
- Short quotes, not a full paragraph
- If you're talking about a person or place, write the name up quickly
- PRINT your words, big, so we can actually read them
- Create very basic maps; most states can be a square or rectangle or a circle (For California, of course, you'll have to use curved lines and thirty-seven colors)
- We love stick figures! You really do not have to be an artist.
- You can write the title or topic of your talk, along with your main points

If you want to put more detail on the board, do it *before* the speech so that it doesn't take too much time during the talk. You don't want to spend two minutes drawing a bargraph on the board, especially if you are not talking and you have your back turned to the audience. You might turn back around and find that everyone left! If there is a screen that pulls down over the blackboard, you could do a detailed quote/chart on the board behind the screen, and then just raise the screen in the middle of your speech. You never want to reveal any visual aid before you are ready to use it, because your audience will be looking at it and wondering about it instead of listening to you.

Please note that all of these suggestions apply to all the different kinds of visual aids. If you ignore them with blackboard use, however, it just seems to be more noticeable.

Electronic

Electronic sensory aids can be as complicated as blackboards are simple. These are the aids that create the most stress for a speaker, because of worry that they won't work. When I say, "Have backups for your backups," I'm talking about electronic aids because all the other types usually work fine. The upside, how-

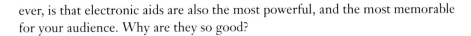

ever, is that electronic aids are also the most powerful, and the most memorable for your audience. Why are they so good?

- The color on electronic photos is more vivid than on transparencies or in books.
- You can project photos/videos for free (once you have a computer/projector).
- You have access to endless photos and clip art you can add to enliven your lists.
- You can access music and videos on the same machine as your PowerPoint.
- A USB/memory stick is easier to carry around than a briefcase full of slides.
- Electronic aids can appeal to more of our senses at one time = better memory!

So electronic aids can be Superman, but sometimes they are also Kryptonite. Caution:

- Be sure your computer/projector is working; need extra cords/connectors/bulbs?
- Electronic aids can lead to standing in one place with a monotone voice.
- Most electronic aids show better with the lights off; "danger, danger."

Most of you know Murphy's Law: If anything can go wrong, it will. Murphy, I imagine, was a public speaker . . . using electronic aids. If you have ever watched even a handful of speeches, you know what I'm talking about. You must keep your sense of humor, laugh it off somehow, and move on. It's easier to move on if you have played the "What If?" game: "What if the computer doesn't work? What if I can't get it synchronized with the projector? What if a bulb burns out? What if the wireless Internet doesn't work in this room, this day? What if there is a power loss? What if my computer battery runs out? What if I don't start planning for retirement today?!!?" (That last question is actually part of a real-world

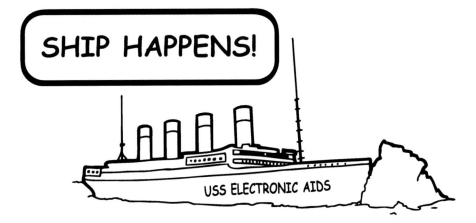

game you should be playing, thanks to our Social Security system, but that's a different speech.) Just remember the Titanic!

There are numerous **types of electronic aids,** especially when I define electronic as "anything that plugs in" (except overhead projectors with transparencies, which I put in a separate category). I often see speeches that incorporate several of these:

- *Lights:* Black lights, strobe lights, mood lamps, motion lamps, emergency beacons. I've had film majors give speeches on the effect of lighting in movies, and they turned the classroom into a stage set to illustrate use of shadows.
- *Objects:* I've seen clocks, griddles, coffee pots, smoke machines, and fans.
- *Musical Instruments:* During a talk on the history of rock and roll, Tyler played some Jimi Hendrix on his electric guitar. Keyboards are common, too. Remember, if you can play any instrument, find a way to do it.
- *Cassette Players:* Yes, people still use cassettes sometimes; you can set them exactly where you want them to start and not fight with them during the talk.
- *CD Players:* Most people use CDs today, or they play music on their iPods and laptops. (Make sure you have speakers.) Be careful; some people spend a lot of time searching for the start of the song.
- *VCR/TV:* Yes, some (old) people still use VHS tapes. Like music cassettes, you can preset them to the exact scene you want and just "plug in and go."
- *DVD:* Most people use DVDs today, or they play videos on their laptop. Be careful; some people spend a *lot* of time searching for a clip. (ooh, Deja vu?)
- *Digital Camera:* I see more and more students plug their cameras into the TV and share personal photos/video they shot or they run them through their laptops.
- *Computer/Projector:* This is by far the most common electronic aid I see. Just make sure you know how to make your computer "talk" to the available LCD (Liquid Crystal Diode) projector. Not every computer works the same way.
- *16mm movies and 35mm slide shows:* Huh? What are those?

It amazes me that I don't hear more music in speeches. My daughter, Shannon, who is the same age as many of my students, won't back out of the driveway without music screaming in her car. I have to remind students sometimes to please quit listening to their iPods and pay attention to their friends' talks. Yet music is the last electronic aid they use in speeches. You can find music to fit in with most topics, even if it's just a favorite song you use in ten-second sound bites to help transition between main points. If I want to evoke patriotic feelings, I play

John Philip Sousa music, especially *Stars and Stripes Forever.* If I want to inspire teamwork, I play *One Shining Moment*, which is played each year after the college basketball championships. If I want to induce vomiting, I play bald Britney Spears singing *One More Time.* Oooh, hit me baby. When you hit us with music, thirty seconds at a time is usually plenty, not the whole song. Do not play background music while you talk, even if the volume is low; if you have to compete with music... you will lose.

Videos should also be limited in time. In *Successful Presentations for Dummies*, Malcom Kushner says, **"Video is so powerful that it should only be used in small doses."** The danger is that it will take over your presentation. It will make the non-video portion (in other words—you talking) seem boring by comparison. That's exactly what you don't want. Use videos in short bursts to emphasize key points and heighten audience interest." Videos, without a doubt, create the longest-lasting memory from your speech. When I ask students to comment on a peer's presentation, the first critique is usually, "Cool video, man!" When I ask a group a week later what they remember from a particular speech, it is *always* the video that is mentioned first, with very few other comments to follow. This should be no surprise if you remember the way we use our senses: 88 percent of what we keep in our little pea brains comes through our sight and hearing, and videos capture both senses! It's like the old double whammy from an old comic strip called "Li'l Abner" by old Al Capp which only old people remember. (I must be needing a Baby Boomer bond.) Here are some **HINTS** to tame the wild, video beast:

- Limit a video clip to sixty to ninety seconds for a ten-minute talk
- Make that limit five minutes total for a forty-minute group speech
- Several shorter clips mixed throughout is better than one long clip
- Tell us beforehand how long the video clip is if it's over a minute
- Tell us the background of the clip if it's important to the topic
- Tell us what to watch for specifically if you want to stress a point
- Have the video cued up exactly where you want it; don't waste our time
- Don't ever let the video talk for you

I had a student once who gave a talk on extreme snow skiers. He said, "I love extreme skiers; let me show you why." Then he showed us seven minutes of an awesome Warren Miller film with some of the coolest extreme skiing ever seen, with heart-stopping music pounding all the while in the background. Then he said, "Now you know why I love extreme skiers." That was the end. I asked the class what they thought, and several people immediately said, "Wow, dude, that was the best speech we've heard in this class yet! Powerful, man!" I had to agree it was a great video, but that's all it was—just a video. No speech whatsoever: no introduction, no body, no conclusion, no research, no support (CENTS), and only one type of visual aid. He let the video do his entire talk for him, and he honestly didn't see anything wrong with that; he wanted something exciting for his classmates, and he did provide that. We talked more after class, and he came in the next week and did a real speech on the same topic, which was fine. After that lesson for me, I learned to ask people to stop their videos after two minutes and talk to us. I say, "*I want to hear your voice*, since it's your talk, and not the video's voice."

The really good critical thinkers will make their own videos. One of my students gave a speech on Labradors, which sounds like a fifth-grade topic, doesn't it? I tell my students, however, that they can show "college level" effort with their sensory aids, and Rob did not disappoint. When he compared labs with other dog breeds in terms of intelligence, he did not just say, "Labs are really smart." He said, "Let me show you a trick I taught my dog in forty minutes." Then we watched a ninety-second video clip of this dog getting him food and drink from the kitchen, while Rob sat in front of the TV. The dog opened the refrigerator twice, while music blared in the background, "Who let the dogs out, Who Who?" That was seven or eight years ago. I still show that video in lecture.

Like videos, **PowerPoint presentations** are also good and bad, or maybe I should say fabulous and horrible. There are many strong feelings:

- From *A Pocket Guide to Public Speaking* by Dan O'Hair, Hannah Rubenstein, and Rob Stewart: "It's a speech, not a slide show. Some speakers may become so enamored of generating electronic aids that they forget that their primary mission is to communicate through the spoken word and their physical being."
- From Tom Diamond, former public speaking instructor at Montana State University: "Don't fall in love with the bells and whistles of PowerPoint." He always cautioned us all to not lose sight of the message due to the medium.
- From *Pocket Keys for Speakers* by Isa Engleberg and Ann Raimes: "Don't become one of those speakers who prepares a speech by preparing a series of slide images. Begin with your ideas, not with computer software. Outstanding speakers prepare their presentations *before* creating their presentation aids."
- From Me: "Do your outline first, then build your PowerPoint. Many people do the PowerPoint first, putting way too much detail on their slides, and then they back in the outline requirement for this course. That is exactly back-asswards."

- From *Presentations Plus* by David Peoples: "You are the message; you are the prime medium. . . . Your power to project as a human being, to interact warmly and intelligently with the audience . . . cannot be duplicated by any kind of electronics. . . . The bigger the electronic extravaganza, the smaller the presenter becomes. . . . You may be viewed as an usher in your own theater. . . . The credibility of you as a human being can decline as your reliance on high tech goes up." I say, "Wow."
- From totalcommunicator.com, an August 2008 reprint of a 2004 article entitled "Visuals Can Power Your Presentation—If you know how to use them." (no author): "Lately, magazines have been popping up with titles like 'More Power than Point' and 'Friends Don't Let Friends Use PowerPoint.' Some critics even want to eliminate PowerPoint or other visuals altogether. Why the backlash? Because too many presenters simply fail to use visuals correctly."
- From my favorite article on this topic, "Absolute PowerPoint; Can a Software Package Edit Our Thoughts," by Ian Parker, published in *The New Yorker*, May 28, 2001: "Before there were presentations, there were conversations, which were a little like presentations but used fewer bullet points, and no one had to dim the lights. . . . Because PowerPoint can be an impressive antidote to fear—converting public-speaking dread into movie-making pleasure—there seems to be no great impulse to fight this influence. . . . Instead of human contact, we are given human display."

As that last article indicates, we all crave another human's touch. If PowerPoint is beginning to alienate audiences and remove this human "touch," we must revisit its purpose. I am sensing a type of revolution "out there, somewhere" which is *screaming:* "If you turn out the lights one more minute, and turn your back on me one more time, and read another busy slide to me once again, I shall kill you." It might be my imagination.

> *"PowerPoint is not the answer to giving a good speech; I am.*
>
> **—Blaine Towles, MSU student**

Here are some **hints for the PowerPoint equipment:**

- Do NOT plan your entire presentation in PowerPoint; mix in other types of aids to better create movement, audience interaction, and vocal variation—and it gives you a reason to turn the lights on and off.

- Do NOT depend on it for critical sections; have a backup for Murphy's Law.
- DO bring in your own laptop, and make a backup of your slides on a USB mini-driver (memory stick) so you could borrow a laptop if necessary.
- DO have "backups for your backups" for real-world, professional presentations.
- Hopefully, the school/business can provide the LCD projector; if not, you may have to bring one yourself from a friend, your own department, or a rental.
- Always, always, always *test your equipment before the day of the speech!*

And some **hints for the actual PowerPoint slides** (also transparencies.)

- Every expert source I've seen says to just use ONE main idea per slide.
- Landscape (horizontal) layouts are generally preferred over Portrait (vertical).
- I think a dark, big font on a light background is best for slides; if you use a dark background, you usually need to turn off all the lights to view the presentation.
- Most books talk about a six and six rule; no more than six lines on a PowerPoint slide, and no more than six words per line.
- Try to keep the text in the upper two-thirds of the slide; leave the bottom blank.
- Definitely avoid full sentences; use "key words" or sentence fragments so the audience can digest them more quickly and you will read less from them.
- Keep things simple; avoid too many colors, font changes, or clip art clutter.
- In most professional presentations, the background for each slide will be the same, usually with some company logo or symposium theme in the corner of each.
- Try to use some photos or artwork to enliven the "dry" lists.
- DO YOUR OUTLINE FIRST, and THEN PLAN YOUR POWERPOINT. You may think you're saving time, but you'll have more effective slides if you plan them on paper first. An edited product is always better than a first cut.

I assume most people know the basics of building a PowerPoint presentation, since most people have to use it in high school today. If you need help, ASK. Friends can usually get you started, and then computer lab technicians can clarify the fine points. Jump in and get your hands dirty now because PowerPoint is clearly the norm in the real world. When used properly, electronic aids really can make your presentation "sharp."

Costuming

The first hint of a "sharp" speech will come directly from you, for **YOU are the first visual aid the audience will see.** My old buddy, Randy Durham, used to say, "Nothing is as important as looking good. If you look good, you act good, and if you act good, people think you're good and treat you good, so nothing is as important as just looking gooood."

A common line in public speaking is "Dress to Impress" or "Dress for Success." I stress to at least dress "nicer than normal" for academic speeches. In many business classes, instructors require students to wear coat and tie or a dress for graded speeches. In the real world, people always usually most likely dress up, but that's defined by the situation. What I do know is this: If you put on your favorite outfit, you will stand up straighter and act more confident, I promise. The audience will note the extra effort on your part, and they will also sit up straighter and pay more attention. Some of them.

"Costuming" per se is good because it touches the Halloween child in all of us. It's fun, and it can help to loosen up both speaker and audience. Here are some costuming hints:

- The most common "costume" I see is just dressing up; It says, "I'm an adult."
- *Sports* Costumes: If you're talking about a particular sport or a famous athlete, you might dress up as a soccer player or wear that #23 Chicago Bulls jersey.
- *Rodeo:* Does it surprise you that I hear a lot of speeches about rodeo in Montana? I love to see the gold in the buckle and the boots and chaps and cowboy hats, and the spurs and the latigo, and they call the thing rodeo. (Thank you, Garth.)
- *Hunting:* Does it surprise you that I hear a lot of speeches about hunting in Montana? Those people wear camouflage clothing, so I can't always see them.
- *Fly Fishing, Snow Skiing, Hiking, Biking, Kayaking, all those "ings."* Does it surprise you that all such outdoor activities lend themselves to good speeches and fun costuming? One of the main points is often the clothing required.
- *Professions:* If you're telling us to donate blood, you might dress up like a doctor or nurse. If you're telling us not to drink and drive, you could dress up like a policeman. I've seen lawyers, professors, car mechanics, cooks, and soldiers.
- *Gimmicks:* It does not fit most people's personalities to wear a full costume, but I see many gimmicks that are worn that relate to the topic. If you persuade us to vote, you could wear a big "Vote!" button. Some people

wear a funny nametag. If it's a nerdy (smart) topic, I might see a pocket protector full of pens. I had a group speech once about Dr. Seuss, and the whole group wore Cat-in-the-Hat hats. We-thought-it-was-fun fun. Another group wore clothing made of duct tape.

- *Hats and T-shirts:* Very common, since they can reflect the school, state, or band you are describing. They can also be special ordered with a particular slogan that could match your topic directly, such as "Free Tibet!" or "Drink Water!"

Yes, costuming can be cheesy, but **a little cheese goes a long way in a speech.** If you have never tried costuming, why not try it in academia first? Experiment. Be brave. Remember, you're only limited by your own imagination. Whatever you decide about costuming, the caution is *don't wear something that would create a distraction* for your audience. I'm thinking of clothing with rips and tears, dirty clothing, terribly wrinkled shirts, short shorts that are too short, sunglasses and hats that hide your eyes, huge hoop earrings, too much "bling," and t-shirts with profanity on them. Nose rings and multiple piercings can be fascinating for a college audience, but very distracting around young kids or senior citizens. You don't want to get objections from your fans. Hey, let's talk objects!

Objects

I like to define "objects" as anything you can hold in your hands, or at least touch. There are some very good reasons why objects are good for a speech:

- Objects are another way to "bring out the child" in us
- 3-D objects make us think of toys, and we still like toys
- Objects remind us of "Show and Tell" in grade school; we smile
- Objects include "presents," like candy or handouts, and we like presents
- Objects can relax the speaker: bring your favorite stuffed animal with you, or a framed photo of your family, or that fishing rod that defines your weekends
- Objects can help set the mood of the speech: If you're describing yoga, you might burn some incense or light some candles. A cooking/health topic could cover a tabletop with objects from the kitchen. Shovels and rakes leaning against a table that is holding plants could help set the mood for a talk on gardening.
- If your speech was about an object, it would be nice to show that object. My classroom has held bikes and kites, canoes and kayaks, pots and paintings, tools and tires.
- If you pass an object around class, you can appeal to our sense of touch.

Some of the more common objects I've seen in speeches:

- *Posters:* Anything that can be put on a slide or transparency could also be put on a poster. You might use a poster to emphasize a main point by leaving it up while you cover some sub-points with other aids. A poster could display definitions that you might use several times or a map that shows several places you'll describe. Because they are hard to see, posters work better with smaller audiences, like twenty to thirty people. I like posters because they give the speaker a reason to move out from behind the podium; it gives you something to point to and touch, which creates natural gestures. Posters can showcase the *speaker's* artistic talent rather than the talent of Microsoft engineers. (If you have a talent, find a way to use it.)
- *Flipcharts:* These are the large pads of paper that sit on an easel, seen more in real-world business meetings than a classroom. You can write on it ahead of time, like a poster, or you can use it like a blackboard and emphasize information as you talk. It tends to get the audience more involved because you are flipping big pieces of paper close to them. Have you watched Demetri Martin, a comedian who uses flipcharts? Very funny guy.
- *Handouts:* If you really want us to remember your information, give us a handout. You can make handouts "busier" than a slide because people can study them later on their own time. For that reason, **don't give out handouts until after your presentation**. ("Here, I took notes for you; this is the key information I think you need to remember.") If you give them out before the talk, make sure they are simple, more like an outline or a note-taking device to better follow your speech. Otherwise, they might read the material rather than listen to you.

- *Pamphlets:* These are usually commercially made handouts, and they can vary quite a bit in length and detail. When you do your research, you can obtain pamphlets from an organization that promotes the given cause. The Red Cross does pamphlets on donating blood; dentists do pamphlets on tooth care. These type items can be nice "presents" for your audience—*after* your talk.
- *Maps:* Maybe it's the old navigator in me, but I love maps! I'm talking about an actual map, one you unfold, making some noise! Tack or tape it to the wall. It might also go on posterboard on a tripod, or maybe you can have some friends hold it up. You can move around and touch it, or maybe draw on it.
- *Pictures/Paintings:* These can be big or small; original or copies; commercial or private. If *you* took the photo or did the painting yourself, the object means more. I think it's okay to pass around a few small photos because they don't take much attention away from you. I often see original work from my photography and art majors, and it always gets a great reaction. (If you have such talent, display it!)
- *Models:* I had a student talk about Maryland crabs, and she built a large, cardboard model of one and asked two friends to hold it up. As she described how to eat a crab, she removed the "shell" and showed us the insides. "You can eat the green stuff here, but not the yellow stuff here!" Very fun speech; memorable.
- *Food:* If you talk about organic farming or your grandmother's cheesecake recipe, you need to show us some food. And, hopefully, you'll feed us! I tell my students, "If you feed us, it's probably an 'A' speech." Don't just tease our sense of taste, give us some chocolate! One gimmick that's fun is to ask a few direct, simple questions to get the audience involved, and reward answers with candy.
- *Animals:* Some places will not allow animals, but remember that it's easier to beg forgiveness than to get permission. I've seen snakes and spiders, falcons and ferrets, turtles and tomcats, mice and men.
- *People:* Yeah, I classify people as objects under my BECOT formula. Friends can display dance moves, judo kicks, or proper weight-lifting techniques. Friends could be actors in a short, cheesy skit about "No means no!" I've had parents bring in their special needs children during talks on the Special Olympics. I saw a sober roommate packed into a duffle bag once. Just once. You, yourself, are not only the first visual aid we see, you are the best one. Get excited! Be a little animated! Don't just "tell us" if you can also "show us." Have some fun. Smile. (This brief commercial for Chapter Six was brought to you by your phobias.)

There are some definite **cautions** to consider **with** the use of **objects**:

- *Animals and small children don't always act the way you want* during a speech, in front of a bunch of strangers. You must be prepared to clean up their messes and perhaps remove them from the room. It's best to have a friend available to do this.
- *Animals can really scare people*, or touch off their allergies. I've had several talks on how harmless pit bulls are, and I've had audience members who wanted to leave the room when the pit bull came in. Always ask your instructor/audience for permission a day or more earlier before you introduce an animal to them.
- *Practice with your friends* who might help you demonstrate something. Let them know exactly what you want. No one wants to be surprised by your impromptu comment, "No, no, that's not right. Here, let's do it again." (Yes, I've seen that.)
- *DO NOT PULL PEOPLE FROM THE AUDIENCE:* No one wants to be "volunteered" for your speech. I've seen real-world speakers pull people up on the stage with them: "Come on up! Come on! It will be okay; I won't hurt you." That might be acceptable in a Vegas nightclub act, but not in a normal speech. If you talk to the "volunteer" beforehand and agree to make it look spontaneous, okay.
- *Don't stop talking* while using the object. Especially in demonstration speeches, I've seen people just stop talking while they add ingredients and stir the pot. That's okay for ten seconds or so, but not a full minute. Think of those cooking shows on TV and, "BAM!," you'll be okay. (Thank you, Emeril.)

I hope all this advice on sensory aids has been rather "transparent." Hang on, there's only one more letter in the BECOT alphabet.

Transparencies

Note: Everything I say here about transparencies also applies to Elmos, those very cool document projectors that display books, papers, and any object. An Elmo is very expensive, however, so don't expect to see one in small classrooms. That's why overhead transparency projectors are still very popular.

Some of my students think it's really "old school" that I still use an overhead projector with transparencies or an Elmo in my lectures, rather than using 100%

PowerPoint. Part of my rationale is that, well, I'm old. I'm simply not as comfortable with PowerPoint as they are, and you have to be comfortable with your sensory aids. There are other reasons why transparencies are still good for me:

- *Currency:* I often read an article in the paper at 8 A.M. that I can copy onto a transparency for use in my 10 A.M. lecture.
- *Local Media Photos:* I often copy a photo from a local source, especially if it shows one of my students in lecture that day. Such photos might not be online.
- *Theft:* I regularly steal transparencies from students, which I easily slide into my stack of lecture or classroom aids that I might use an hour later.
- *Time:* I do use PowerPoint at least 50% of the time, but I . . . am . . . really . . . slow making the slides. If I'm only adding/changing one slide in a lecture, transparencies are faster for me.
- *Multiple Screens:* I always use two screens when I lecture, sometimes three. I like to get eyeballs moving around, and I like to have a side screen displaying a main point while I use the center screen to show sub-point examples. If I did that with PowerPoint, I would need two whole different systems; that's expensive.
- *Personal Items:* I might display an overhead photo of my daughters, Morgan and Lindsay (and my son-in-law Aaron), in their band uniforms if I tell the story about their band going to the Rose Bowl. I might display a copy of my college transcript if I want to prove to people I am not an engineer. (Yes, I could scan such items into my computer, too, if I had time. . . .)
- *Writing Notes:* I can use an audio-visual pen to write on a computer-generated transparency to make a point or even a reminder to myself to do something. I also put yellow sticky notes right on my transparencies for such personal prompts.
- *Hand-Drawing:* I can also write an administrative note on a clean transparency if I think of something just moments before lecture: "Who left the Little Mermaid lunch box in class?" I could draw a sketch of the mermaid with color pens.
- *Cover Ups:* I can put a piece of paper over the transparency and cover up portions I don't want the audience to see yet. PowerPoint has a "slide in" feature that essentially does the same thing, but you have to push more buttons.
- *Flexibility:* This is the biggee for me. Transparencies allow me to better think on my feet and edit my presentation as it's happening. If I decide to delete/reinforce something, I can easily pull out a slide or grab an earlier slide and use it again. It bothers me to see speakers get rushed for time and click through numerous slides without explanation so they can get to their conclusion aids.

I can't think of any unique cautions for transparencies, except don't drop them and mix them all up, and don't spill water on them. Oh, and I suppose you can spend too much money on them if you get them all done in color at a commercial copy center. Learn how to print them on your own printer at home. Just be sure to get the right kind of transparencies; some are for copy machines and some are for your printer. Ask. Finally, if you're not using the overhead projector, turn it off. Note: The hints for making transparency slides are identical to the PowerPoint hints shown earlier in this chapter, on page 74.

PowerPoint gurus would argue that their program can really have all the same good points I just described for transparencies, and I would not debate that. (But I would have to say transparencies have fewer mechanical problems, and therefore less stress.) I love the impact of transparency overlays for comparisons, for example, but computers can do that, too, if you know how. Overall, I try to get people to use both mediums, mainly because it causes a shift in audience's eyes and senses, and it creates movement for you. In other words, *use as much BECOT as possible to "Mix Up the Air!"*

GUIDELINES (PRACTICAL)

Malcolm Kushner, author of *Successful Presentations for Dummies*, quotes Allatia Harris, Dean of the Communications Division at Mountain View Community College, Dallas, Texas:

> *There are two things to remember about visual aids. Number one, they should be visual. Number two, they should aid.*

Those are probably the only two guidelines you really need, but here are some more specific, practical hints that apply to all of the BECOT items:

Do I Need a Sensory Aid?

- Have at least one aid for each main point, if not each sub-point
- If you find yourself making a list of things in your outline, make an aid
- Always use an aid for your purpose, preview, and summary statements
- Always try to work in a short video clip, and maybe some music
- If you're talking about dates and key events, make a timeline aid

- If you're talking about a person, show the name in writing and maybe a photo
- If you're talking about a place, show us a map
- If you're talking about a comparison, show us a chart or a graph
- If you're talking about an object, show us that object
- If you're talking about an animal, show us the animal or a picture of it (Be sure to obtain permission to bring in an animal)
- If you're talking about beer or wine or alcohol, probably don't show it (You could bring in "simulated" booze: water in empty containers)
- Do not bring in any weapons or something that could seem like a weapon
- If it's really important data, consider making a handout, and definitely have a backup aid to display the information during the speech
- Definitely dress up for your speech, or maybe use some costuming
- Overall, what are you comfortable with? What do you like to use?

Making/Planning Sensory Aids

- **Check Spelling!** Use spell check, but also use friends. Spell check won't catch it's vs its, there vs their, effect vs affect, to vs too, or your vs you're. (See page 243 for a spelling test!)
- Mostly, flip back to page 74 and review hints for PowerPoint slides
  - Keep aids simple! Key words only, six lines only
  - Use big, dark fonts with simple print, not fancy script
  - Mix in photos and clip art a little bit with your words
  - Consider light backgrounds vs dark ones
- Use color when possible, but avoid yellow or orange lettering
- Practice with your aids, especially electronic aids
- Make sure you have all the equipment you need (See Chapter Two, "Where Will It Happen?", page 31)
- Overall, what do you have the time, money, and expertise to make?

Using Aids During the Speech

- Position your aids before the speech to create natural movement and to ensure everyone can see the objects, especially posters
- Make slides easy to see; put them high on the screen and get out of the way
- Talk about your aid, don't just show it
- Talk to your audience, not the aid
- Don't let the aid talk for you
- Don't just read the aid to us; try to explain it in your own words (Exception: Do read cartoons to us . . . and don't try to explain the humor)
- If you made the aid, drew the picture, or took the photo, tell us. If you are in the photo, show us.
- Don't reveal the aid until you use it
- After you use it, remove it (It's very common to leave an aid showing for too long)
- Pointers, both traditional and laser, can be helpful, but don't bang them on the podium or in your hand, and don't point lasers at the audience.
- Generally, do not pass things around the audience during a short speech (Simple items that don't require concentration might be okay, like photos)
- "Busy" items, like handouts/pamphlets, should be given after the speech
- Overall, use a variety of aids to enhance understanding and retention

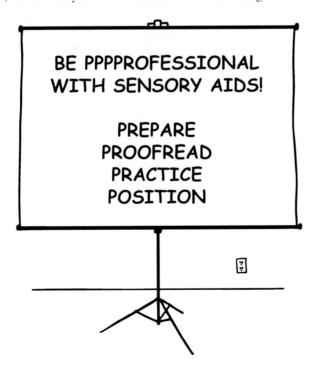

Your mission, should you choose to accept it, is to boldly go where no speaker has gone before, to explore new worlds of sensory aids, to show me the money and Aim High and ask not what your audience can do for you, but what you can do for your audience. If I can mix metaphors and story lines, you can mix sensory aids, probably more effectively.

SUMMARY CHECKLIST FOR SENSORY AIDS

Principles (Theory)

- ❏ Sensory aids are the cure-all for all the ills of public speaking
- ❏ With aids, you can cover more material more effectively in less time
- ❏ Aids help delivery, understanding, credibility, and the "human factor"
- ❏ Sensory aids appeal to the left brain and right brain in all of us
- ❏ They can appeal to all five of our senses, sight being the most important
- ❏ Aids "Make Me A Memory!"
- ❏ Variety is the spice of life

Variety of Sensory Aids (BECOT) "Don't BECOT without Sensory Aids"

- ❏ **B**lackboard: Traditional, simple; good to list topic, preview, names, numbers
- ❏ **E**lectronic: Modern, complex; PowerPoint; TV with DVD, VCR, or digital camera; CD and cassette player; lights, electric instruments, and anything that plugs in
- ❏ **C**ostuming: Dress to impress, not to distract; anything on your body that relates to topic, like t-shirts, hats, ties, buttons, pins; could wear sports/outdoors clothing
- ❏ **O**bjects: Bring out the child in us; any 3-D object you could hold up; includes posters, handouts, pamphlets, maps, books, models, food, animals, and people
- ❏ **T**ransparencies: Much the same advantages of PowerPoint, in a simpler form; can be handwritten or made with computer and printer; can also print on copy machine
- ❏ Video/Music extremely powerful: Think Michael Phelps video with Rocky theme
- ❏ Variety is only limited by your imagination

Guidelines (Practical)

- ❑ Do the outline on paper first, THEN build your visual aids
- ❑ Edit, edit, edit
- ❑ Keep It Simple, Stupid (KISS); see Chapter Eight
- ❑ Keep it visual; make sure everyone can see it
- ❑ Keep it human; *Look at us* and *Talk to us* rather than look at screen and read to us (Remember that it is a speech, not your granpappy's 35mm slide show)
- ❑ Practice with your aids and ensure you have all the equipment you need
- ❑ Check the spelling so that ye shall not have to play the phool

I want you to be an expert, so let's move on and talk about organization!

Chapter 5
ORGANIZATION

PLAN THE FLIGHT, FLY THE PLAN!

Note: I flew airplanes for ten years, and I have been teaching public speaking twenty-five years. I see many similarities between the two activities (I could be biased), especially in terms of the "checklist mentality" that is vital to both. I am talking basic organizational skills. You MUST "stay ahead of your airplane," or you crash.

Plan the flight, fly the plan. That was one of the first, and most important, lessons I learned at Undergraduate Navigator Training. (It's also great "antithesis," but that's another story for another page.) Navigation is a science, but it also has a lot of "art" mixed in. In other words, there is "procedure" you *must* follow, but also "technique" you *might* follow:

- Procedure: You must have an outline—(a plan), to follow before you give a speech.
- Technique: You can use your own style to develop the outline that works for you.

I think Public Speaking is an art (technique) with some science (procedure) mixed in, and that science is clearly reflected in the outlines. "Plan the outline, then fly the outline." (A speech can't be on autopilot, so yes, you have to hand-fly it.) In the Air Force, we used to do "arm-chair" flying before a mission. We would plan out everything, spending maybe four hours planning for every one hour of flying. Then we would literally sit in a chair and fly the mission in our minds. We would "What If?" everything, discussing how we might react if things went wrong. In speech, we call this "practice your speech before you give it." Speech, like flying, is not magic. It's not Harry Potter buzzing around on his old Nimbus or new Firebolt. It's mostly organizational skills.

GENERAL ORGANIZATION

"ORDER MARCHES WITH WEIGHTY AND MEASURED STRIDES; DISORDER IS ALWAYS IN A HURRY."
- NAPOLEON, MAXIMS (1804-1815)

If you procrastinate, if you wait until the last minute to put your speech together, you will be in a hurry, and you will crash and burn. (That's my scary metaphor for the day.) I'm not telling you anything different here than what your parents have told you all your life. In college, however, your parents aren't around. Some new freshmen, on their own for the first time, do not make the transition to college very well. They party too much and study too little, and they procrastinate on everything. The biggest single reason for poor college speeches, and nervousness, is . . . (drum roll, please) *procrastination!* It is, quite frankly, epidemic. Rather than see you fall victim to an epidemic, we instructors would love to see you . . . become . . . epic.

The greatest enemy of procrastination is organization! The biggest difference I see between good and poor students is organization. To keep with the flying analogy, organization is the way you combat the flying monkeys from the *Wizard of Oz*. I hate those monkeys! (That's my fun metaphor for the day.) Organization is not easy.

> *It takes two weeks to organize a great ten-minute talk.*
> *It takes one week to plan a good one-hour talk.*
> *If you want me to talk two hours, I'm ready to go right now.*
>
> **—President Woodrow Wilson**

The most obvious sign of a disorganized speech is that it goes way, way too long. Most people can get up and "ramble" their way through a speech, but to do it effectively in the time allowed takes solid organization/planning. The audience knows when you are organized, and they will listen better and remember longer. They will also like you better because you did not waste their time. I regularly hear that students spent four to six hours to put together a good eight-minute talk, but it's not unusual to learn that someone spent twelve hours. Some of those long planners love their topics and just keep researching, and some are teaching themselves how to do PowerPoint, but some are simply not that organized in how they research or plan a speech. Here are some basic steps to follow:

Twenty Overt Speech Steps

Surveys
Media
Internet
Library
Experts

1. Learn all the assignment requirements/parameters
2. Get a general idea of the topic
3. Start your research
4. Determine the main points for your body

5. Gather good support (CENTS) with more research (SMILE)
6. Narrow your topic/purpose
7. Brainstorm good sensory aids (BECOT)
8. *Outline the body*, with audience in mind
9. Get away from it for a while; have some fun
10. Edit/delete to streamline the body
11. *Outline introduction* and *conclusion*
12. Add some style points (Chapter 11)
13. Edit/delete outline one more time
14. Prepare sensory aids
15. Add prompts for aids, cites, delivery
16. Do bibliography
17. Practice (once or twice, out loud)
18. Pray (once or twice, out loud)
19. Deliver the speech
20. Receive wild applause

Comparisons
Examples
Numbers
Testimony
Stories

Blackboard
Electronics
Costuming
Objects
Transparencies

Twenty **O**vert **S**peech **S**teps. Hmmmm? "TOSS" those around a bit and see if they don't make sense. Please note that you do the introduction *after* the body. (I'll come back to that thought later.) Those steps are procedure, I think, but the order you do them in could certainly be technique. The time you spend on each step is certainly up to your style. Let me offer some random ideas that might help you stay organized in general:

• Once you start a speech/writing assignment, keep some paper handy where you can jot down ideas *as they happen* . . . even in your dreams.

• As you research, jot down the bibliographical data you'll need from each source at the top of a page, and then take notes on that page, so you'll always know what material came from what source. Disorganization can ruin a bibliography.

• Take actual notes to record your CENTS vs copying whole pages off the Internet, which are very difficult to organize. You could also highlight sections of pages you think you'll use, and then cut those out like separate notes.

• Once you decide upon main points and sub-points, cut and paste your research notes (CENTS) under those headings. If material does not fit, you might need to create new sub-points or delete part of your research or outline.

• Find a place (including the trash) for all your research, and then sit back and see if you have too much or too little material for each section.

• Staples and folders do a nice job of compartmentalizing your notes and thoughts by sub-points, then you can stack up your piles in order and write your outline.

YOU MUST OUTLINE!

Each semester I ask my students a question: "Do outlines save you time?" Every semester, several people quickly say, "Yes!" Then I ask who actually does an outline prior to a speech or paper, and only 10–20 percent of the hands go up. Outlines *do* save time because they organize your thoughts more quickly and allow you to catch errors that eat up time later, so why don't more people use them? The left brain says it's logical and organized to do outlines, but the right brain says it's too hard and unnecessary. The instructor says that better speeches have better outlines.

Why Do Outlines?

Ken Alstad and those *Savvy Sayin's* had some great advice: "Before you go into a canyon, know how you'll get out." Outlines will help.

- *Logic:* Put your topic/purpose at the top of the outline, and then bounce everything you want to say off that purpose. Does it fit? Does it answer the mail? Does each part of your CENTS actually make sense?
- *Flow:* Do the main points flow well from one to the other? Can you connect the points with smooth transitions, or are you jerking your audience around? Have a well-planned introduction/conclusion to smoothly get in and out of the speech?
- *Balance:* Does each main point have roughly the same amount of material and will it take roughly the same amount of time? If one main point is two pages and another is two lines, something is wrong. The long one might actually be two or three main points; the short one might just be an example, not a main point.
- *Time:* Outlines should easily show you if you have too much information for the time allowed. From my experience watching thousands of speeches, one page of double-spaced notes is roughly five minutes. If you use the same style outline for three speeches, you'll have a great idea of what a page of notes means for you in terms of time. You can put time ticks on your outline and think in terms of three short speeches (three main points) vs one long talk. Ask yourself, "How long will it take me to do each section of my outline?"
- *Notes:* Your outline becomes your best notes to deliver the speech

The whole **purpose of an outline** is to **help you remember "most" of what you want to say.** It is *your* outline to help you, not an outline for your audience or instructor. (I don't look at student outlines during a speech; I listen. If it's a good talk, it will be a good outline.) **It's a guideline, not a mandatory checklist.** If you leave something out, we won't know it, and it probably wasn't that important. So, let your outline become your notes. I am very suspicious of neat, clean, perfect outlines hot off the printer. I love to see dog-eared outlines with pen and ink changes, some lines scratched out, and coffee and ketchup stains. That is a plan you have carried around a while, thinking about it, and editing and polishing into a better speech. Please don't think of outlines as an extra step. Some people can actually "outline" in their heads, but most of us need to put pen to paper to better see the big picture (skeleton) before we start adding the support (meat). As one of my students said, "Outlines are like my little invisible friend." (Thanks, Kyle.)

Types of Outlines

Before you decide on the type of outline to use, you need to decide which delivery method you will use. A combination of these methods, which is often the case, actually calls for a combination of outline types. I will go into more detail on **delivery methods** next chapter, but here are your basic options:

- *Manuscript:* You read every word to us, so you must write out every word
- *Memorization:* You memorize every word, so write out every word
- *Impromptu:* On the spot, no real planning, so you plan out no words on paper
- *Extemporaneous:* (Pick me! Pick me!) The best delivery method because it is the most natural, most effective, and most audience centered. Use key words.

Some people think extemporaneous and impromptu are the same, and if you look those words up in a dictionary, you can build a case for that argument. All speech texts today, however, clearly separate the two: **Impromptu means little or no planning, while extemporaneous entails much planning.** In my mind, extemporaneous is the only delivery method to use in a speech class, mainly because you don't have to be totally politically correct (which is why politicians read their speeches), and it allows you to be more spontaneous and therefore adapt better to your audience. You can still employ the best aspects of each method, so you can read some short sections of an exact quote or company policy, you can memorize a short poem or joke, or you can even offer a totally impromptu example or story if something spurs your imagination. Mostly, the extemporaneous style makes you talk more naturally since you only have key words to look at—so *every time you give the speech it would be different* from the time before. Some people equate it to jazz music; the basic form and content are always the same, but the style and exact wording can change as you get feedback from the audience. I like all that jazz . . . and I bet you hard rockers like it when the band just jams a bit, right?

Some people believe the best way to create a speech outline is to write out every word, and then go back and underline just the "key words" you think you need to remember most of what you want to say. Then list those underlined words on your outline, and speak from that. If you want to teach yourself how to outline, try that method; it does work. Getting most students to actually write out every word, however, is like pulling teeth. Just use key words, but use all **four types of outlines** below, in order:

1. *Brainstorm Outline:* Your initial listing of any ideas; random order
2. *Rough Draft Outline:* Basic order of main and sub-points in body; place the CENTS under each category; plan some BECOT; edit and revise
3. *Speaker Outline:* The finished product of what you'll actually use, complete with introduction, body with main points, conclusion, and prompts for where you'll use sensory aids and when you'll cite your sources out loud. Add bibliography.
4. *Audience Outline:* Whatever words you may share with the audience directly, either on a slide or a handout; these lists could look much different than your speaker outline

Outline Steps

Outlining, like any building project, is best done in steps, with a break in between major steps. Your first big step is to **brainstorm** everything in your head that has to do with your topic; get it down *on paper!* Show it to some friends; what do they think? When they think of your topic, what main points and what type of support would they expect to hear? Then, start some *exploratory research*. Get online and spend an hour to see if your brainstorm ideas seem to work; change them if you find something better. Then get away from your brainstorm outline for a while. Go to the gym instead of McDonald's.

Your second big step is to do a **rough draft,** focusing just on the *body* of the speech. Do some *serious research*, looking specifically for a variety of CENTS. (Comparisons, Examples, Numbers, Testimony, Stories.) Put each small piece of support on a separate small piece of paper, and spread them all out on a table. It should look like a puzzle because that's really what an outline is. Instead of grouping all the blue pieces together in one pile and all the edge pieces with straight lines into another pile, however, you will group together pieces that seem to support the same lesson, the same sub-point in your outline. Then, you can better align the sub-points under the appropriate main point. You can see if you have too much support overall (time control), and you can see if you have too much support in one area (balance). You can see if the support really fits with your topic (logic), or maybe you got some pieces from another puzzle box by mistake. Oops. You can see if the pieces will really fit together without forcing them into place (flow). You can start brainstorming what sensory aids you might use. It's not a finished picture yet, not by a long shot, but you're seeing the structure, and you feel better. You know you can do this now. Your rough outline is done, so you deserve another break to clear your head, at least a few hours. Go work on a puzzle of Yellowstone Park. . . .

Breaks are very important. You *need* to get away from your research/outline for a while in order to clear your head and "back away" so that you can still see the mountain in spite of the trees. You will always have a better product if you come back to your outline with a fresh mind and edit/revise again. (**Your hardest task is deciding what NOT to say.**) Therefore, if you procrastinate and rush every-

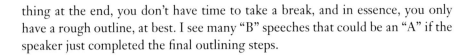

thing at the end, you don't have time to take a break, and in essence, you only have a rough outline, at best. I see many "B" speeches that could be an "A" if the speaker just completed the final outlining steps.

Your third big step is to develop your **speaker outline,** the one you will actually use during your presentation. You'll probably do a bit more research and "polish" the support in your rough draft. Make most of your sensory aids (but wait on your "lists"). Add your handwritten prompts to remind you of aids, citations of sources, and any delivery cues you personally want. Add the introduction and conclusion, and write your bibliography. You might also add some extra "style" points by planning your transitions and some clever word use, like similes or metaphors, if that's your style.

Your last step is to make your **audience outlines,** which are the "lists" you will share with your audience. Most of them will be on overhead or PowerPoint slides; some could be on note-taking devices or summary handouts. The slides and note-taking devices should be even more edited/ streamlined than your speaking outline (please don't show us your whole outline on a transparency), but the handouts could have more detail since the audience will get them after your speech and can study them on their own time. All audience outlines, *especially PowerPoint*, should be done after your own speaking outline, and after some thoughtful editing, or they will simply be another type of rough draft, usually too wordy or "busy" with graphics, often distracting, and sometimes illogical. This order of events is my biggest complaint with PowerPoint.

> PowerPoint is NOT your outline!
> It is an aid to your speech, done after your outline.

Note: Let me add a note here about note cards. *Note cards, also, are not your outline.* (I want you to note this.) People who use note cards to speak usually prepare them at the last minute, with way too many words and scribbled additions on them, so the cards are sloppy and hard to fol-low. Therefore, speakers concentrate on their cards more than on the audience, and their heads are down more than up. They tend to hold the cards with two hands, which pulls their shoulders together and for-ward more, hurting their posture. If you do your speaker outline first, note cards can be very effective for such things as verbatim quotes, exact statistics, or reading a short passage from a government document. In other words, think of note cards as another "aid" to your speech instead of your whole speaker outline, and you'll be fine. Justine said this in a course critique: "I love outlines! Prior to this class, I was under the impression I had to use note cards, which always gave me trouble. They got mixed up or they were too small, and I had to look too closely at them. With outlines, I always know where I am and can quickly find my spot without being overtly obvious." I did not pay Justine to say that.

Wow. You've done a lot, taken a lot of steps. This is where you take a full twenty-four-hour break and really get away from your speech. Then come back and practice the speech once or twice (not ten times, so it won't be memorized and mechanical), make a few minor adjustments, eat a nice dinner, think nothing but positive thoughts about your speech tomorrow, go to bed early, and get a solid eight hours of sleep. (That Disney ride is called "Fantasy Speech.") Your outline is done, baby! Wanna know what it looks like?

Outline Mechanics

Since 1977, one of my best bibles for communication has been *Tongue and Quill*, the Air Force book used to help standardization in both speaking and writing. I have often preached a section of that book on outline formats:

> It's not necessary to be overly concerned with form in outlining. **Use any form that works!** Although most writing texts lay out elaborate formats for topic and sentence outlines, your purpose in outlining is to *arrange main and supporting ideas in a visible framework that permits you to see and test your logic on paper.* **There are no "absolutes" for organizing;** everyone has his or her own mental approach to the task.

Having said that, be aware that many instructors do mandate format. Just know the rules and follow them. The ones I see the most are fairly standardized, listed below. They do make sense, honest. I highly recommend them. I would call this list **PROCEDURE**:

- Use some symbols, and keep them consistent throughout
- If you use roman numerals, they should be farthest to the left
- If you use numbers and letters, alternate them at each level
- Don't use the same symbol at different levels

- Indent sub-points and sub-sub-points
- Points of equal value should be aligned throughout
- If you have an A, you must have a B; if you have a 1, have a 2
- Most experts say to start each line with a capital letter
- You should only have one idea per line
- Bibliography must follow proper MLA or APA format

What most of that means is your outline probably looks like this:

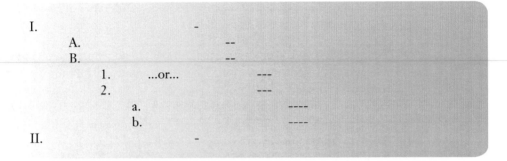

More important and practical, here are some great **<u>TECHNIQUES</u>** for outline mechanics:

- Key words, mostly! If you use full sentences, you'll read to us (Short readings are okay for verbatim quotes, so write those out)
- Make sure the main points are roughly balanced in length
- Plan the five parts of an introduction (coming soon, this chapter . . .)
- Plan the four parts of a conclusion
- TYPE your outline, always; it will then be engrained in your brain better and you won't have to use your outline as much during the talk
- Leave at least one-inch margins all around
- DOUBLESPACE some, at least between sub-points
- Use a BIG, **dark** font for easier reading
- Type on only one side of a page; slide your pages instead of flipping them
- Do not staple your outline (due to the "flipping" thing, again)
- Number your pages (if you drop them, they aren't stapled, duh)
- Definitely number note cards if you use them to supplement the outline (But anything that can go on a card can go on the typed outline paper, and three pieces of paper on a podium or table are easier than thirteen note cards.)
- Definitely use prompts

Prompts (also called delivery cues, or reminders) are little notes to yourself to remember to do something. They are the yellow stickies on your refrigerator and that string around your finger. Some people type their prompts on the outline, usually off to one side. They can be typed in **bold** print or *italics*, they can be <u>underlined</u> or in (parenthesis), and they can be BIG or little. Most often, I see handwritten prompts. Use your favorite colors! Sometimes I see yellow stickies come off the fridge and mark an important portion of the speech. Another favorite method is highlighters. (Be careful not to highlight too much, or nothing will be highlighted, don't ya know?) Some people use different colors for different **<u>types of prompts</u>**:

- *Sensory Aids:* Use a prompt for each sensory aid you'll use. Some folks just write VA in the margin for Visual Aid; some write OH for OverHead transparency; some use PPt for PowerPoint slides. Most people write out the name of the object they might use, such as book, hiking stick, or life-sized Jessica Alba poster :) "Video" and "Lights" are two common prompts.
- *Citations:* You should use a prompt for each citation you'll give, and all of your research sources should be mentioned, out loud, in the body of your speech, as you use them. More on this in Chapter Nine, Ethics.
- *Delivery Prompts:* If you know you need to work on eye contact or movement, you can write a prompt that says "Eyes!" or "Move!" I regularly see prompts that say "Smile" or "Be Louder." Sometimes I see "Pay Instructor." President Gerald Ford was giving an address once upon a time, and in between scripted lines he accidentally read a delivery prompt out loud on TV, "Look right into camera." You normally don't want to read your prompts out loud.

Before I leave the subject of outline mechanics, I want to mention **bibliographies.** I bet that 70 percent of the bibliographies I see are wrong. I often write, "Be more exact with format, even punctuation and spacing." Here are the most **common errors**:

- The entries are not listed in alphabetical order
- The second and third lines are not indented
- Entries begin with the author's first name, instead of last
- I see only the URL (Uniform Resource Locator) Web site address

Proper bibliographical format is just one of those awful, boring things you ultimately have to teach yourself. When I pick up a student outline, the first thing I look at is the bibliography. If it is formatted properly, it's usually a nice outline and speech. In other words, if a student cares enough to correctly complete a picky portion of the assignment, I know the big stuff will take care of itself. It's a great "first impression." Get a Modern Language Association (MLA) handbook, or go online at *http://mla.org*. Many textbooks show samples, and many instructors offer extra handouts. You can go to your local Writing Center for help, or ask your favorite English teacher. Maybe your roommate? I don't know. ***If you want to do a proper bibliography, you will.***

By the way, I prefer the label "Works Cited" for a speaker outline. I think it reinforces the thought that you should actually "cite" each source out loud. Just my opinion.

Whatever overall outline format you decide upon, try to develop some consistent, effective habits in school that will carry over into the workforce—habits that promote a more natural *extemporaneous* speaking style. Remember this analogy:

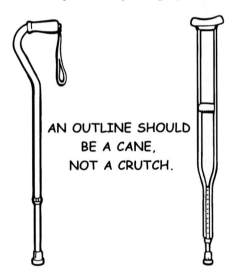

AN OUTLINE SHOULD
BE A CANE,
NOT A CRUTCH.

If you have to rely completely on your outline, it's like having to put your full weight on a crutch. A memorized or manuscript outline is a crutch, so if you forget the next line or lose your script, you fall down. You shouldn't try to memorize a whole speech, but it is possible to memorize the important parts of a key-word outline. You'll know the next big thing coming up (story; video clip) and you have sensory aids to offer you extra prompts. Glance down at your outline for quick reminders, and then your eyes are back up, with your audience. If you do that, the outline is a cane: nice to have for a little stability, but you won't fall down if a kid knocks it away with his skateboard.

LOGICAL PATTERNS

> EVERY DISCOURSE OUGHT TO BE A LIVING CREATURE; HAVING A BODY OF ITS OWN AND HEAD AND FEET; THERE SHOULD BE A MIDDLE, A BEGINNING, AND END, ADAPTED TO ONE ANOTHER AND TO THE WHOLE

We communicators love Plato, but we usually butcher his great quote and give this rather secular advice when we talk about the logical organization of a speech:

1. Tell 'em what yur gonna tell 'em (a beginning, the introduction)
2. Tell 'em (a middle, the body of the speech)
3. Tell 'em what ya told 'em (an end, the conclusion)

This very basic pattern is quite logical and easy to follow, and it's used in planning papers as well as speeches. In execution, however, there needs to be a different focus. If a reader gets confused with a writing pattern, he can stop and study it a while. If a listener gets confused with a speech pattern, she cannot stop the speaker (normally) and ask for help. Therefore, speakers need to be clearer and more overt with their organizational patterns and more conscious of their **logic flow.** In a very broad sense, your information should flow as follows:

- Big → small
- General → specific
- Known → unknown
- Simple → complex
- Old → new
- Past → present → future
- Least → most

- Worst → best
- Agree → disagree
- High school → college
- Pop → beer
- Popular → unpopular
- Common → uncommon
- First → last

You get the idea: Take us from what we can more easily understand into the brave new world of your more challenging ideas. Take us slowly. Take us in some logical order. As the King said, gravely, to Alice in Lewis Carroll's epic *Adventures in Wonderland*, "Begin at the beginning, and go til you come to the end; then stop."

BODY FIRST

Organize the body of your speech first, NOT the introduction. After all, "How ya gonna tell em what yur gonna tell 'em until you know what the heck yur gonna tell 'em?" I think Plato even understood this street wisdom, for he mentioned "body" before head and feet, and "middle" before beginning and end. I might be wrong; never talked to the man.

When you're working on your rough draft outline, you should have a pretty good idea of your main points. The classic academic speech has three main points, but I often see very credible talks with two or four main points. (If you have five points and only a ten-minute time limit, you have less than two minutes per point after you factor in intro/conclusion, and that's not easy.) Once you decide on your main points, you have to decide what order to put them in. Some popular **organization patterns** for the body are as follows:

- *Topical* (not tropical...): This is the most common pattern. Uses natural, logical divisions in a topic, and the *exact order is not critical*. If you're talking about why Auburn is such a great football team, you might discuss the players, the fans, and the coach, or you might want to start with the fans and end with the players. It really doesn't matter; any way you look at it, Auburn is still a great team. Yep.
- *Time:* Great for history explanations (how something evolved over time, like the wolf issue in Yellowstone Park). You can go past to present or present to past, but go in order; if you skip around on a timeline, you'll confuse us.
- *Order:* Great for demonstrations (basic first, second, third steps for making or doing something, like "How to Change Oil in a Car.") Uh, be sure to go in order. . . .
- *Spatial:* Great to explain how something is structured; start at some point in space and go in a logical sequence to other points. (Describe a rifle by talking about the sight, barrel, trigger housing, and stock. Describe a house by talking about upstairs, then downstairs, then the basement.) Be logical by going top to bottom, left to right, inside to outside, clockwise, or any of those opposite directions.

- *Geographic:* Used to explain the actual location or proximity of something. (Where are all the Air Force bases in the world? Where can you encounter mountain lions on a hike? Which countries affect our oil crisis?) If you show us a map, you are using geographic organization. If talking a sequence of places, you should go north to south or east to west vs. just jumping around the map.
- *Reason:* State an opinion ("You should stay in college") and then list the reasons (friends, money, respect). The reasons might be ordered according to other logic patterns, such as the least important reason to the most important.
- *Story:* Present information/opinions through one storyline, maybe even using characters, setting, and plot. (How I spent my fourth-grade summer vacation.) Could be real or fictional. A series of separate stories can also be effective, such as the impact of the WWII Holocaust told through the eyes of three different survivors.
- *Pro-Con:* Tell both sides of an issue (Abortion; pro-life vs pro-choice). If you just tell us each side, it's an informative speech. If you tell us both sides, and then tell us which side is best, and *why* we *need* to choose, you have a persuasion talk.
- *Cause and Effect:* Could talk about a cause and the effects, or an effect and its causes. (Drinking and driving can cause increased insurance costs, property damage, and death. Obesity is caused by lack of exercise, fast food, and big bones, right?)
- *Problem–Solution:* Define the nature and significance of a problem and offer solutions. (Steroids are hurting sports, so increase steroid danger education.)
- *Gimmick:* Look at your main points and create some mnemonic (memory) gimmick that makes it easier for your audience to remember your points. Remember why you should stay in college? Instead of saying Friends, Money, and Respect, you could re-label those points and create an alliteration gimmick pattern: Fun, Fortune, Fame. Put those three words on the board; we'll smile.

Story: I wanted to give a short speech on lecture hall etiquette. I brainstormed the rules I wanted to stress and then thought about a good order to present them. I ended up with a gimmick pattern (an acronym—a word created by the first letters of each main point), and then I asked students to get into the HABITT of good lecture etiquette:

Hand: Raise your hand at any time if I lose/confuse you, or you want to speak.

Asleep? If you're sleeping, I'll wake you up somehow, OK? It will be fun.

Bathroom: This is college; you don't need my permission to go to the bathroom.

Itch? If you itch, you may scratch; just be politically correct in your actions.

Trash: This is college; you can bring in drink/food, but clean up your trash, please.

Time: Please scream/yell or throw something at me if we are going overtime.

I need to stress that **very few speeches use just one of these organizational patterns.** You might have one big pattern for the main points, but each main point could have its own unique pattern for the sub-points. These patterns are not your only options; I bet you could think of one I did not describe. I see very few logic problems with organizational patterns. People may not know the technical name for a pattern, but they just seem to know a good, common-sense way to order the body of their speech. Knowing how to order the introduction and conclusion of a speech, however, is a different story.

Transition Commercial: Did you notice my last two sentences? One mentions my last point (body) and one mentions my next point (introductions). There is a contrasting transition word (however) that helps to connect the two. If you use some sort of transitions in your speech, the audience will move with you better into the next point—especially if you also use a visual aid to help the move. Most people seem to do fine with transitions, but again, they may not know the technical name for the types:

> **Four Cs**
> **C**omplementary
> **C**ausal
> **C**ontrasting
> **C**hronological

- *Complementary:* (Not complimentary) Adds one idea to another; words like *also, and, in addition, just as important, likewise,* and *not only.* Complementary transitions are good, *and* so are causal transitions.
- *Causal:* (Not casual) Emphasizes a cause-and-effect relation between two ideas; words like *as a result, because, consequently,* and *therefore.* I just described causal transitions; *therefore,* contrasting transitions must be next.
- *Contrasting:* Shows how two ideas differ; words like *although, but, in contrast, however, in spite of, nevertheless, on the contrary,* and *on the other hand.*

Chronological transitions, *on the other hand*, would use more time-related words.

- *Chronological:* Shows the time relationships between ideas; words like *after, as soon as, at last, at the same time, before, later, while.* (I also include some words here that other texts call **signposts,** which are much like transitions but technically tell the listener where you are in your speech: *first, second, third, finally.*) I like giving examples of transitions, but *at the same time,* I must move on. *Finally.*

I want to thank George Grice and John Skinner and their text *Mastering Public Speaking* for the "Four Cs" gimmick description of transitions. The gimmick is theirs, as well as the words in *italics.* The examples are mine, so it's Grice and Skinner's procedure and my technique. Some people, by the way, do actually use the technique of planning their transitions, in writing, on their outlines. If so, they might be the last item to format in your body.

INTRODUCTION/CONCLUSION LAST

Now that the body is done and you know exactly what your speech is really about, you can organize your introduction and conclusion. Here are the basic steps:

Five Steps of an Introduction

1. Attention Step: Do something quick to grab attention
2. Purpose Statement: Tell us the specific purpose of your speech
3. Motivation Step: Why should we listen to the *topic?*
4. Credibility Step: Why should we listen to *you?*
5. Preview: What are your main points?

Four Steps of a Conclusion

1. Restate Purpose: Same as your purpose statement above
2. Summary: What were your main points? (Same as preview)
3. Remotivation: Why should we remember your speech?
4. Closure: Do something quick to end on a positive note

As you can see, **a conclusion is much like an upside-down introduction, minus the credibility step.** Your credibility will soar in the body if you seem excited and organized, have convincing CENTS and interesting BECOT, and you cite your sources as you use them. Your credibility will take a nose dive (aviation analogy again . . .) if you sound bored and give only rambling generalities with no visual support or expert citation. Either way, credibility is a done deal after the body, so there is no need to repeat it in the conclusion. Other than that, you get into a speech by doing certain things, and you get out of a speech by doing those same things again. It seems redundant . . . and it is . . . and it works.

In general, the **purpose of an introduction** is to **focus your audience** and **get them ready to listen** to the body of your speech, the "meat." Therefore, do NOT get into any real detail in the introduction. Keep it simple; keep it short. Most experts say it should be **10–15 percent of your total talking time**, so let's call it **60–90 seconds** for a ten-minute talk. You have to be organized to do those five items in that amount of time; visual aids and practice help. Some experts advise you to write out every word of your introduction, but I plead with you NOT to do that. The introduction is too important to have your eyes buried in a script and to be reading in a monotone voice. It's like a first date; **you never get a second chance to make a first impression.** You MUST look us in the eye or you will not capture our attention and our souls. Therefore, I stress to **"almost memorize" the introduction.** Practice it several times (more than you practice the body), but please don't try to memorize each individual word, which is so mechanical. Be human. Be extemporaneous. Trust yourself. You can do this. Here's how:

Attention Step

Remember, this is *fast*, ten to fifteen seconds. You only have ninety seconds for the whole introduction, so if you think your clever attention step will be a two-minute joke, three-minute story, or four-minute video clip, you better take a few minutes and think again, cowboy. I've seen students use more than half their total allotted time on a supposed attention step. What they've really done is lost their audience before they even began. Also, it's "nice" if the attention step has something to do with the topic, but that is not mandatory; it's technique. The procedure of an attention step is just that: get their attention! **Get them to just shut up and look at you** for a second so that you can then motivate them to listen further. The attention step itself does NOT have to be motivating. You could just turn off the lights or jump on a table or yell at them or throw something at them (something soft . . .). You don't have to be clever here; be direct and forceful. If you don't believe that, then you have never been a substitute teacher for a bunch of seventh graders. Don't ask me.

I know some people sweat and sweat over their attention steps. It really doesn't have to be that hard; most likely it will be kinda fun to do. Here are some proven **techniques**:

- *Ask a Question:* Probably the most common attention step. *Rhetorical questions,* ones that don't demand an overt answer, are good to make us think, but not so great to make us shut up. ("How would you describe the type of wedding you want?") *Direct questions* <u>do</u> ask for a physical/vocal response, so they make better attention steps. ("How many of you ride motorcycles? Wear a helmet?")
- *Startling Statistic:* Scare/amaze us with some crazy number. "90,000 people are on the organ donor waiting list; 90,000 people who need your help."
- *Vivid Photograph:* Turn off the lights for a moment and show a scary photo of a car crash ("This was my friend's car; please don't drink and drive.") or a beautiful, color photo of a sunset ("I took this photo during my vacation to Hawaii; I want to describe the different islands there.")
- *Emotive Video Clip:* Show us fifteen seconds of an avalanche ripping down a mountainside, then say, "I'm here to talk about avalanche safety."
- *Objects:* Bounce a basketball to start your speech on LeBron James. If you want to talk about donating money for cancer research, you might show a framed photo of your mother; "This is Mom, who has cancer."
- *Quotes:* One of my favorites! Dig out that expert quote on your topic or that celebrity quote that's just funny. Not everyone likes quotes, however. As Emerson once said, "I hate quotations; tell me what *you* know."
- *Personal Knowledge:* If you know how to ride a unicycle, why not ride it into class? Can you juggle, sing, dance, paint, yo-yo, speak another language, or play some musical instrument? If you have a talent, try to incorporate it somehow into your speech, and the attention step is a fun place. Personal confessions can also be effective. ("My name is John Daly, and I'm an alcoholic," or "My name is Barney Fife, and I'm *really nervous* today.") Audiences react well to such openness.

There are endless ways to start a speech. You can arouse curiosity, be funny, stimulate imagination, give promises, refer to the special occasion, make fun of the boss or a coworker, reference a special event we all know, bash the "enemy," or even suck up to the audience with compliments or candy. Yadda yadda yadda. Once again you are only restricted by your imagination, but remember your primary goal is to "get their attention."

Purpose Statement

As a quick side note, if you were not introduced by someone and if the audience does not know you, this is the time to also introduce yourself. Just tell your name and state your job/title and your relationship to the audience or company involved. (You can tell more about your expertise during the credibility step.) Then make your purpose clear, which is best done with a visual aid. Look closely at your body and all its support and ask yourself one final time, "What exactly am I saying with this speech?" Now, for sure, you can let them know if you are there to inform or persuade, and what the topic is. If it's a persuasive speech, be sure to tell them exactly what you want them to do or think at the end of your talk. In the business world, this is known as "putting your bottom line up top." Your aid might say:

- To inform Montana teenagers about the state's new driving rules
- To persuade all American college students to vote

Note that those examples included a specific audience. When you develop your purpose statement, it should be aimed at the particular audience you have in mind. (Go back to Chapter Two, page 19, to review some earlier advice on purpose statements.) Keep your purpose statements as short and direct as possible, and visual.

Motivation Step

Give the audience a reason to listen to your topic. (Don't explain here why *you* picked it.) Why is it important to them; what "value" does it touch? If it's an informative talk, we might listen just because it's fun, interesting, unique, current, popular, local, or curious. Persuasion speeches, however, beg for stronger reasons, ones that touch us at our basic needs. According to Abraham **Maslow**, author of *Motivation and Personality*, our **basic needs** are physiological, safety, belongingness and love, esteem, and self-actualization. So, will your topic help me eat or sleep better? Will my pimples go away? Will it save me time, money, or energy? Will it save my basic life or promote my love life? Is it the smart or ethical choice? Will I be proud of myself when I'm done? Is this a way to fulfill my potential and give back to America all that it's given me? Could I be . . . the next . . . Batman? How about . . . the next . . . Barack? Barack Obama engaged this country in 2008 partly because he and his staff knew how to motivate us, how to touch our values and needs. We were hurting for change, and he said,

"We can change; yes we can." Simple. Powerful. Okay, your speech doesn't have to save the world, but can't you at least nudge us in that direction? Give us a reason to listen!

Credibility Step

Give the audience a reason to listen to you. **This step has two main parts: your research and your connection with the topic.** Let us know when you did your research, so we know it's current. Tell us how and where so we know you did not just sit in front of a computer for twenty minutes. Did you remember to SMILE? (Chapter Three, page 40) Tell us why the research is credible; was it a government or educational source with a known, published author, or maybe just Wikipedia? Also let us know if you have any personal or professional connection with the topic. If you want to tell us why you picked the topic, do it here, not with the motivation step. Maybe it's aligned with your major, summer job, family interests, or personal hobby. Maybe you chose the topic on diabetes because you have that disease, or you want to talk about the Beijing Olympics because you got to go there! Go USA! How big is your passion for the topic?

Surveys
Media
Internet
Library
Experts

Preview

Just list your main points on a visual aid, and you're done with the Introduction. **Keep the words simple; hopefully just one to three words per main point.** Do not show full-sentence main points; we cannot read them quickly. Also, do not show your sub-points; too much detail for the introduction. "Tell us what you'll tell us." (Note: In the real world, this is also a good time to clarify how long you'll talk and whether or not the audience can ask questions.)

Save those aids you made for your purpose statement and preview because you will show them again in the conclusion, when you restate the purpose and give the summary. In general, the **purpose of a conclusion** is to **summarize key lessons** one more time and to provide a satisfying sense of closure. Like the introduction, keep it short, direct, and visual. The recommended time is **5–10 percent of the total**, so **30–60 seconds** for a ten-minute speech. "Almost memorize" the conclusion, because you MUST look us in the eyes. We tend to remember best what we heard last, so the conclusion is even more important in a persuasion speech when you're trying to influence the way we think or act. **You should NOT introduce new material/concepts** in the conclusion; just repeat and reinforce the lessons you already covered. (A new quote or new statistic is fine for motivation or closure; those are quick and probably reinforce lessons from the body.) If you're running short on time, cut minor sub-points from the body, but **never cut** the conclusion. An abrupt ending is like a fairy tale without a moral or a flight with a crash landing. Have a "hip-pocket" conclusion ready, four clear points you can share on short notice:

Restate Purpose

Put up the visual aid from the introduction and simply repeat the reason you gave the speech.

Summary

Show the visual aid you used for the preview, and "tell us what you told us." The better summaries go a bit beyond just reading back the main points again. They pick the most important "lesson" or sub-point under each category, and they re-mind us of that one more time. Maybe you've heard speakers stress during their conclusion, "If you only remember one thing from my speech today, I want you to remember _____!" If used, that line is normally in the summary.

Remotivation

Give the audience a reason to remember your speech. Whatever motivation worked in the introduction will probably work again here, but you could cer-tainly add a new quote/statistic/photo that tugs at our heartstrings and pumps us up. For persuasion, attack our value system again and mention our *needs*. This step is sometimes referred to as the "Call to arms!" As an old military guy, I like that term. It smacks of volunteer forces in the Revolutionary War. I can hear Paul Revere galloping by my window: "The British are coming! The British are coming!" (Maybe I shouldn't write late at night.) Tell us "WHY" we "NEED" to act, now. How exactly will we be better off because of your speech? Answer the question "What's in it for the audience?"

Closure

Also called the "clincher." Upbeat. Positive. We *know* you're done, instead of leaning forward in our seats wondering if you're done. Concise. Like the attention step, this should be quick; maybe ten seconds. **Everything that works well as an attention step works well for closure.** (If you do the same thing, it's called a "circular closure" because it makes the audience feel like they've come full circle. Very satisfying technique; try it.) Do NOT read a two-minute poem or tell a three-minute story or show a four-minute video, cowboy. (Didn't it feel good to hear that line again?) Do NOT surprise us, and say, "You know that little girl I told you about at the start of my speech, the one who was abused by her father? Well, that little girl was me." What?! Arrgh. That type of closure really jerks your audience around. Tell us during the introduction-credibility step that you have personal experience with child abuse (put your bottom line up top) and I *guarantee* you we will listen to your speech much more intently. Do NOT say, "That's all I got," which is boring and shows no planning or thought. Finally, closure is NOT saying thanks or asking for questions; those are two things you should always do *after* the proper, well-planned, satisfying, inspirational closure. No pressure on you at all.

I think it's procedure that you do the five parts of an introduction and the four parts of a conclusion, but there is much room for technique in how you do them and in what order. You can combine steps, too. I've just given you a starting point. Experiment.

Please flip back to the end of this book, Appendices F and G, to see Sample Outlines. Ask your instructor to see sample outlines, too. Most people look at a few speaker outlines, see how intro/body/conclusion/CENTS/BECOT/prompts/transitions/bibliography all fit together, and say, "Hey, I can do that." **Remember that outlines are more for planning than for execution.** The better outlines are hardly looked at during the speech.

SUMMARY CHECKLIST FOR ORGANIZATION

General Organization

- ❑ Think procedure vs technique; what do you *have* to do vs *want* to do?
- ❑ The greatest enemy of procrastination is organization
- ❑ Follow steps: research CENTS, outline, edit, add aids/prompts, practice

You Must Outline!

- ❑ Check your plan for logic, flow, balance, and time control
- ❑ Outline for extemporaneous speaking, not manuscript reading
- ❑ Do four types of outlines: Brainstorm, Rough Draft, Speaker, Audience
- ❑ Outlining is like building a puzzle
- ❑ PowerPoint and note cards are aids; they are NOT your outline
- ❑ Mechanics are mostly technique; use any form that works for you
- ❑ Should be typed (so it's in your head) with key words (so you don't read)
- ❑ Strongly recommend big print, double-space, on one side of the paper
- ❑ Definitely add prompts for aids, cites, and delivery
- ❑ An outline is a cane, not a crutch

Logical Patterns

- ❑ Introduction, Body, Conclusion
- ❑ General: big to small, simple to complex, least to most, known to unknown
- ❑ Specific: topical, time, order, spatial, geographic, reason, story, pro/con, cause/effect, problem/solution, and gimmick
- ❑ Transitions help to connect the points smoothly

Do Body First, Then Introduction/Conclusion

- ❑ Body has two to five main points, evenly balanced and full of CENTS and BECOT
- ❑ Introduction has five parts: attention, purpose, motivation, credibility, preview
- ❑ Conclusion has four parts: restate purpose, summary, remotivation, closure

Plan the flight, fly the plan. Pretend you're a pilot taking your audience on a trip. The airplane gets their *attention*, but they want to know the *purpose* of the trip, why they should go (*motivation*), why they should trust you as the pilot (*credibility*), and what cool things they might see along the way (*preview*). During the trip, be sure to fly smoothly (*logical flow*), not circle one place too long (*balance*), and stay on schedule (*time control*). Make the flight memorable (*CENTS*), point out the beautiful places (*BECOT*), and don't turn too fast (*transitions*). During final descent, remind them why they took the flight (*restate purpose*) and what they saw (*summary*), encourage them to fly with you again (*remotivation*), and, for gosh sakes, touch down safely (*closure*)! AIM HIGH!

Chapter 6
DELIVERY

TALK LIKE YOU TALK

Image © Yuri Arcurs, 2012. Used under license from Shutterstock, Inc.

Note: It's no mistake that the phrase "Talk Like You Talk" became the title of this book. Of all the components of public speaking, "delivery" is the one people worry about the most. The best advice I can give you is to just *talk like you talk* . . . like you're talking with your friends.

L et's pause for a moment and see where we are along this trip called "Public Speaking." You know why you're giving the speech and who the audience will be (Chapter Two). You have a great topic that is well researched and supported with CENTS (Chapter Three), brought alive with BECOT (Chapter Four), and unbelievably logically organized (Chapter Five). In other words, *all your hard work is already done!* You have the plan all laid out in front of you; all you have to do is follow it. Easy. Now is the fun part, when you get to share all the startling statistics, vivid visuals, and words of wisdom. You know the audience will like it okay, because *you* like it. I know you're still a little nervous (Chapter One), but those are good nerves! You can do this! (You know you can.)

Comparisons
Examples
Numbers
Testimony
Stories

Blackboard
Electronics
Costuming
Objects
Transparencies

You students need to keep speech delivery in proper focus. It is not your whole speech. In fact, it is actually a very small part of your course grade. Look at the peer evaluation form in Appendix E. If you do good research, put together good support/aids in a balanced outline, and give the speech when scheduled, you probably have a "B" at worst. Good students also do great with written assignments, exams, and attendance. Out of the total points in our course at MSU, "delivery" (your huge fear) is only about 10 percent.

You real-world speakers have more to worry about in terms of delivery, but it's still not as critical as you might think. Audiences are very forgiving of delivery if they sense you have the knowledge they need and are "giving it the old college try." If they know you "worked for them" (good CENTS and BECOT), they will work harder to listen to you, no matter how shy/quiet your delivery style is. It really helps if you are sincere (more on that in a couple pages), and the best way to show sincerity is to *talk like you talk*.

TALK LIKE YOU TALK

Don't you just love local TV commercials? You know the ones I mean. A married couple stands very stiff and serious and scared looking, and they use a very mechanical, monotone, memorized delivery: "Hel-lo. We are Al-li-son and Ro-ger at Vac-u-Wor-ld, your neig-bor-hood store for all your vac-uum needs." (Come on, read that line out loud this time, no one is listening.) You hear every single syllable quite distinctly . . . but you don't want to. They don't smile, move, or use gestures, of course. I suppose they didn't have the money to practice the commercial several times before they had to "go final."

Why is it that people change their voices and demeanor when they have to talk in front of a group (especially a TV audience)? If this were a psychology book, I might get into the theory some more, but suffice it to say I think people have an image of how they should act in front of a group based upon the speeches they have heard. If you have been influenced by professional speakers (preachers, professors, politicians, and pundits), you might subconsciously try to model their behavior. In other words, you might try to be someone you're not. If you don't have much speech experience yourself, you don't know your own style yet and might not even know the most basic speech principles, so you're just guessing what to do. You'll naturally be more awkward. Delivery takes time.

It doesn't take a psychologist to tell us we don't like robots! (Remember the cartoon on page 7?) I mean, we like R2D2 and C3PO, but we don't like "robotic" speech delivery. We want people to be more natural and spontaneous, like they are during a regular conversation. The goal today is to become more "conversational" in speech, more informal. Just talk like you normally talk, not like how you *think* someone wants you to talk. Granted, some old-school instructors are still teaching the way they were taught, and I certainly had many teachers who demanded we be more formal in our speech delivery. Some other countries/cultures and some older American audiences would still expect a more "proper" delivery, for sure. And they would not be wrong, just different. In general, in American public speaking today, we need to remember what Bob Dylan tried to teach us: *The Times They are A-Changin'*. (Sing along with me!)

Sometimes I get students who tell me, wide-eyed, "I'm no good at speech! I can't talk!" I ask, "Can you talk with your friends?" I'm serious. Instead of pretending you're that professor or politician in front of strangers, why not pretend you are yourself in front of a bunch of friends? You're sitting up in the dorm, all excited about something *you* know that they don't know: "Guys, ya gotta hear this!!" Capture the moment.

Sometimes I get international students who tell me, wide-eyed, "My English is horrible! No one will understand me." I say, "I just understood you." I'm serious. Instead of worrying about your English, worry about your research—CENTS, BECOT, and outline. You, international friends, are truly fabulous students, because you, no kidding, appreciate the value of an education more than many Americans. Your English is always better than you think it is. If you're still concerned about your English, follow three suggestions: use less content, use more visual aids, and slow down your rate of speech.

Sometimes I get students who ignore all my ranting and raving about extemporaneous speaking, and they flagrantly read every word of a manuscript outline. I am wide-eyed. I give them about three minutes, and then I say, "Okay, Megan. I've let you *read* to us a while, but it's not a reading course, so I want to hear you *talk*. Please turn over your outline, come around to the front of the podium, sit down on the table, and just tell us what you want us to know about urban architectural needs." I'm serious. I do that maybe twice a term, out of 600 talks. After they throw their manuscript at me and throw up, they do fine. In fact, I am NOT kidding, they do much more than fine. I'll ask a question or two to get them going, and someone in the class usually joins the lesson and asks a question, too. Then they are off to the races! We all get to see the *speaking* facade fade away and get replaced by the *talking* reality. The speaker's whole delivery style changes; more inflection, more gestures, more effective. This nervous student who thought she had to depend on a script transforms in front of us into an approachable speaker with a heartbeat. I swear, it's truly one of the coolest things I get to see as a speech instructor. Afterward, when the smoke has cleared and the native drums have silenced, the "victim" thanks me for the most important lesson in her life, and we write a movie script together.

Delivery is really the least of my concerns with speech students. (You may have gathered last chapter that procrastination is my biggest concern.) I honestly see very few serious delivery problems, and the minor problems all improve with a little awareness and practice. Most people seem to innately know what good speech delivery is because they know what they like/dislike from other speeches and lectures they hear. The vast majority of my students grasp the concept of "Talk Like You Talk" very quickly, especially after we cover some helpful hints:

- Use some humor! Make yourself smile, and then we will smile
- Do something early in the talk to get a reaction, then you'll relax more
- Focus on the audience (How can I help you?) vs. yourself (How do I look?)
- Think "helpful" speech instead of "persuasive" = more sincere/friendly
- Find a friendly face or two and don't forget they are out there
- Have some water to sip; loosens up lips and creates natural gestures
- Fight hard to be yourself instead of an actor upon a stage
- Tell a story! Everyone's delivery is more natural when telling a story

- SensoryAidsSensoryAidsSensoryAidsSensoryAidsSensoryAids
- The best sensory aid to teach you delivery is a video of you giving a speech

As I said in Chapter One, you never look as nervous as you feel. Most people don't believe that until they see themselves on tape. If at all possible, tape one of your talks. In *Successful Presentations for Dummies*, Malcolm Kushner says:

> *It's amazing what watching a videotape of yourself will reveal. That's the quickest way to improve your body language—because the camera doesn't lie. It will show you movements and gestures that you may not be aware you were making. . . . Watch the video with the sound off. Common sense will tell you most of what you need to correct.*

I videotape at least one speech for every student, and then they complete a written self-evaluation after they watch their tape. Those papers convince me it's a powerful exercise and well worth doing. I tell students they will forget most of our course eventually (one month?), but they will never forget their own video-taped speech. One of my students was aghast when he watched his own tape. He was mad at how boring he seemed:

Kyle actually wrote that, and then rewrote his delivery style. He had a great sense of humor, and he unleashed it on us. Most people are happy with their videos in terms of not looking nervous, but it's very common for them to still want to improve movement and gestures. They'll say, "I'm using more visual aids next speech!" As I said in Chapter Four, sensory aids are the "cure-all" for everything evil in public speaking: boredom, complexity, understanding, time control, sense appeal, and retention. In terms of delivery, sensory aids create natural movement, gestures, facial expressions, and vocal variation like no written prompt can. Aids will definitely help you talk like you talk, but nothing helps more than just good ol' down-on-the-farm, home-style *sincerity*.

SINCERITY

Audiences are kinda like dogs on the hunt; they can flat out smell insincerity, and when they do, they'll rip you to pieces. You cannot fake sincerity, and no Hollywood delivery or slick sensory aids can cover up insincerity. (Wow, I guess I was wrong; sensory aids can't cure everything.) People are smart that way; we've trained all our lives watching our parents and our friends. And we watch soap operas, and Oprah. We are ready for you.

SINCERITY IS EVERYTHING. IF YOU CAN FAKE THAT, YOU GOT IT MADE

I found that great Groucho Marx quote in a 2008 textbook, *Public Speaking; Building Competency in Stages*, by Sherry Devereaux Ferguson. She inserted an article by Brian Creamer, who is an author himself: *Successfully Speaking: Seven Keys to Unlock Your Speaking Potential*. He offered some hints on how to be more sincere:

- Be ourselves; appear to be who we really are
- Speak from personal experience
- We must be willing to share and risk ourselves as speakers
- We must focus on the audience
- Say what we mean and mean what we say

I loved that article, probably because it reinforces timeless lessons I have tried to teach for years. I tell students to "put your heart out on your sleeve," to "open a window to your soul," and "don't let anchovies ruin that perfect Colombo's pizza." If you share a piece of yourself with the audience and tell a personal story, there is NO way your delivery will be robotic. No way. You will talk like you talk, and you'll be sincere.

Here are some other things I know to help you evoke sincerity:

- Pick a topic you sincerely care about
- Pick a topic you sincerely *want* to research more
- Get excited! If you like your topic, you can do this; if not, you can't
- Pick a topic you sincerely believe will interest or help the audience
- Don't talk *down* to the audience; talk *with* them
- Don't talk *at* the audience; talk *with* them
- Don't read or memorize your speech; *talk like you talk*
- If you sincerely care about your audience, "delivery" will be fine

> *The people who make a difference are not the ones with the credentials, but the ones with the concern.*
>
> —**Max Lucado**, *And the Angels Were Silent*

METHODS OF DELIVERY

I feel obligated to tell you there are twenty-something books scattered around me on the floor, and every single one of them lists four methods of public speaking delivery. I "sincerely" believe there is only one, or at least, there *should* be only one: Extemporaneous. If you sincerely care about your audience more than anything else, then you would never use any other method as your primary choice. I recognize, however, that some speakers have other **priorities,** which are higher on the food chain than just a mundane, average, run-of-the-mill, common audience. I'll discuss those priorities shortly. I also recognize that the other methods do have **potential**. Therefore, I shall, alas, include all four delivery methods in my book . . . but I won't go into much detail. If you want to know the many particulars about these lesser methods, come borrow one of the other books on my floor.

Manuscript

You write out every single word you plan to say (the manuscript), and then you read it to us. Manuscript delivery is known best for putting us all to sleep, due its lack of movement, eye contact, and vocal inflection. Most audiences sincerely *hate* manuscript speeches, and if they go on for fifty minutes, the audience can actually learn to hate the speaker. I speak from experience. When I was a student at the Air Command and Staff College, we regularly had fifty-minute lectures from guest experts. Many were quite good; many were quite bad. The worst, in my biased opinion, were the politicians from Washington, DC, who would just pull out a script and read it to us. No visual aids; no humor; no stories; no personality. We would all sleep, 500 of us! I would fight to stay awake just to watch everyone else fall asleep. It was funny. I learned absolutely nothing from the information in those awful, awful briefings, but I did take copious notes about ineffective speaking techniques, at least until I fell asleep myself. Just thinking about those days makes my neck hurt. I bet you know the feeling, too. So, why would anyone choose a manuscript delivery style?

PRIORITY

The only professional reason for manuscript reading is political correctness. The president, and most politicians, must be extremely careful with their word choice so that they don't offend any groups, or nations, due to a "slip of the tongue." High-ranking officers in any organization might feel similar pressure. Funerals might be too emotional to choose another delivery method. Some other personal reasons might be nervousness ("I'll forget what to say if I don't write it all down."), time control ("I know I talk too much, so I must control my words."), or laziness ("I'm lazy. I'll just read my speech so I won't have to think about it much during the talk.") Whatever the reason, manuscript speakers normally do not think of the audience first.

POTENTIAL

I like to actually pick up a book and read a passage from it during my extemporaneous lectures. If you're worried about the exact wording or the precise statistics in some study, by all means read it out loud. Reading "a little something" to us is a good way to get variety into your speech pattern, and that's a good thing. Just keep it short, maybe a minute. Student manuscript readings can also help in a speech course to practice vocal variation and allow us all to compare different reading styles.

Memorization

You write out every single word you plan to say (another manuscript), and then you memorize it; every . . . single . . . word. This is exactly like memorizing your lines as an actor in a play, but how many actors talk for ten minutes at a time? My biggest complaint here is that memorization speakers do not even see the audience; they only "see" the mental script scrolling in front of their eyeballs. This method is more for entertainment than sharing information. **This is by far the most time-consuming method.** Not only do you have to write out every word, but imagine how long it would take to memorize it all. And you still might forget the words. Panic city! Who would do this!?

PRIORITY

I have rarely seen this method in real life. I have seen people memorize a 5-minute, formal introduction of a guest speaker so they would seem more professional, but it usually made them seem stilted or mechanical. I've seen people memorize long toasts at a wedding so they will be "smoother," but there always seems to be an awkward pause in there somewhere. I guess some other countries still employ this old method (technically called *oratory*), and some American schools still use it as a form of speech competition, like debate. I have seen students memorize their whole speech, but it usually is not done with a full script. It's the result of practicing with an extemporaneous outline so many times that the speech becomes memorized. These students are striving too hard for a perfect speech and a perfect grade, and this goal becomes more important than the audience. Again, if you love your audience, don't memorize your whole talk.

POTENTIAL

I am impressed when speakers memorize a short portion of their speech. This can happen with a poem (I really emphasize *short* with poetry), a song verse, or a paragraph out of a familiar story/movie. I have been known to recite (part of) the prologue to *The Canterbury Tales* in old English, just because I can. My tenth-grade English teacher made us memorize it. It makes me smile. Some people recite something they wrote themselves; it adds a nice, personal touch and makes them closer with the listeners.

Impromptu

You jot down a few notes, at best, because you have little or no time to prepare. There is usually no introduction or conclusion and no sensory aids, although some skilled speakers can make that happen. It can be a very conversational method of delivery, but it usually takes more of the audience's time and gives them less useful information. It can't be planned well, so it can't be as "tight" or effective as an extemporaneous speech. Most people only choose this method if they have to.

PRIORITY

Sometimes, you have to. You're sitting in a board meeting, and the boss says, "Hey, Nic, why don't you give us all a status report on the opening of that new restaurant?" Your priority here might be on saving face ("Oh, my gosh, I don't want to look incompetent!"). For most professionals, however, the impromptu priority actually *is* the audience; you want to give them good information on the budget, schedule, and personnel involved with your project. (Note the three main points you could use to quickly outline your short talk in your head.) You don't have to do research; you truly are the expert in most impromptu situations. Effective delivery, per se, would just have to take a back seat, and that's okay. Time is money in the business world, so the boss doesn't need a long speech, just five to ten minutes. He wants you to adapt to the moment and just give the facts. If you forget something, or it's not clear, they can ask questions. If you start to "ramble" and waste time, they'll let you know, and I don't mean in a bad way. They know you're more nervous and disorganized than you would be if you had time to prepare an extemporaneous speech.

POTENTIAL

I think impromptu speeches are great for a speech class. They get students to think on their feet and gain the confidence that they can do so, preparing them a bit for longer talks. Sometimes people think of something in the middle of an extemporaneous speech, which is not on their outline. It might be important information, or it might just be fun. It might be a reaction to a question/comment, or maybe you notice a nonverbal cue from a listener that tells you to clarify your point with another example. It is certainly okay to stray from your outline, because outlines are not mandatory checklists, remember? Just be aware of time and don't stray too long. Maybe a minute.

Extemporaneous

(Pick me! Pick me!) You list key words and prompts on your outline to help you remember "most" of what you want to say. You might also use full sentences for short sections of verbatim reading, especially quotes and interviews. This method employs more sensory aids than the other methods, and more movement, which means better audience interaction. It's very well prepared, but appears more natural and spontaneous. You can edit/delete on your feet to adapt to the listeners and time restraints. It's definitely a conversational method of delivery, allowing you to actually "talk like you talk," providing you are sincere in your concern for the audience. Focus on this truth: extemporaneous delivery allows you to incorporate the best parts of any other delivery method you want, in short bursts. **When you have a choice, this is the only choice.**

PRIORITY

The priority of extemporaneous speaking is the audience, as it should be. It also helps the speaker be more relaxed since it removes the pressures of a "perfect speech" (manuscript and memorized speeches have that word-for-word perfection criteria written all over them) and an "awful speech" (impromptu talks can really make you feel stupid, especially if you find nothing in your brain and no one helps you out with questions). Extemporaneous speeches are also just more fun, on both sides of the podium. These are all noble priorities; carry their flags high!

Overall, your choice of delivery method comes down to the Golden Rule (Chapter Nine): Do you like robots reading to you? No? **Then don't be a robot when you speak to others.**

KEY ELEMENTS OF DELIVERY

The two broadest areas of delivery are **verbal and nonverbal.** Verbal is anything that is spoken (consider word choice, voice quality, articulation, and pronunciation), and nonverbal is everything else (such as appearance, sensory aids, eye contact, and movement). Words are certainly important, but I heard a rumor the other day that "actions speak louder than words." All of my communication research indicates that when your nonverbal actions don't match your verbal words, we tend to believe the nonverbals. As Steven and Susan Beebe say in their textbook, *Public Speaking: An Audience Centered Approach,* "We usually believe nonverbal messages because they are harder to fake." I think this is true, because when I was a child and my mother did not believe something I said, she would grab my chin and say, "Look me in the eyes and tell me again where you got the money for that candy bar." You been there? Done that? Your words need to be truthful, and then you need to deliver them in a way that we understand and believe you.

I tend to put more emphasis on the nonverbal area of delivery, because I subscribe to the public speaking magazine that says, "How you say something is more important than what you say." Now, we could argue this point for a while, but we would probably just be arguing semantics. Speakers must have both content and delivery, but if I have to break the tie, I would give the edge to delivery. You may disagree, and that's fine, but I bet you would agree with the following statement:

You cannot NOT communicate.

Your nonverbal body language tells a story that your words cannot. You can fake the words and the statistics of a speech, but you cannot fake the effort and sincerity. If you mumble and look at the floor, you might be nervous, but you're probably just not prepared. If you're not prepared, you will note some nonverbal communication from your audience: restlessness, fidgeting, falling asleep, texting on cell phones, and definite lack of eye contact. That's why I say *my biggest concern with student speeches is procrastination.* If you put time and effort and concern into your speech, your delivery will be fine; trust me. The audience will know you tried, so they'll try harder to listen. Your delivery will be even better when you learn how to minimize audience noise.

Basically, **"noise" is anything that hurts communication,** heard or not heard:

- *Speaker:* tapping podium, mumbling, lack of eye contact, crowded visual aids, talking too fast, low volume, repeating words too often, no movement, gum
- *Environmental:* hallway traffic, hot room, uncomfortable seats, poor lighting, weird smells, overhead projector fan, campus construction, peeling paint
- *Audience:* private conversations, phone beeping, listening to iPods, rustling papers, shifting chairs, asking too many questions, falling asleep, hungry
- *Mental* (speaker or audience): school stress, family worries, money concerns, sexual fantasy, boredom with topic, planning ahead to your next speech

That list may "SEAM" like a lot of "stress" to worry about, and it is, and some of it is totally out of your control. A lot of it, however, can be overcome if you follow good speech advice. **Everything you are taught about public speaking is ultimately designed to cut through the noise in the audience, so that you will have a better chance to influence them.** If you follow the guidelines I discussed in earlier chapters for good CENTS, BECOT, and organization, you will already be removing much noise, at least the daydreaming stuff. Now, with good delivery, you can better override the environmental and speaker noise.

Speaker
Environmental
Audience
Mental

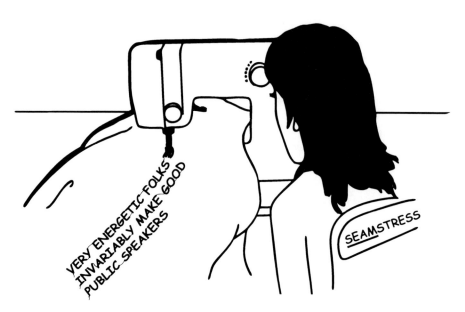

As you might guess, that cartoon sentence is another mnemonic device I created to better remember the key elements of delivery: *V*olume, *E*yes, *F*ace, *I*nflection, *M*ovement, *G*estures, and *P*osture. The "S" at the end stands for *S*incerity (already discussed) because that's really the rudder that keeps the whole boat moving in the right direction.

> **V**ery **E**nergetic **F**olks **I**nvariably **M**ake **G**ood **P**ublic **S**peakers.
> **V**olume-**E**yes-**F**ace-**I**nflection-**M**ovement-**G**estures-**P**osture-**S**incerity

Volume

The number one rule in delivery is: **WE MUST HEAR YOU!** It doesn't matter what you do or how you do it if they cannot hear you. I see this rule violated frequently in the real world. Just last week, I attended a wedding and once again "watched" a series of toasts. Even though there was a microphone, people did not use it properly, so the audience was largely cupping their ears and straining to listen, often looking at the people around them and asking, "What did he say?" You've been there.

Story: I was asked to be the guest speaker at a Veteran's Day ceremony. It was outdoors at the cemetery, in November, in Montana, wind howling, no PowerPoint, no microphone, and about seventy-five people, most of them older, with hearing problems. It was a recipe for failure. I wore my uniform, kept the speech short (seven minutes), and focused on WWII so I could relate to the audience and tell a story about my father, the ol' Marine who won two purple hearts. Mostly, I was LOUD!! I got a nice applause, but I'll never forget the group of three women who came up to me immediately and said, "Thank you SO much. You're the first speaker here in ten years who we could hear!"

Volume is a relative thing. If I spoke in lecture as loudly as I spoke at the cemetery, I would scare my students. If I spoke in class with twenty people as loudly as I speak in lecture with 150 people, I would bother everyone. Asians like less volume than Americans. It all depends on the situation. Two constants, however, are (1) be sure they can hear you, and (2) vary your volume some. (Yes, I just said variation should be a constant.) It's funny to hear speakers in a large auditorium ask, "Can everyone hear me?" Usually there's someone in the back who turns to his buddy and asks, "What did he just say?" Next time you're in front of a big group, try this comment: "Those of you in the back, please raise your hand if you can hear me." Then you know. Don't hesitate to use a microphone if you know you need one, and most large audiences really *want* you to use one. With a microphone, you can really vary your volume, and they can still hear you. Sometimes, the best way to emphasize something is not to yell it out, but to whisper it.

> *You can't hurt a tongue by speakin' softly.*
>
> **—Ken Alstad,** *Savvy Sayin's*

People often worry about speaking too fast, but that's rarely a problem because we can listen at a much higher rate than people can talk. If you talk fast, however, it's harder to keep your volume up, especially at the end of sentences. Just be aware.

COMMON CRITIQUES I WRITE ABOUT VOLUME

- Can you get louder if you have to?
- Soft spoken; okay for this size audience
- Deep tone; easy to hear
- GUM! (Take gum out so we can hear better)
- Strained some to hear you
- Loud! But not too loud

Eyes

The number two rule in delivery is: **you must look at us!** We simply won't believe you if you don't look at us. I have an old handout from one of my Human Relations courses, based upon an article titled "U.S. Mainstream Culture," which says:

> *In mainstream U.S. culture, people feel that there is no human contact without eye contact.* ***People are expected to make eye contact 80% of the time when they are listening.*** *Lack of eye contact is judged as lack of attention, lack of interest, low self-esteem or dishonesty.*

I also know that some cultures might judge American eye contact as rude, aggressive, or even flirtatious. Social eye contact, however, is not the same as public speaking eye contact. I think all audiences want a speaker to look at them. Put your head on a swivel and look left and right, including all audience members at some point in your speech. Try to look individuals *in the eye*, directly, but only for a second or two. If you want to experiment with this recommended time, try looking at a person for ten seconds straight during a speech. I guarantee their eyes will go away from yours in five seconds or less.

There is some old public speaking advice for nervous folks that says to look just over the top of the people's heads, or maybe at their foreheads. My experience says you'll do better if you find those friendly faces in the crowd and hold eye-to-eye contact with them a bit longer than you normally would, from time to time. They will give you positive nonverbal feedback, usually with a smile or nod of the head, and you will feel better.

Eyes truly are powerful. Have you ever been driving on the highway and caught the eye of a driver coming at you from the opposite direction, at 70 mph? It might only be a nanosecond of eye contact, but your head will whip around and you'll say, "What was *he* looking at??!!" In *Mastering Public Speaking*, Doctors Grice and Skinner emphasize:

> *Your face is the most important source of nonverbal cues as you deliver your speech, and your eyes carry more information than any other facial feature.*

For this reason, I make students **take off** their **hats** when they give a speech. Any hat, especially a baseball hat, can hurt your eye contact or detract from your facial expressions. Sunglasses, of course, are outlawed in the state of Montana speech awareness. (Any glasses stuck up on the forehead or on the back of your head also create unnecessary noise.) You should want to have good eye contact with your audience in order to get nonverbal feedback so you'll know if you need to change your "delivery swing." You know, you might have to widen your stance, choke up on that bat a bit more and really keep your eye on the ball. (Public speaking can be like a sport, kinda.)

COMMON CRITIQUES I WRITE ABOUT EYE CONTACT

- Bit much on me (Don't look at your instructor/boss/parents too much)
- Take your hat off!
- Solid eye contact; very natural
- Look more at us, less at the screen
- Don't turn your back on us too long
- Eyes on floor, or eyes on ceiling
- Expressive eyes! You liked your topic!
- Looking at your watch too much
- Try to hold eye-to-eye contact longer
- Looked left/right very well

THE EYES HAVE IT!

Face

We tend to listen to attractive, positive people more seriously than messy, sad people. Face it, that's the truth. So, wash your face, brush your hair, and put on a smile. I tell students, "If you can smile, you can give a speech." The three authors of *A Pocket Guide to Public Speaking*, O'Hair, Rubenstein, and Stewart, say it this way:

> ***Few behaviors are more effective for building rapport with an audience than smiling.*** *A smile is a sign of mutual welcome at the start of a speech, of mutual comfort and interest during a speech, and of mutual goodwill at the close of a speech.*

The smile is the most important part of your facial expression. A smile makes us smile, and we love to smile. Mother Teresa said, "Every time you smile at someone, it is an action of love, a gift to that person, a beautiful thing." If you google "smile quotes," you'll find hundreds of such happy statements about smiles. Many have unknown authors but sound like common sense we've heard all our lives, like: "Everyone smiles in the same language." As I traveled to about fifty different countries, I learned that the smile is one nonverbal sign that cuts through all language barriers. As the great comedienne Phyllis Diller said, "A smile is a curve that sets everything straight."

I have been known to stop a student smack dab in the middle of a speech, and just say, "Hey, I bet you can smile." They always do, and I always say, "I knew you could. Nice smile." Find something to make yourself smile during your own speech; the audience doesn't have to know what it was. I often see handwritten prompts on outlines that simply say, "Smile!" (You may add little smiley face drawings or expletives if needed.) If you tell a personal story or show a personal photograph, chances are you'll smile. A smile makes you human, and remember, we like humans, not robots.

While you're improving your face with a smile, don't forget some other actions:

- Seriously, try to get a good night's sleep; your face will be brighter
- Brush/comb your hair; get it out of your eyes
- Wash your face; at least splash some cold water on it right before the talk
- Brush your teeth; use floss to get that spinach gunk out
- Guys, shave, or trim/comb your beard
- Girls, use a little make-up (but don't overdo it, or it becomes distracting)
- Consider removing excessive jewelry, especially lip/nose/tongue rings; college-age audiences can handle that, but most others find it distracting, and you don't want young kids and senior citizens staring at you instead of listening to you
- Acne medicine or cover-up is good
- A runny nose is bad (runny ain't funny; have tissues)
- Superman band-aids can be funny

Overall, act like you're getting ready for a job interview, and "clean up." You'll feel better if you do, and probably smile more.

- Can you smile?
- Brush hair out of your eyes
- Seemed friendly/happy
- Contagious smile!
- You looked bored; if you're bored, your audience will be bored

Inflection

One of the biggest signs of a boring speech is a monotone voice. When people say a speaker "droned on and on and on and on," they mean there was no voice inflection. I looked up the word *drone* in my *Webster Dictionary* (thanks, Noah):

> **Drone:** to make a low, heavy, dull sound; to hum; to snore; to talk in a dull, monotonous voice; to live in idleness.

Man, none of that sounds interesting. I don't want to *drone*, do you? If you understand how pitch, inflection, rate, and pauses help you to speak with variety, you'll be okay.

- *Pitch:* how high or low your voice sounds, like notes on a musical scale; you may have a high or low voice, but it's usually not a problem in speeches.
- *Inflection:* changes in pitch, using several tones (multitone) vs one (monotone); helps you give meaning to your words, like *oh!* (surprised), *oh* (sad), or oh? (confused). I hope **you** understand that (you, personally), you **understand** that (comprehend?), and you understand **that** (the lesson on inflection). So, you can use the same words, but your inflection emphasis can alter the meaning. If you get excited, inflection is usually not a problem. Monotone speakers, however, make nothing sound important, and if nothing's important, why should we listen?
- *Rate:* how fast you speak, or how slow. If you speak too fast, we can follow, but we'll get tired after a while and think you don't like us since you're not giving us a break. In addition, your inflection suffers, and you tend to mumble more, which means your meaning suffers. Know what I mean? If you speak too slowly, we're all silently waiting for the punch line, please! Just mix it up, k? Let it happen, like a normal conversation. If you get excited, you'll talk faster. To emphasize key points or get more serious, you'll talk slower. Variety is the spice of life.

- *Pause:* Ah, the power of the pause! Gives us a break from our job, thank you, and helps you catch your breath, maybe even snatch some cool, clean, refreshing agua. **Pauses are like punctuation in writing, preventing run-on sentences.** They can set the suspense for something you're about to say or clarify your transition into a new point. They slow you down so you can use better inflection. A perfect example is Senator Fred Thompson's speech about John McCain at the 2008 Republican National Convention. (Yeah, Thompson's also that guy from *Law and Order.*) Pauses are normal in any conversation, so (*pause . . . wait for it . . .*) be normal.

COMMON CRITIQUES I WRITE FOR INFLECTION

- Can you get a little excited?
- Well-paced delivery; not rushed
- Too slow; need to talk faster, but great inflection!
- Loved the "squeaky" voice you used with that story
- **Do not read to us Do not read to us Do not read to us Do not read to us**
- Deep tone; you have a good "radio" voice
- You sounded bored; if you're bored, your audience will be bored

I really believe there are no boring speeches, just bored speakers.

Movement

Audiences enjoy movement. If you stand in one place the whole speech, you can appear "tied to your notes," which indicates you're nervous or unsure of your material. From the speaker's standpoint, you will actually be *less* nervous if you move, because movement allows you to work out some of that nervous energy. Besides, I was always taught in the military that it's harder to hit a moving target.

You can have monotone inflection, but have you considered that you can also be "monotonous" in your rate of speech and movement? If you move while you're talking, your tone and rate will more naturally fluctuate, and your gestures will soon follow. (Experiment: try to move around and talk at the same time with a monotone voice and no gestures.) Therefore, **find a reason to move!** The best way to create movement is to use sensory aids. Set aids up around the room and then move toward them during use:

- Go over and physically touch the poster on the tripod
- Actually touch the screen to point out an item on your PowerPoint slide
- Touch the spot on the map you're talking about, rather than use a laser pointer
- Move around to give us a handout
- Go over and hit the light switch a couple times
- Move to the edge of the table to hold up that object you brought
- Move over to the TV to start that video instead of using the remote
- Step out from behind the podium to show us that "costuming" item

I bet you could add to that list right now. I see many good outline prompts that just say "Move!" I think most people move more naturally back to the screen behind them and up to the podium in front. It's harder to move left/right of the podium, so work on that. If you are on the same level as your audience, and the screen is behind you, you will block some views of your visual aids if you don't move left and right. It's a real special treat when the speaker can move into the audience. If you get closer, you appear friendlier, and we can all use more friends. During my lectures, I usually walk up the aisles (about halfway) a time or two, especially if I want to get closer to a student who is beginning to doze off. I increase my volume and get more emphatic with my inflection, as well, and I casually work in some comment about listening skills, and the sleeper always rises from the dead and somewhat smiles. It's funny. It works.

CAUTION: Like anything else in public speaking, you can overdo it. You don't want to *constantly* move, and you don't want to move in a monotonous way, such as madly pacing back and forth, back and forth along the same path. The movement should match your style, so don't try jumping on a table and lighting your hair on fire if that is not your personality. In short, you do NOT have to be Dane Cook in his "Vicious Circle" comedy routine, although I believe the man is a giant genius in terms of movement and gestures.

COMMON CRITIQUES I WRITE FOR MOVEMENT

- Were your feet nailed to the floor?
- You were blocking the screen
- Move more left/right
- Don't hide behind the podium
- Your movement had purpose
- Natural movement; not awkward/forced
- You touched the screen! That's good.
- Use more sensory aids to create more movement

Gestures

Gestures are basically anything you do with your hands, but certainly include arms and legs. Shy people tend to use fewer gestures; energetic people use many. I want to stress that gestures can really have different meanings in other cultures, so if you find yourself speaking in a foreign country, be *sure* to practice your speech with your local hosts so that you don't offend anyone. In America, we love gestures.

I like to see gestures that are *wider than your shoulders*. It opens your body up to the audience more, which in turn opens their hearts, for it's as if you have let your guard down and made yourself more vulnerable to them. If you stand in front of a group with your arms crossed, it could send the nonverbal signal that you are "blocking" people from getting too close to you. The big caution here for audience members is that one brief nonverbal signal does not necessarily mean anything; you have to look for "clusters" of signals. So, if you stand with arms crossed for a long time, plus tightly clinched fists, plus stiff posture, plus clinched teeth and no eye contact, the overall "cluster" image says you're not happy with the situation.

Gestures, like all other key elements of delivery, should be natural. Think about how you gesture in a conversation with friends, and try to do that up on the speaking stage:

* If you use the word *circle*, make a circle motion
* If you use a number, hold up that many fingers (numbers less than 10 . . .)
* Describing a "quiet" moment? Touch one finger to your lips
* Saying it's an "OK" thing to do? Make the OK sign (Here's a good example of cultural gestures. Apparently the OK sign is obscene in some parts of Asia.)
* Stressing something important? Bang a fist into the palm of the other hand, or maybe stomp your foot or slap the podium
* Talking about money? Rub your finger tips with your thumb for the "money sign"

If such gestures are natural and consistent with your words, they will enhance your communication. Gestures should reinforce your message, not be a **distraction:**

* Playing with fingertips, pulling on fingers, rubbing hands
* Playing with jewelry and glasses too much
* Holding a pen or pointer too long, tapping it on table, jabbing at audience

- Holding an elbow or wrist too long
- Fidgeting with objects, like twisting paper clips all around
- Guys cram hands into their pockets or hook thumbs into belt loops
- Girls play with their hair a lot, and touch their ears and earrings
- Rattling loose change or a big wad of keys in a pocket

I know you can add to this list. Take advantage of the academic speech class with its open critiques to learn what your distracting gestures might be. And be sure to watch a videotape of yourself; gestures are probably the first thing you'll notice and correct. Most folks seem to correct delivery distractions just by becoming aware of them.

COMMON CRITIQUES I WRITE FOR GESTURES

- Put the pen down after you've used it
- The podium is not a drum
- Loved your wide gestures! Wider than most!
- I thought you might twist that button off
- Mostly, I highlight the distractions listed previously

Posture

You want to have good posture so that you appear more confident and can physically deliver your speech more effectively. You want to roll your shoulders back, face your "enemy" straight on, and speak *out* rather than *down*. Do not stand in one place too long, or any posture can start to be annoying. It's okay to lean on the podium a little bit, but don't fall asleep there. It's okay to put your hands into your pockets some, but don't glue them there. Some people stand with their hands behind them (the military "parade rest" position), and some stand with their hands held together in front (the biblical fig-leaf position). Some football players "stiff arm" the podium, some dancers curl their right leg around their left leg, and some politicians flip-flop from one foot in the mouth to the other. The key is to use a variety of postures and avoid the extremes; don't be too stiff or too sloppy for too long.

COMMON CRITIQUES I WRITE FOR POSTURE

- Face us, not the side wall (be "squared" to the audience)
- Rocking and/or swaying a bit
- Death grip on podium/lectern/table

- Bit stiff today; try to move more
- Hands on hips a lot; mix it up more
- Confident demeanor
- Came across relaxed/natural

Yep, *Very* (Volume) *Energetic* (Eyes) *Folks* (Face) *Invariably* (Inflection) *Make* (Movement) *Good* (Gestures) *Public* (Posture) *Speakers* (Sincerity). That is the gimmick to remember the key elements of speech delivery, but it also speaks directly to another critical aspect of public speaking: **energy!** If you are truly excited about your topic, your natural energy will take care of most of your delivery concerns, except maybe words.

WORDS

I can't talk about "talking like you talk" unless I talk about the actual talk—the words. There are some things people get away with in conversations with friends that would not go over well in a speech. It's a larger audience, so you have a larger chance that someone might be offended or distracted by your word choice or use. I will discuss offensive words under Ethics (Chapter Nine), so let's concentrate here on potentially distracting words.

Being Too Formal

Don't try to sound smarter than you are. Don't grab a thesaurus just to throw in "big" words. In their textbook, *Public Speaking*, Suzanne and Michael Osborn have an excellent chapter called "The Speaker's Language." I hope I'm doing their lessons justice by summarizing/paraphrasing them below:

- Use familiar words
- Use shorter words, including more contractions
- Slang is okay
- Shorter thought units; sentence fragments are okay
- More personal pronouns (*I, you, we, our*)
- Use more words that refer to human beings and relationships
- More repetition of key lessons

I love that list because I think it all reinforces the thought, *Talk Like You Talk.*

Poor Grammar

If your normal talking style includes poor grammar, you might want to correct that. I don't make a big deal out of this because it really can be a nice style for some personalities (technique), and it's mostly "young talk," which can be exciting. In a professional sense, however, some grammar is flat out wrong (procedure), grates on people's nerves, and will hurt you in a job interview. In a speech with an older audience, it will make you seem a bit "slow." Here are some of my favorite examples:

- "They have ran that play before." (They have "run" that play, please)
- "Tristan could have came to see me." (He could have "come," please)
- "Kaitlyn could have took the book." (She could have "taken," please)
- "Her and me have speech class together." ("She and I" have class, please)
- "Me and Chris love the Gators!" ("Chris and I" love the Gators, please)
- "Ivy should have went to Seattle." ("She should have gone to Seattle," please)
- "David and Deb have boughten another dog?!" ("bought," please)
- "Maggie don't hardly talk." ("She hardly talks," please)

Wrong Words

I personally have to slow down every time I use the word *prescription*, because I'm afraid I'll say *subscription*. When you confuse words that sound similar, it's called a **malapropism.** (Named after a fictional character named Mrs. Malaprop who always mixed up her words.) I've heard students say seductive instead of deductive, density vs destiny, Pacific vs. specific, and contraception vs contradiction. Those can be funny, and it's usually a one-time mistake, and most audience members will just "listen through" them because they know what you meant. Some people, however, use words that don't even exist. President George Bush invented words like *sublimanible* (vs subliminal) and *misunderestimate* (vs misjudge, underestimate, or Iamtalkingtoofast), but hey, I like to invent words, too, and I'm not even the President.

Articulation/Enunciation Errors

These problems refer to the process of forming sounds, and it's worse if you mumble. With articulation, you might leave out sounds and say "libary" instead of "library," or you might add sounds and say "athalete" rather than "athlete." You may have heard people say "ax" instead of "ask" or "expesically" instead of

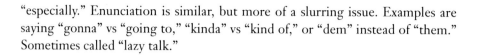

"especially." Enunciation is similar, but more of a slurring issue. Examples are saying "gonna" vs "going to," "kinda" vs "kind of," or "dem" instead of "them." Sometimes called "lazy talk."

Pronunciation Errors

Pronunciation is knowing how to say the word correctly. As the old saying goes, "Don't put the wrong em-**fass-**is on the wrong syl-**lob-**le." (Shucks, I wish you could hear how my Dad used to say that.) Some people even say "pro*nounce*iation" instead of "pro*nun*ciation." The presidential candidates got in trouble in 2008 for talking about "New-clee-ar" (correct) vs "Nook-you-lur" weapons. (Does it really matter if the meaning is clee-ar?) One that I often hear is "Illinoise" instead of the great state of "Illinoy." (Sorry, I had to misspell Illinois twice to make a point.) My dad was born in Decatur, Illinois, and that mispronunciation drove him crazy. Two of my daughters graduated from Cottey College in Nevada, Missouri, but it is pronounced "Nuh-*vay*-da" instead of "Nuh-vah-da" or "Nuh-vat-a." Do you know which pronunciation is correct in Reno? I'd be nervous to give a speech there. If you are not *positive* how to pronounce a word, especially people's names, find out. (I personally really struggle with Meghan and Megan, which can both be pronounced Maygun, Meegun, or Mehgun. Makes me want to get out me gun.......) In most cases, you can just use another vocabulary word if your mouth don't work. (Uh, bad grammar and wrong pronounceiation *can* provide some humor, ya think?)

Filler Words

Yeah, like, uh, you know, what are those, um, filler words, and stuff like that? I mean, that kinda thing can get, uh, really annoying for your audience, see, if you use filler words to just fill a void (a pause), you know, like, too often, okay? Actually, interestingly enough, you can, um, get rid of most of those filler words, and such, if you, uh, you know, practice out loud a couple times, okay, like, ah, twice. My favorite filler word is "and." Some people use "and" at the end of every sentence, *and* if you read a verbatim transcript of the speech, it would be one long sentence, *and* that can be stopped if you'll just use the power of the pause, *and* you can also count the "ands" on your videotape, *and* that will drive you crazy, *and* then you'll improve, *and* that's all I've got today, okay, about filler words. (*Pause.*) You know what I mean?

Repeat Words/Phrases

These are the "kissing cousins" of filler words, so most of the distracting words I hear repeated too often are ones used in the previous paragraph. Some words form a personal, favorite phrase, however, that simply becomes a bad habit. If you use the same word/phrase over and over, "and so forth," it can start to feel like a hammer blow to our pea brains. In 2008, John McCain was critiqued for saying "my friends" too often in his political speeches. A favorite word in student speeches lately is "awesome." My favorite in this category is "basically." Basically, if you use "basically" too much, it basically starts to basically drive us basically crazy, basically. We want to keep speeches simple and short, but people who overuse the word "basically" often follow it with too much detail. Other problems that I see repeated:

- "I'll talk about that later." After I've heard that the third time, I *really* want them to talk about it *now*. Besides, if it's a short speech, you don't have time later.
- "Real quick now. . . ." It never seems to be real quick.
- "To make a long story short . . ." I've learned to expect a long story.
- ". . . and what not." And I'll scream if you say that one more time!
- "You know what I mean?" We probably don't.
- "That kinda thing." That kinda thing, too often, gets old
- "Don't ja know?" I'm not sure, unless we're from Minnesota
- ANY WORD REPEATED TOO OFTEN IS DISTRACTING

Gum

Take the gum out. It will improve your volume, inflection, articulation, pronunciation, and looks. "Smacking" gum is not polite. Take the gum out.

PRACTICE

I bet you've heard the old axiom, "Practice makes perfect." Well, forget it. It's nice alliteration, but that's all it is. **Nothing makes anything perfect.** Perfection is a goal, not a real condition in life. There are no absolutes in life, not even this one. Please remember my initial advice from Chapter One: Their is no such thing as a purfect speech. Most of you reading this book are probably college freshman taking a basic speech course. You don't need to think "perfect." You need to think "survival."

You need to practice your speech, but don't practice too much.

If you don't practice at all, then you're just "going for it," and that usually isn't a good speech. Please don't waste our time. Besides, practice will make *you* more confident, no argument. Most people at least practice "in their heads," and that is usually good enough. Get thee to a nunnery, Shakespeare, or some other quiet place, and mentally go through your speech, using the actual outline and visual aids you have planned. I feel strongly that practicing out loud is even better, because it will better approximate the time involved and bring your word choice closer to the top of your brain, decreasing the *uhs* and other filler words during your actual speech. If you **practice out loud, twice,** I think you've got it. By George, you've got it! (Please increase the volume on the background music here, *The Rain in Spain* from *My Fair Lady.*) And try to find an audience.

Your practice audience should not be animals, stuffed or alive, unless they talk. Your audience should not be a mirror. Some books recommend that you practice with a mirror, and it might work for you, but will you look at yourself during the real thing? Don't practice in front of your mother; she is simply too biased: "Oh, darling, that speech is just perfect! If David doesn't give you an A, I'll come down to that MSU campus and kick his little ol' behind." Find a few of your speech class friends and listen to each other's practice talks. In the real world, use coworkers. People who relate to your situation are usually fair, objective critics. They can help, really. That's why we call them friends. (Change background music to *I'll Be There For You*, by the Rembrandts; theme to *Friends* TV show.)

Time yourself, then add 20 percent, to check the time limit.

Most people talk slower and elaborate more extemporaneously during the graded speech, so add 20 percent to your practice time and you'll do fine. If your first practice is twenty-five minutes for a ten-minute talk, delete half your outline and start your two practices over again, because you'll have a whole different speech. I say two times, because ten times is absolutely too many. If you "overpractice," your delivery will become too memorized and therefore too mechanical. Trust yourself. With a good outline and some good sensory aids, you will remember most of what you want to say. That's almost perfect!

SUMMARY CHECKLIST FOR DELIVERY

Talk Like You Talk

- ❑ Use a conversational, natural delivery style, like talking with friends
- ❑ We don't like robots!
- ❑ Focus on audience rather than self
- ❑ Use some humor; tell a story; use sensory aids
- ❑ Be **Sincere:** Sincere concern is more important than credentials

Delivery Methods

- ❑ Manuscript: Reading every word; for political correctness; mechanical
- ❑ Memorization: Memorizing every word; like a play; mechanical
- ❑ Impromptu: Little or no preparation; content/delivery must suffer
- ❑ Extemporaneous: (Pick me!) Combines best facets of all styles; human

Key Elements of Delivery (Verbal and Nonverbal)

- ❑ "Noise" hurts communication; delivery elements cut through the noise
- ❑ *Very Energetic Folks Invariably Make Good Public Speakers*
- ❑ Volume: We *must* hear you!
- ❑ Eyes: You *must* look at us!
- ❑ Face: I bet you can smile
- ❑ Inflection: No monotone voice; vary pitch and rate; use power of the pause
- ❑ Movement: Find a reason to move
- ❑ Gestures: Natural, consistent with words; avoid distracting gestures
- ❑ Posture: Speak *out*, not *down*; face your audience square on, not sideways
- ❑ Sincerity: Worth repeating; be sincere and the delivery follows . . . naturally

Words

- ❑ Don't be too formal: "Talk Like You Talk" with your own vocabulary
- ❑ Wrong Words: If in doubt, dictionary; be aware of malapropisms
- ❑ Articulation: Do not mumble! Speak clearly and distinctly

- ❏ Pronunciation: Like spelling and meaning, when in doubt, check it
- ❏ Filler Words: uh, um, ah, like, yeah, and, stuff like that, you know?
- ❏ Repeat Words: *Any* word is annoying if repeated too often

Practice

- ❏ You need to practice, but don't practice too much
- ❏ Add 20 percent to practice time for a good feel of actual speech time
- ❏ Practice out loud with friends, especially for a group speech. Next Chapter!

Image © Yuri Arcurs, 2012. Used under license from Shutterstock, Inc.

YOU can do this!

FALL INTO THE TEAM TRAP!

Be:
There
Ready
Attentive
Polite

Image © iQoncept, 2012. Used under license from Shutterstock, Inc.

When you're part of a team working on a speech, it really helps if you fall into the TRAP for your weekly meetings: be **T**here, be **R**eady, be **A**ttentive, and be **P**olite.

My master's degree is in Human Relations, which is basically, well, "relating to humans." In other words, I learned about the theory of getting along with other people. As a member of the Air Force team for twenty-five years, I also got to practice that theory with a few real people. Now I'm writing a book, and I'm very tempted to expound upon the virtues of teamwork and all its glory (rah! rah!) . . . but you, dear readers, are the wrong audience. You might not even have to do a group speech in your speech course. If you do, it's probably a minor portion of your class. If you really needed to know about teamwork, you would enroll in a Group Dynamics course or an upper division communications course about small groups. If groups become a serious part of your real-life job, you'll most likely attend some team-building seminars or a leadership symposium. Therefore, this little chapter will deal mostly with some simple, practical hints about teams. You don't have to know much of the theory behind the hints for now; just trust me when I say they work. Then, whenever you have time, I strongly encourage you to take a formal course in group dynamics, especially if you want to stay married more than six weeks. My name is David Calvin McLaughlin, and I approve this message.

I will assume that my audience today is a small team of three-to-five freshmen who will meet once a week for a month to prepare a nice thirty- to forty-minute presentation. Go Team!

WHY TEAM TALKS?

Many of my students do not like group projects, so they'll ask, "Why do we have to do stupid group speeches?" (They don't say "stupid," but I can hear the brain cells rattling around.) I just tell them to shut up (I don't say "shut up," but they can hear my age taking a long, deep breath), and then I chain them into their seats and show them videotapes of all the North Carolina basketball championship games. Then we watch clips of the Thunderbirds, Tom Hanks on the beaches of Normandy looking for Private Ryan and in space with Apollo 13, and maybe some Irish line dancers. I make them all give two-minute impromptu speeches on the importance of their family, including pictures of their dogs. (In the background I play songs from the *Sound of Music*.) Finally, I show them the Appalachian State football victory over Michigan in 2007, or maybe the Boise State Fiesta Bowl victory over Oklahoma the previous season, and we remember the Titans. (I love football.) If you cannot get excited about groups excelling under impossible odds, then you either have never been on a team of any kind, or you're dead inside. Only loners would question the validity of an academic group exercise.

> *People acting together as a group can accomplish things which no individual acting alone could ever hope to bring about.*
>
> **—Franklin Delano Roosevelt**

If you have ever been on a team, you know what President Roosevelt was talking about. If your coach or band leader or yearbook advisor was worth his or her salt, he or she probably went to the blackboard at some point and wrote, in bold letters: **There is no "I" in team!** Old, trite, and very valid. Some people say they don't like groups because they don't like to lose their individuality, but if they were ever in a "good" group, they would know about synergy. **Synergy is that magic juice that makes the total greater than the sum of the individual parts.** Your individuality will not suffer in a group; it will grow in leaps and bounds! Teams can pull great stuff out of you that you could never pull out by yourself. As the old saying goes, "The Wizard of Oz never did give nuthin' to the Tin Man that he didn't already have." The Wizard just created a situation for three loners in which *teamwork* pulled leadership out of the Scarecrow, bravery out of the Lion, and heart out of the Tin Man, which resulted in a better ending. (At least I thought the melting wicked witch was a better ending than the monkeys pulling straw out of the Scarecrow.) Teams can give us hope that we can make fiction reality. Therefore, I always say:

**If you want something done faster, do it yourself.
If you want it done better, do it in a group.**

Unless you plan to live on an island by yourself, you will have to work in groups. As for team talks, per se, they *are* common in the real world. For longer presentations, it's better to "break up the voices" and "mix up the air" with different styles of public speaking so the audience will pay better attention. Plus, a team can bring more expertise and knowledge to one place than any individual. This classroom small-group experience shows folks how such a real-world presentation might look. It also allows people another opportunity to better comprehend how to enhance group work in general. One of the keys is "influence." Teams form due to a common interest and similar motivation, and they grow due to an acknowledged influence that they have on each other. Once you realize that someone is your wingman or your homie, you know you must perform better to keep him or her safe. (Some people never comprehend this truth until they hold their own baby in their arms the first time.) I was at a leadership conference in 1984 in St. Louis, and a guest speaker gave a moving presentation about influence. He gave us all stickers with the following quote, and I still have my sticker on my desk:

> There *are* people whose feelings and well being are
> within my influence. I will *never* escape that!

I wish I could remember that man's name so I could acknowledge him, but I'm guessing he knows he had an influence on at least one person (me!) at that conference. Bottom line: **You Cannot NOT Have Influence.** (If you miss a team meeting, you still have influence, probably in a negative way. Who do you think they are talking about.....?) Remember that, and learn about group communication whenever possible. I know your speech group is not the most serious organization in the world, but take advantage of the situation and at least try to learn a little bit about yourself and how well *you* work with other people. For example,

many of my students who didn't get any real leadership experience in high school find out during our group exercises that they have some hidden talents. You won't use those talents to save the world this year, but maybe the lessons can serve you later on.

> *On the fields of friendly strife are sown the seeds*
> *that on other days and other fields will bear the*
> *fruits of victory.*
>
> **—General Douglas MacArthur**

General MacArthur was one of our great WWII leaders, and he was referring to his football playing days at West Point and how that "friendly" teamwork competition prepared him to later lead men into combat. If you are too young to relate to that example, then maybe you would like an *Extreme Makeover: Home Edition.*

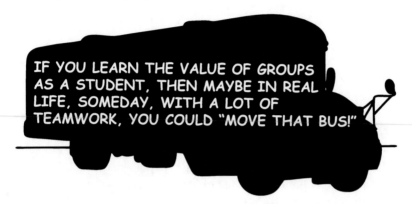

We are all better and stronger because of our groups. No argument. Rudyard Kipling wrote a famous poem called *The Law of the Jungle* where he said, "The strength of the pack is the wolf, and the strength of the wolf is the pack." So pack it up, and let's get to work on that stupid team talk you have to do.

ADMINISTRATION

Before you can start a group speech, you have to get some administration junk out of the way. If your instructor or boss gives you all the following information, fine. If not, I suggest you ask, or at least discuss them with your group members before you travel very far. Don't leave home without these items!

- How will you determine group members?
- What's the date/time/location for the presentation?
- Does everyone get the same grade?
- Any special format for the talk?
- Focus more on content or delivery?
- Where/When to have meetings?
- What's the topic?
- Make a contacts list

This would be a good time to scan through *Chapter Two, Getting Started*, again. Your group needs to know the Why, Who, What, Where, and When of the assignment. Now, let me elaborate on the unique focus of these items for team talks.

Determine Group Members

If the instructor/boss puts the group together, so be it. If you have a say in the matter, you might be tempted to get into groups with your friends, people who think like you. Let me offer this strong advice: **Look for people who are different from you.** You will question each other more and end up with a better presentation. (I'll discuss "groupthink" later, on page 159.) In most classes, you don't know each other, and the instructor doesn't know you, so it can be a very random selection. I like to use the following criteria: age, gender, international culture, and left/right brain orientation. I like each group to have the experience of age and the energy of youth, the aggressiveness of men and the patience of women, and the wisdom that comes from awareness of other people and places. Then I check their brains:

- *LEFT BRAIN:* More objective, mechanical; major in technical areas like engineering or accounting. Loves a "bottom line." Never loses car keys; balances checkbook.
- *RIGHT BRAIN:* More subjective, artsy; major in humanities like English or music. Loves the "gray area." Often misplaces car keys; doesn't the bank know my balance?

Okay, okay, okay. Don't get too sensitive about being put into a category. (I'm speaking to the right-brained people.) These are just gross generalities, which have some truth. We all use *both* sides of our brains, but some of us really do lean heavily toward one side. The right brainers tend to be better with generating ideas and discussion; left brainers are better with organization and implementation. The bottom line here (I'm speaking to the left-brained people) is that **a good team needs both brains!** P.S. I also favor odd-numbered groups (five is best), so that you can vote on things without getting a tie.

Date/Time/Location

Decide the speaking date early so the group can set up some milestones. Unlike individual work, team talks do not allow you to procrastinate until the last possible moment. You have to show your teammates enough work, early, so they are comfortable with your preparation. Know the total time limit allowed for the actual speech so that each individual can talk equal time. Location dictates equipment.

Everyone Get the Same Grade?

I hate groups like this, and most students do, too. When everyone gets the same grade, not everyone will do the same work. Haven't you been in a group where you did all the work, and your lazy teammate got the same grade? That's simply not fair. I can easily see differences in my groups with quality of outlines, research, support, visual aids, and delivery. I also have students complete peer reports so they have a chance to give me feedback on how everyone did in the group, including themselves. Having such a peer report tends to keep academic groups honest. In the real world, don't fool yourself and think the boss won't find out you did not pull your own weight. I tell my groups they can tell me if they want to "fire" a group member with a poor attitude, and then I'll talk to that student. I think the real world works like that, too. So, if you have instructors who give everyone the same grade, I suggest you talk with them and see if they'll be open to some kind of peer feedback, at least for the extreme individuals. As students, you shouldn't have to deal with difficult people during a temporary group assignment. As I learned from Ken Alstad's *Savvy Sayin's:*

> Never approach a bull from the front, a horse from the rear,
> or a fool from any direction.

Special Formats

The average academic group presentation is one person talking after another, each for the same amount of time. That's fine, but some groups want to be more creative. Some individuals find a way to get up three times, two minutes each time, rather than talking their allowed six minutes all in one shot. Sometimes two people talk together, back and forth, for twelve minutes. I've seen symposium and forum presentations, as well as panel discussions and debates. Skits can be fun, but I don't recommend you structure a whole team talk around a skit format because it can start to sound like a play for entertainment instead of a talk for information. "Town hall meetings" seem to be a current trend, since the media uses that format with politicians. Overall, you are probably only limited by your imagination. Ask your instructor/boss if a certain format is required.

Content or Delivery Focus

In the real world, I think the focus is always on content, but delivery is important. In upper-division major courses, I think the same is true. For 100- and 200-level speech courses, however, I think delivery and teamwork are more important for team talks. Just be sure to know what your instructor believes.

Meeting Location/Time

When you are first put into groups, find a time/place to meet that matches everyone's schedule, then treat that meeting like another class and be there. Most of my groups say they meet once a week for about an hour. You can coordinate many things by phone and e-mail, but "face time" is ultimately required.

Topic

The first meeting should only be thirty minutes, just to determine the topic. (Review page 38; brainstorming topics.) Of course, if the topic is given to you, the first meeting could be a pizza party to get to know everyone better. Hey, maybe you could do both?! So, come to the meeting ready to suggest topic ideas . . . and maybe topping ideas.

Image © Raywoo, 2012. Used under license from Shutterstock, Inc.

Contacts List

Very important! Learn everyone's *full* name. Record phone numbers and e-mail addresses. If you're running late to a meeting, call. If people "no show," call them. If you have questions/ideas between meetings, call. Every person doesn't have to be at every meeting to do well, but you do have to **keep in touch!**

TRICKS OF THE TRADE

Once you have the administrative details answered, you can get to work. Here are some street lessons I've gathered through the years, working with many teams:

Be:
There
Ready
Attentive
Polite

- Pick a Leader!
- Followers, recognize your informal leadership strengths
- Mix task and social aspects of the group
- Everyone talks equal time during the speech, so have a time-control method
- Everyone does individual research, outline, bibliography, and sensory aids
- Do introduction and conclusion as a team
- For meetings, fall into the team TRAP

Early on in the group process, discuss the items listed. You may agree to disagree, but at least talk about them. If everyone understands these "tricks of the trade" up front, I promise you there will be fewer problems. One subtle trick is to **call yourselves a team instead of a group**. "Group" sounds a bit vanilla, pedestrian, ordinary, and blah. "Team" implies more commitment, teamwork, uniqueness, and hurrah! For example, my "group" saw that new movie last weekend, but my "team" built a house for Habitat for Humanity, won a gold medal at the Olympics, and found a cure for cancer! Go Team!

Pick a Leader

Not all groups have leaders, but all teams do. **You NEED a leader.** Some academic groups fight this. No one really wants to be the leader, and they think they'll just sorta kinda maybe somehow muddle along with all of them being leaders. "Muddle" would be the operable word here, like a body wandering around without a head. There are many ways to select a leader, and I love to ask my teams how they did it. Here are the most common methods I hear:

Pegge was the smartest; Mike was the oldest;
Kelly kept us relaxed; Chris had the idea for the topic;
Becca seemed the most confident; Rachel had actually
read the group instructions; Anita was the most organized;
Bill had good visuals; Bob had more ideas
than anyone else; Shawn arrived last to the meeting.

You guys probably know who the leader will be after one meeting. Just admit it. It really doesn't take much debate. You're just doing a speech, not crossing the Atlantic in a sixteen-foot boat. Then, **let the leader lead!** Here are some basic leader duties:

- Set meeting times/locations
- Determine the agenda and stick to it
- Basically guide the discussions
- Get everyone involved
- Summarize the meeting
- Contact lost souls as needed
- Keep the Peace. Amen.

It helps if the leader is more democratic (Roosevelt) than autocratic (Hitler). The leader of an academic team talk doesn't really have any more power and usually doesn't get paid any more money than the followers. Here at MSU, we don't even give the leaders a reserved parking spot or guarantee them an "A." I also hear it's lonely at the top.

Followers Lead, Too!

The good news for the formal leader (with position power) is that everyone else can be an informal leader (with knowledge or charisma power) at any given time. At the least, leaders should pick a deputy dog to rule over the masses in their absence, when they skip to the south of France. Every team member can cross-check the leader on his/her duties; everyone can keep an eye on the clock and a focus on the agenda. In addition, every person brings some unique knowledge or talent to the team, so they can "rise as a leader" when those skills are used. For example, there is probably someone on each team who is the best at one of the following group needs:

- Outlining skills, including how to do a proper bibliography
- Computer skills, especially PowerPoint knowledge
- Research skills; will get more research than others and share it
- Visual aid skills; someone has more artistic talent or creative ideas
- Organization skills; see agenda needs early; suggest milestones; take notes
- Social skills; positive attitude; laughs out loud; calls people; makes others smile; keeps the peace.
- Devil's advocate; asks great questions; makes team evaluate more closely

Good team members will recognize their unique skills and use them to improve the team. Some books list fancy names for people who help to accomplish tasks (Left brain, like *initiator, orienter,* or *evaluator*) or who enhance relationships (Right brain, like *harmonizer, encourager,* or *coordinator*). Teams need such people, but they don't need folks who inhibit progress (NO brain, like *blockers, aggressors,* or *dominators.*) I don't think you need to know the labels, but certainly be aware of the actions that the labels represent. What kind of team member do *you* want to be? I know you don't want to be the "#!@?&!%^!?#!!" Basically, you have three choices on a team:

1. Lead
2. Follow, or
3. *Get the Hell Outa' the Way!*

Task and Social Teams

In the Air Force, we used to have what I called "Mandatory Fun." There would be some social activity that we were "highly encouraged" to attend, which really meant "be there." I often resisted such social events, but once I arrived, I would have fun. It was always interesting to see my coworkers and commanders in a different light: off base, casual clothes instead of uniforms, and with spouses. If you can play with your teammates, it usually makes it easier to work with them. For your academic team, try to meet off campus once or twice, maybe at a coffee shop or pizza place. My groups that meet at someone's house with food and drink always seem to be more cohesive on the day of the team talk. At least take a few moments at the start of each meeting to get to know each other a bit better; show some concern for each other's classes, jobs, friends, and family. If you act like you know each other and actually like each other during your graded presentation, we will listen better.

Talk Equal Time

I often hear group talks, and it's *extremely* common for one person to dominate the time. It's usually the first speaker. It is SO annoying to watch one person talk for twenty-five minutes of a forty-minute presentation, leaving his four team-mates fifteen minutes total to rush through their portions. You should all agree that you will each talk roughly the same amount of time in the body of the speech, but many groups have a "long talker" who seriously has no concept of time. You MUST discuss this phenomenon at one of your meetings and agree upon an overt **time-control method.**

- Someone needs to be the official time keeper for each section and give a signal
- Try a subtle time signal, like time cards, or gestures (tap watch, slashing throat)
- If subtlety fails, do NOT hesitate to stand up and slowly move toward the speaker
- Finally, if that fails, agree that it is not mean and cruel punishment to more overtly get the long talker to shut up, such as touching her shoulder or duct taping his mouth

The long talker is usually the result of poor planning/procrastination. It is MUCH easier to give a rambling twenty-minute talk than a short, concise, effective five-minute talk. Therefore, I allow my groups to throw things (soft things, dry things, painless things) at the offensive long talker. I am not kidding. I wish real-world groups would do this, too; it's funny, it wakes up the audience, and it works! Most groups are in the "polite stage" and will simply allow one member to ruin time control for everyone else, which ultimately ruins the presentation for your audience. If every audience in every world were armed with ping-pong balls to fling at a speaker who went grossly overtime, I would smile.

Everyone Does Own Work

This sounds so common sense, but again, I see this violated with many groups. "Teams" understand and embrace this trick of the trade. At the first meeting, individuals can be quick to volunteer: "I'll do the group outline. I'll do the group PowerPoint. I'll do the introduction or conclusion." What those statements sometimes mean is: "I don't want to do any research or any real work. Y'all give me your work, and I'll just format it. I certainly don't want to talk much during the speech." Today, I am older and wiser and combat tested in the heated arena of laziness, so I make sure that each individual on the team does his/her own research, bibliography, outline, and visual aids. (If your instructor does not enforce this, your team should discuss it.) The team can certainly help individuals with their work.

Team Introduction/Conclusion

Before I learned to enforce the "equal work" ideal, I heard people talk for two minutes during the introduction of a group speech and then never talk again. Afterward, I would say, "Where's your outline and bibliography?" and they would say, "Oh, I didn't need to do that. The only thing the group gave me to do was the introduction." Uh-huh. If you have a particularly weak team member, you might be tempted to assign him bare minimum tasks so he won't make your team "look bad." Fight this temptation, and challenge that individual to do more. Remember this is an academic exercise, and the goal is to learn and grow (the process), not to give the perfect group presentation (the product). One fun way to get everyone working together is planning the introduction and conclusion.

Flip back to page 104 right now and review the steps of introduction/ conclusion. You might each take one of those steps ("I'll do a visual aid and talk about the purpose statement."), or maybe each of you can talk during the preview or the credibility steps ("I'll be discussing the safety issues of our topic, and I interviewed a nurse.") If the audience sees all of you up front together, they can more easily grasp who you are and what parts you'll cover. It also makes you seem more like a team if you all participate in the beginning, rather than just a random group of individuals who happened to show up at the same place and time. This is where you show us that you really know each other and like each other, you're excited about your topic, and you did good research/preparation. In other words, we're ready to listen to your team! After the body of the speech, I highly recommend you all go back up front to do the conclusion as a team, too.

Most teams plan the introduction and conclusion at their last meeting, usually the night before the graded presentation. For a thirty- to forty-minute talk, the introduction would be about three minutes, and the conclusion about two. You probably want to practice these sections out loud once to see if you're in the ballpark on time.

As a guide for team meetings, you should fall into the TRAP.

FALL INTO THE TEAM TRAP

Some people just hate group work, mostly due to poor meetings. In *Public Speaking, An Audience-Centered Approach*, Steven and Susan Beebe list the most cited meeting sins:

Getting off the subject	No goals or agenda
Too long	Poor preparation
Disorganized	Poor leadership
Irrelevant information	Wasted time
Starting late	Interruptions
Rambling discussion	Dominant individuals

I concur, completely. These sins are a reflection of weak leadership and poor teamwork, and I hear them so often that I must assume we could all use more work in this area. For that reason, I created another mnemonic device to hopefully guide people toward more productive team meetings, a simple device that addresses all the sins listed: TRAP (Be *T*here, Be *R*eady, Be *A*ttentive, and Be *P*olite). Whether you know it or not, when you agree to be part of a team talk, you have signed an unwritten agreement to follow these four primary guidelines. They are simply a result of the Golden Rule (coming up in Chapter Nine). You hate it when people violate these guidelines, so don't be the one who violates them yourself.

Be There, on Time

My wife, Catherine, is the aquatics director at a swim school, and her biggest problem is swim instructors who come late to work or do not show up at all. She consistently has stories about rewriting the instructor assignments at the last moment or even having to cancel classes due to employees not showing up. I wish this were a limited problem in the workforce, but you know it's not. Think about the part-time job you have, and think how annoying it is when other workers do not show up, and they don't even call. I think these academic team talks should be treated like a part-time job, and the biggest complaint I hear is people not coming to meetings. It's no secret. Your team should agree on a time/place to meet that allows each member to participate, and then treat that time like another class. Woody Allen once said:

"Showing up" does NOT mean "making an appearance." No one likes the drama queen who blows in and out like Hurricane Katrina because her life is just so much more important and hectic than ours. "Be there" for the whole meeting. If you prove you can come to work on time every day and do decent work, you will be promoted ahead of most other people. If you show up to each group meeting for this exercise, the public speaking gods will smile down upon you. If you're running late, call. While I'm on the topic of time, let me stress some other good group guidelines for meetings:

- Start the meeting *on time*, even if people are missing.
- End the meeting *on time*. This should be the first item discussed at every meeting; "When will we stop?" Agree on a time, and then stick to it! If people know there is a definite stopping point, they will be more attentive and productive.
- No three hour meetings, please! No one is productive at that point. Academic teams should really limit their meetings to sixty to ninety minutes, like a class. We have sixty-minute butts, so take a break!
- Someone must keep an eye on the clock. That doesn't mean you're not listening; it just means you're the time keeper, "keepin' it real."

Be Ready, with Research

Don't you just love the people who show up at group meetings and say, "Sorry, I didn't have time to do my research/work this week; I guess I'm just busier and more important than the rest of you. So, what do you have for me?!" They may use other words, but that's what we hear. A big reason to have weekly meetings for team talks is to make everyone feel better that the flight is "on time and on target." If you do not have your research ready to discuss, you're slowing progress. As I learned watching a *Star Trek* episode or two, "Insufficient data does not compute." (Thank you, Spock.) You will have some homework to do for the team each week, based upon the agenda you'll coordinate. Bring that homework with you, and be ready for discussions:

- Briefly share what research you found; discuss content and credibility.
- How/where can you use the research? It might fit best in a teammate's part.
- Does there seem to be a logical flow to everyone's section and support?
- Is there a good mix of CENTS? Using too many statistics/quotes?
- Deconflict research; be sure two people aren't using the same pie chart.
- What sensory aids would be best to display the awesome research?
- Everyone needs to be willing to evaluate the research; is it good?
- Which means everyone needs to talk, so be ready to talk. That means to have something to talk about, and don't be shy. The clock is ticking . . .

Be Attentive to the Agenda

You have probably heard the three most important words in real estate: location, location, location. Well, for team talk meetings, the three most important words are *agenda, agenda, agenda.* Near the end of each meeting, you should briefly set the agenda for the next meeting so that everyone knows what homework to do. You could look at page 89 in this book to get started, reviewing the basic organizational steps you need to take for any speech. You simply cannot procrastinate in a team, so it's nice if you can set up the big milestones early. The following is just one example of a timeline you might choose. I've made the assumption you have a month to plan, and you will have four meetings, one each week:

- 1st Meeting: Brainstorm the topic. (thirty minutes)
- 2nd Meeting: Have exploratory research done; discuss enough to confirm topic and divide up parts for each member. (sixty minutes)
- 3rd Meeting: Have specific research done for each part; each person has a draft outline for his/her section; confirm order of main points; brainstorm ideas for sensory aids. (sixty minutes)
- 4th Meeting: Each member has outline and aids "mostly" done; convince other members you are ready for the graded speech. Discuss how to do introduction/conclusion as team. Practice as desired. (ninety minutes)

Of course, you're probably allowed to add/subtract to those agenda suggestions to fit your specific team needs. I shall check with my boss. Meanwhile, at least have some kind of plan and a spoken agreement to stick to that agenda so everyone can get home tonight. The leader should make sure people stay "on task" so that you don't end up talking an hour about Monday Night Football. **The world needs more short meetings.** In his book, *Taking Charge*, Major General Perry M. Smith says leaders must know how to run meetings: establish ground rules, stay on track, allow everyone to express views and disagreements, and know how to wrap up meetings on time with a good summary. Specifically, he said, "American leaders especially must fight the cultural tendency to hold long, undisciplined meetings with little useful output." How are we ever going to fight this ugly trend in the corporate world if we don't start now, in the academic world? Remember those twelve "meeting sins" at the start of this TRAP section? Well, at least eight of them will go away if we all pay attention and be attentive to our agendas.

One other thing to be attentive to is poor group decisions. Sometimes, teams will decide upon a poor course of action just because no one on the team was willing to speak out against it. We call this *groupthink*, and even though it might sound like something you want, **GROUPTHINK IS BAD!** It's basically gross conformity with the group just because you don't want to be the one to "rock the boat." The space shuttle Challenger crashed in 1986 due to groupthink; it was a classic study used at the Air Command and Staff College when I taught there in the late 1980s. Sad. Your academic group won't crash an aircraft, but your grade might crash if you allow the group to do something stupid. One of the team members should play "devil's advocate" and poke holes in the group's decisions, forcing them to look at the other side of each *coin*. That practice will *pay* dividends. If you're really attentive, you might even be able to prevent poor presentational puns.

As the great Winston Churchill once said, "Let our advance worrying become advance thinking and planning." I think he was talking about preparing for Hitler's Germany during WWII, but it also applies to team talks. If you plan in advance with good agendas, you'll have less to worry about on the day of the talk. Or, as the great Larry the Cable Guy said, once or twice, "Git 'er done!" Go Team!

Be Polite and Personable

The opposite of groupthink is "open communication," a positive environment where everyone feels free to share ideas. The leader can help set such an open mood, but every team member can reinforce it by being . . . you guessed it . . . polite and personable. Those two words may sound synonymous, but polite means you have "considerable regard for others," and personable means you have a pleasant disposition. In other words, you sincerely care and respect other people, and you can smile, out loud.

If you see the high value of these two qualities in a group, you can see that "selfish" and "moody" don't have much value. Dominant, selfish people need to talk all the time, and they want the group to accept their ideas, or they shut down. "It's my way or the highway." Immature, moody people can be totally distracting to a group with their negative body language and frowns. They don't talk and don't look at people. We all have "baggage" in this life, but we need to consciously leave the bags out in the hallway when we enter a team meeting. Trust me, no one will steal the baggage; it will still be there after the meeting. Meanwhile, bring a smile to the meeting and a willingness to share information and be a good listener. Here are some practical hints to help the team:

- Play fair; everyone should get to talk about the same amount of time at meetings
- Listen fair; listen to the whole idea before you judge it; don't interrupt
- Pause, just a moment, and think, before you critique ideas
- Critique the idea, NOT the person. I know you see the difference between "Your idea might not work, Jonah; let's discuss it" and "You're stupid, Cruz! I'm not doing that!"
- "Share the spotlight" and ensure everyone has an equal part of the presentation
- Think open-minded and open communication vs closed-minded and groupthink
- Remember it's an academic group for one month, not a marriage for life

There is bound to be some conflict in the group. Not every individual will be 100 percent committed to the group or even the topic. Not everyone wants to work hard enough to earn an "A." Acknowledge those differences and don't get too excited. At least agree to disagree. You are not trained, professional counselors, so don't try to manage serious conflicts on your own. Walk away first, and let your instructor know about it. Not every group is like a Norman Rockwell painting of a family's Thanksgiving dinner. Indeed, some groups are more like the South Park episode, *Woodland Critter Christmas*. It all seems to work out okay in the end. Just do the best you can, and try not to kill Kenny.

COMPROMISE

One of the best ways to avoid conflict is to compromise. If you have learned something this chapter about left- and right-brained people, groupthink, and playing devil's advocate, then you know that you don't even want everyone to agree 100 percent of the time. Some conflict is healthy for the group, if it's processed properly. Ruth Graham, the wife of the famous evangelist Billy Graham, said, "If two people agree on everything, one of them is unnecessary." Welcome the opportunity to cuss and discuss freely and openly . . . and fairly. Such discussions keep us honest. We might call this democracy, which at best is a compromise, and in the long run, it usually results in a better product. Just as we hope the democrats and republicans keep the country's interest in mind, we must also trust each team member to keep the team in mind.

> *In order to have a winner, the team must have a feeling of unity; every player must put the team first, ahead of personal glory.*
>
> **—Coach Paul Bear Bryant**

Bear Bryant was the famous coach of the Alabama Crimson Tide football team, and he's often quoted on the topic of team building. Roll Tide! If he were the leader of your team, you would do well, but you'd probably still struggle to beat Auburn. War Damn Eagle! See how I compromised and represented both schools, who sometimes act like they don't even like each other? A cornerstone of compromise is this truth:

> YOU DON'T HAVE TO *LIKE* EACH OTHER
> TO *RESPECT* EACH OTHER.

If you respect your teammates, you can probably just discuss conflicts and decisions until you reach an acceptable compromise that everyone can live with. If you are pinched for time, you can just put it to a vote. If it's a tie, allow the leader to break the tie. Keep the "big picture" in mind and don't get hung up on minutia, which sounds a lot like "manure" if you say it fast. You can avoid a lot of crap if you'll just remember the *four most important words* in the English language, which you first heard on page 28: **"I MIGHT BE WRONG."** Say these words out loud. If you want to be a good team member and open the door for the inevitable compromise, say them once at each meeting. The complementary phrase **"You Might Be Right"** also works well. Try not to say, "Here's your sign." (Thanks, Bill Engvall.)

One last thought on compromise. Just as there is no such thing as a perfect speech or perfect audience analysis, there is no such thing as a perfect group, and certainly no perfect meeting. When you work with other people, there is always something a touch annoying lurking about. That's normal. So, you need to have a gimmick I learned about while flying tactical airlift missions around the world, missions full of broken schedules and broken promises: **RIGID FLEXIBILITY!** It's a *paradox*, a statement that at first appears contradictory but upon closer inspection bears great truth. (If life is a paradox, I want two pair....) Remember Murphy's Law: If something can go wrong, it will. So, stay loose as a goose. Expect the unexpected. Smile all the while. Take one shot of whiskey. These words of wisdom help with all aspects of public speaking, especially team talks.

PRACTICE AND PRESENTATION

During your last team meeting, you'll want to develop the introduction and conclusion together, and then you should practice it . . . out loud. I believe in that, because as I said on page 105 when I talked about introductions, your team should "almost memorize" this opening few minutes so you can deliver it in a direct, confident manner. As for practicing the entire team talk out loud, you probably don't need to. I think most of you knights can just sit at the round table and walk the team through your talk: "I'm going to do some of this, then that, and finally those. I've got these four visual aids. I'll mention these two sources out loud. I have three examples, two statistics, one expert quote, and, oh yeah, do I have time to show this video clip? Let me show you the clip!" Just take a few minutes to convince the team you are all that and a bag of chips. If they have doubts, they'll ask to see/hear more. If you would like to practice your section out loud in front of your team, just ask. I'm sure they would be happy to listen and offer feedback.

If the group agrees to practice the whole thing out loud, fine. Try to do it in place with all the same equipment as the real deal, if possible. This is a good time to review my advice about practicing on page 139. For teams, once is okay; twice, maybe; three or more, never.

During the *actual presentation*, consider these *guidelines*:

- Do not all stand up the whole time; sit down and be comfortable until you talk. Standing up does not support the speaker; it is actually quite distracting.
- Do sit up in front of the class, but probably to one side of the speaker.
- Do not be so comfortable that you fall asleep; the audience is watching you, too.
- Help each other out as necessary, especially with sensory aids.
- Be very aware of your nonverbal body language; if you look bored or angry or really confused, or you cover your mouth to laugh, it won't help your teammate's talk.
- Pay attention to each talk; Do NOT work on your own speech.
- Give your friend nonverbal support, like smiles, head nods, thumbs up, and money.
- Quick side comments to a buddy sitting next to you might be okay, especially during transitions between speakers, but keep it short!
- Don't fidget too much. If you have to scratch, don't make it memorable.
- Keep an eye on the time; help enforce the time-control method.

In short, be a good listener (Chapter Ten). Don't be a distraction.

During *transitions* between speakers, be polite. Introduce the next speaker, by name and maybe topic. Say "please" and "thank you," just like your mother taught you. Say "good job" and "awesome" like your dad taught you. Do not pat each other on the butt like your coach taught you. These little words of praise and friendliness are just natural parts of a team, and they certainly don't have to be said loudly enough for the audience to hear. Any audience enjoys watching people who seem to like and respect each other.

Go Team!

SUMMARY CHECKLIST FOR TEAM TALKS

Why Team Talks?

- ❑ Teams do things an individual never could, and they do them better
- ❑ The team synergy will enhance the growth of individuals
- ❑ Most of us live and work with teams; we do have influence on others

Administration

- ❑ If possible, form your team with people different from you
- ❑ Confirm: date, time, location, grading system, and special formats
- ❑ Agree on time/place for meetings; plan at least one meeting a week
- ❑ MUST have a contacts list; keep in touch!

Tricks of the Trade

- ❑ Definitely pick a leader
- ❑ Allow everyone to emerge as a leader at times based upon special talents
- ❑ Mix in some social aspects with the task requirements
- ❑ Everyone talks equal time in speech; MUST have time-control method
- ❑ Everyone does own research, outline, bibliography, and sensory aids
- ❑ Plan introduction and conclusion together; present these parts as a team

Fall into the Team TRAP (for meetings)

- ❑ Be There, on Time; 90% of success is just showing up; start/stop on time
- ❑ Be Ready, with Research; share info; deconflict content; good CENTS?
- ❑ Be Attentive to the Agenda; keep an eye on the clock; fight groupthink
- ❑ Be Polite and Personable; listen and critique fairly; open communication

Compromise

- ❑ Compromise is a normal and necessary part of all teamwork
- ❑ You don't have to like someone to respect them
- ❑ Have Rigid Flexibility

Practice and Presentation

❑   Practice a little as a team, especially the intro/conclusion; coordinate a lot
❑   Be a good listener when your teammates are giving their speeches

Andrew Carnegie said, "No person will make a great business who wants to do it all himself or get all the credit." That's a clear, simple lesson. Let's Keep It Simple, Stupid!

GO TEAM!

Chapter 8
KEEP IT SIMPLE

K.I.S.S.

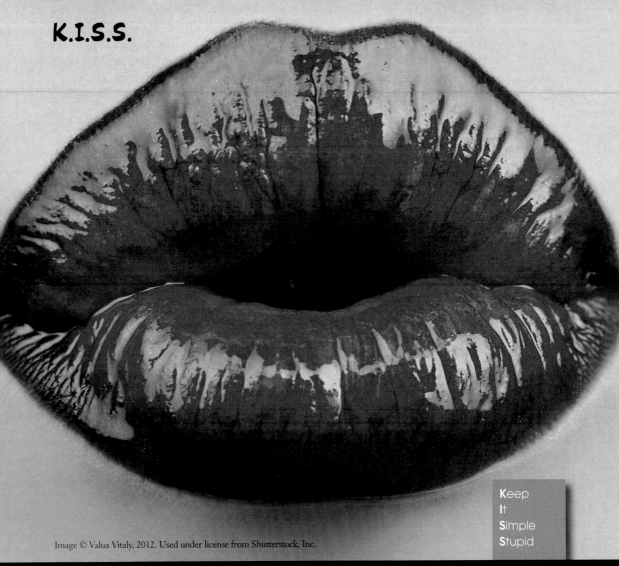

Keep
It
Simple
Stupid

Image © Valua Vitaly, 2012. Used under license from Shutterstock, Inc.

Note: "KISS" is an acronym that I have heard throughout my life and seen in numerous textbooks. It applies to any professional or social endeavor I can imagine, especially public speaking. The letters stand for "Keep It Simple, Stupid." If you need to be more politically correct, the last "S" could stand for student, silly, or even Stan, if your friend Stan-the-man just needs a gentle reminder to shorten his very long jokes or stories.

was in the seventh grade when the Beatles invaded America. I watched with a big smile and wide eyes as they sang on the *Ed Sullivan Show.* Some people hated their long hair and the crazy "noise" they made that could not be real music like Frank Sinatra or Andy Williams. Surely the Beatles could not make music that would last. We all can now laugh at those initial reactions from the "Big Band" generation, because all of us (even you second generation Beatles fans) have some words from Beatles songs playing around in our happy brains, forever! Quick! Tell me a Beatles song. Quick! What's the first thought in your head?! When I ask that question, I rarely get something like *A Day in the Life, Fixing a Hole,* or *Being for the Benefit of Mr. Kite!* I usually get answers like *I Want to Hold your Hand, Love Me Do, All You Need Is Love,* or *Yellow Submarine.* What's my point? Okay, you're right. I should quit my reminiscing and rambling and get to my point, and make that point clear and concise and simple. I offer the *sub*lime message that follows.

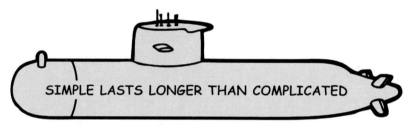

SIMPLE LASTS LONGER THAN COMPLICATED

The early Beatles songs were much simpler than their later songs. Simple words, simple phrases, repeated more often. They simply stick in our heads better, even if we all don't live in a yellow submarine. In contrast, when I read the words from *Being for the Benefit of Mr. Kite!,* I'm still scratching my head about the meaning. (I'm old.) If I just listened to the words once, without a visual aid or explanation/ comparison, I would be even more confused. If it's a song with music that's more entertaining than the words we don't care so much. However, if it's a speech with words that should convey "meaning" and not just entertainment we care much more. **A speech audience is much different than a concert audience.**

The shortest, simplest text I researched to write my book is *Making Presentations,* by Tim Hindle. In his first chapter, the first highlighted point to remember is this: "Your presentation should be relevant, simple, and to the point." I see the importance of that advice every week "out in the field." For example . . .

A student gave a ten-minute speech this week on examining films for hidden themes. He quoted Descartes and Maslow, discussed what it means to live, described the archetype splinters of the human mind, debated whether an author is God, and answered the question, "Is destiny immutable?" (I could not make this up.) When he was done, the whole class just sorta stared at him, and I must admit, I think I stared, too. There was a big, awkward pause, and I said what I usually say when I have nothing to say: "Uh, Phil, so, how do *you* feel about your speech?" He immediately said, "Oh, man, I think I went into too much detail. I'm always making things so complicated!" And we all nodded our heads in wise agreement. I asked Phil if he knew the word *esoteric*. Of course, he did.

> **Esoteric:** Understood only by those few with pertinent interest or knowledge; belonging or pertaining to an inner or select circle; private or secret.

If Phil had given his talk to a group of senior-year film and TV majors, it might have been fine. With an audience of mostly freshman-year, general knowledge survivors, he lost us. Too much film philosophy and too many long quotes from experts with big words; not enough familiar film examples and video clips with simple messages. My class, probably like yours, is about *short* speeches with more general knowledge that hopefully reach a wide range of people, not just a very narrow, esoteric audience. **Short means simple.**

All speech texts stress simplicity, and some even use the KISS acronym, but I have never seen an author dedicate a whole chapter to this topic. I decided to do just that because I think it is that important. I see this guideline violated often, both in the academic and real world, and it creates unnecessary problems for both the speaker and audience. The problem categories basically reflect some chapters of my book, so I will structure this chapter in that order: Purpose, Time, Content, Sensory Aids, Organization, and Words.

PURPOSE

In Chapter Two, I said one of the first questions you must ask yourself to get started on your speech is, "WHY am I giving this speech?" In other words, what is your purpose? This would be a good time to review page 19. Pick ONE purpose, not three. And what type of speech will it be: Persuade, Inform, or Entertain? Pick ONE type, not all three. Make your purpose direct and simple and visual.

Compare these two purpose statements, both from real speeches:

1. I will be speaking to you all today for ten minutes about the recent bill passed in the House and Senate to bail out America's lending firms to a bill of 700 billion dollars so that you can understand it better and maybe invest your money differently in the future without being so scared.
2. To inform Montana residents about the asbestos problem in Libby, MT.

Which purpose statement can you digest better? The first speech did not get into the area of investments or the psychology of "relaxed investments"; it just told us about the bailout bill. Just tell us what you'll tell us, not what you hope might be a residual effect from your speech. Just putting all those words from the first purpose statement on a visual aid would send some audience members into a coma. KEEP IT SIMPLE.

P.S. I suggest you also review Chapter Five, page 107, about Purpose Statements.

TIME

Chapter Two, page 32, introduced the thought of time: How much time is allowed for your speech? Be very aware of this time limit, tell the audience during the introduction how long you will talk, and then stick to it. Since most speakers do NOT stick to their time limit, you will be unique and special and honored and revered if you do.

Time control **is** a common problem. As proof, I gathered some data from student speeches last week. We're doing informative speeches now, and the time limit is seven to eight minutes. Of the forty-seven speeches I heard, only five of them ended within that time limit. Three were under seven minutes, and *all the others were over eight minutes!* That's not a huge problem normally, because I give them a "window" of five to ten minutes before they lose a few points off their grade. I had to stop twenty-one of them, however, who went over ten minutes, or at least "encourage" them to wrap up the speech pretty quickly. After students see how easily the time limit is violated, they do a much better job during the second round of informative speeches the following week. Most people need to see the time violation happening a lot before it really means anything to them. We have to observe the time limit in the academic world, or we won't get all the scheduled speeches done that day. In other worlds, however, it is a different story.

Remember what J.R.R. Tolkien taught us in his story, *The Lord of the Rings:*

I wish shorter speeches could become a Hobbit, uh, habit for all of us. That would be precious. Maybe I just imagined that Tolkien taught us that lesson, but I did not imagine the following sage advice, which I first heard from my seventh-grade English teacher:

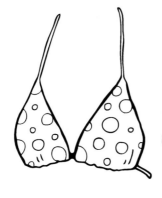

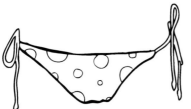

You should also consider the lessons from Malcolm Kushner, the author of *Successful Presentations for Dummies:*

- Don't feel obligated to fill your entire time slot
- It's better to be a little short than a little long
- Don't exceed your allotted time; there are few transgressions that an audience is less willing to forgive
- Twenty minutes is a good length

Twenty minutes IS a good time length for the average speech, but only in the real world. In the academic world, the better time is ten minutes. In the convention or conference or college-lecture worlds, the norm is forty to fifty minutes. In the historical world, you need to remember the lesson from Abraham Lincoln. Most people name his Gettysburg Address as one of the most famous speeches of all time. Why is it so famous? Well, it's a long story . . . but one of the main reasons is because it was short! He followed a speaker who talked almost two hours, and President Lincoln only talked two to three minutes! Think of that comparison, for all those weary listeners at Gettysburg. No wonder people raved about his speech! (Well, it did have some powerful word choice, too.) Lincoln was probably aware of an earlier historical lesson from Thomas Jefferson: **Speeches measured by the hour die with the hour.**

Story: I honestly thought about Lincoln's lesson one night when I was the guest speaker for a Boy Scout awards banquet. There were about 200 people, of all ages, gathered for a potluck dinner at 6 P.M. on a school night. Half the people brought desserts, which the kids ate instead of the real food, and then every single Scout got some kind of an award, presented individually. It took f..o..r..e..v....e....r, and the kids were high as kites from all the sugar and all the fame, and the noise level was incredible as I approached the podium, finally, at 9:30 P.M. I glanced out over Armageddon. Baby sisters were crying, uncles were clutching cousins, mothers were zombies cleaning up messes, grandparents were slapping each other to stay awake, and Scouts had become a living pinball machine. It was a true recipe for disaster. I tried to talk the Scoutmasters out of having the speech, but they swore it was some kind of requirement that had to be filled. So, I took a deep breath and yelled in my best scout leader imitation: "I swear on this Scout manual that I will talk less than ten minutes, and we can all go home!" There was a slight stunned silence, and then the place erupted in applause. One grandfather rose from the front row and came up to shake my hand, and he said, "Bless you, son." He wasn't my father. He was my conscience. Thank you, Lincoln. Oh, yeah, the speech went fine. Nine minutes.

- I told them I would talk ten minutes; if I went fifteen, they would quit listening.
- If your boss asks you to speak twenty minutes, and you go forty, he or she will probably ask you to quit . . . your job
- If you're running for President, and you talk over your time limit during a debate, Tom Brokaw will get upset, and your ratings will go down.
- If you're giving a toast at your daughter's wedding and you've been drinking too much and your wife tells you to shut up, do it. Instantly.

You simply must realize at what point the audience has quit on you. After that point, it does NO good to keep talking. When Elvis has left the building, you gotta face the music, and STOP. Please. Stop. Remember the **Four-S Strategy** of public speaking:

I think that number four might be the most important one. As my parents used to remind me (often), "David, **you don't want to have diarrhea of the mouth.**" You also don't want to be one of those people Ken Alstad referenced in *Savvy Sayin's:*

After some folks tell you all they know, they keep on talkin'.

CONTENT

Closely related to time is content. Yep, Keep It Simple, too, and then time won't be so much of a problem. I mentioned some keys to simplified content in Chapter Three, but I want to add some great advice from David A. Peoples, the author of *Presentations Plus*. In discussing some more sins of speakers, he stresses that you should never tell the audience more than they want to know. "This sin is worse than just boring an audience—it is self-defeating. I would guess that over 90% of all presentations could be given in less time and more effectively. And often in *substantially* less time." No one ever says, "It was a great presentation, but it was too short." He quotes Voltaire, who said, "The secret to being a bore is to tell everything."

Comparisons
Examples
Numbers
Testimony
Stories

I think you should have a variety of CENTS in your content, and for academic purposes I challenge my students to pack as much CENTS as possible into the ten-minute talks, but realistically, you can have "information overload" in your content. Consider the following guidelines to simplify.

Comparisons

Take us from what we know to what we don't know. Start with something local, familiar, and simple, if possible, and compare it to your new, more complicated concept. I had a speech this month on the "Atom Smasher" being built in France, and the speaker used a simple comparison with a V-shaped pipe open on both ends. He rolled marbles down each end so they could crash together in the middle, like atoms will smash together in France. Voila!

Examples

Stephen Lucas, author of *The Art of Public Speaking*, says that people are interested in people, so put people into your examples. He quotes a social psychologist, Eliot Aronson, who explains, "Most people are more deeply influenced by *one* clear, vivid, personal example than by an *abundance* of statistical data." I tell my students, throw away five numbers and replace them with one example. Less content; more impact. Also remember that jokes are examples; make them short, not long; fifteen to thirty seconds.

Numbers

Use one or two numbers per main point; not ten. Don't ever make one of your main points "Statistics" and pack it full of numbers. Always **round off your numbers.** Avoid really large numbers unless you couple them with a comparison so we can understand them. (Review page 53 for examples.) Pie charts and bar graphs help us comprehend numbers, also.

Testimony

Quotes are great, but we don't want to hear sixteen quotes in one speech, especially if they're mostly from one source. Limit yourself to one quote per main point, maximum. Use short, hard-hitting quotes that can fit easily on a visual aid. A student used a quote last week that was a full page and took ninety seconds to read; MUCH too long.

Stories

I found a good line from *Pocket Keys for Speakers* by Isa Engleberg and Ann Raimes. They say to use simple story lines. "Long stories with complex themes are hard to follow and difficult to tell. If you can't summarize your story in less than twenty-five words, don't tell it." For most academic speeches, I think sixty to ninety seconds is a good rule-of-thumb for a story. Most talks would only have one story; two at the most.

Here are some other KISS thoughts from my brain about Content:

- Take a strong look at "Must Know" information vs "Nice to Know"
- You *should* cover "procedure"; you *might* cover some "technique"
- **Don't tell us what you won't tell us.** (Speakers too often say, "I was going to tell you about this and that, but I couldn't find it, or I didn't have time.")
- At the end of your short speech, **we don't need to know everything you know**
- A speaker's **biggest problem is deciding what NOT to say,** so be sure to allow yourself time to make that decision; time to edit/revise/delete information
- You don't need to talk about every single item from a list of items; show us the longer list, if you must, but just talk about two or three of the items.

Keep
It
Simple
Stupid

- If you highlight everything, then nothing is highlighted
- Ask yourself (seriously): **"What do I want my audience to remember?"** Then stress those lessons and don't worry so much about the small stuff.
- If it's a smaller audience, have smaller content
- If the audience is less familiar with your topic, use simpler content
- It's easy to talk long; the challenge is to talk short; make it a game
- Remember what my children remind me of: Too Much Information, Dad. **TMI!**
- What happens in Vegas should stay in Vegas . . . not end up in your speech.

The classic advice about speech content is **"LESS IS MORE."** That's another paradox and another great truth. If you try to cram 100 percent of a topic down our throats, we'll fight you and resist you and quit listening and shut down and forget—all those negative things and probably a few more. If you try to gently spoon feed us only 25 percent of the topic, we'll be your friend and try to listen and remember MORE of the topic overall than with the 100 percent attempt. Tim Hindle, author of *Making Presentations*, says, "Every adult audience has a limited attention span of about forty-five minutes. In that time, they will absorb only about a third of what was said and a maximum of seven concepts." The audience will let you know when they have reached their limit. I see it every week, because that forty-five-minute rule is roughly the same length as my fifty-minute lectures. At that point, in Montana, you have to let the wild cowboys go, or they pull out the guns and knives and bobcats. Out here, in the last best place, we try to remember what John Wayne taught us:

SENSORY AIDS

At Montana State University, we have used the George Grice and John Skinner text, *Mastering Public Speaking*, for the last decade in our Com 110 Public Communications course. I think their advice for simple sensory aids is outstanding, so I'll summarize:

- Focus on a few key points; not every single item needs a visual aid
- Present ideas one at a time; don't let an audience read ahead of your talk
- Use no more than six words on a line
- Use no more than six lines on a page
- Use strong, straight fonts such as Arial and Times New Roman
- Use no more than two fonts per slide or screen
- Use large fonts that can be read from the back row
- Limit the number of colors you use; six maximum per aid
- Avoid *chartjunk*, irrelevant graphics and art that clutter and detract

Some of those items were also covered in my Chapter Four. This would be a good time to quickly review the hints for blackboards (page 67), videos (page 71), and PowerPoint and Transparencies (page 74). Costuming and Objects are two other very simple aids you can add to any speech, so pages 75 and 76 are also worth a short scan.

I want to talk about "busy" charts, graphs, and tables. Don't you hate it when someone puts up an aid that is impossible to read, and they casually say, "As you can easily see, widget A is superior to widget B"—and you can't *easily* see anything? This is usually the result of the speaker copying a chart exactly as it was found. To make it simpler for your audience, you must create your own chart with only the relevant information. Instead of showing a table with 200 numbers and trying to highlight four of them, take just those four important numbers and put them on a new visual aid. You can now make the numbers much bigger and discuss the comparisons more easily. Simple.

You can simplify your explanations and use fewer words if you use sensory aids:

- A picture is worth 1,000 words
- A model must be worth 2,000 words
- A demonstration is surely worth 3,000 words
- So a video must be worth the price of popcorn

David Peoples is really good about stressing simple aids in *Presentations Plus*. He says, "We lose effectiveness and we confuse our customers with the complexity of the subject. A good visual aid looks like a billboard on an interstate highway that people could read going by at 65 mph." He stresses to use no more than three curves on a graph and to never use full sentences on any visual aid. He says, "The world's worst visual aid is a black-and-white transparency of a typewritten page." To conclude his section on aids, he lists the three most important rules: 1. Keep it simple 2. Keep it Simple 3. Keep it Simple.

ORGANIZATION

Can you handle the truth? Can you handle another "Savvy Sayin'" from Ken Alstad?

If you need a map to get all your "stuff" moving in the right direction, go back to Chapter Five and review some lessons on Organization, particularly pages 100–104. If you don't have a simple, logical order to your points, your speech might just wander around, lost.

One of the first signs of a complicated speech is too many main points. Your speech should not be a long laundry list of ideas; it should have the *structure* of some main points, *supported* (with CENTS) by sub and sub-sub points. (If you're starting to think about the Navy or yellow submarines, please come back to me.) If you just have a list where every item has the same value, you have not worked hard enough to categorize items for us. We can remember a few categories; we can't remember the whole list.

I think Jo Sprague and Douglas Stuart say it better in *The Speaker's Handbook:*

> **Include two to five main points.** As a speaker, **you should be able to cluster your ideas around a few main themes**. If every thought is treated as a main point, you will have no opportunity to *develop* any of them. With many random subpoints, you never extract meaning from an unorganized barrage of information. Understand, too, that your audience will not be able to remember more than a few main points.

I think most experts agree: two to five points. In general, the fewer main points, the better, but if you only have one main point, you basically have a topic with no real structure. In *The New Public Speaker*, by George Rodman and Ronald Adler, I learned this tidbit:

> Research reveals that people are best able to understand and remember information when it is grouped into no more than seven categories. Most rhetorical experts agree that the best way to make your ideas clear and memorable is to limit the body of your speech even further, to a maximum of five main points.

Let me offer an example of simple structure. Let's say you had to give a speech about your college. You and your friends might brainstorm the possible topics and come up with the following list of items you want to brag about:

Location	History	Curriculum
Students	Costs	Local action
Campus	Town	Reputation
Weather	Sports	Graduation rates

Assuming you actually had time to discuss all these points (maybe it's a forty-minute team talk you all might present to high school students), what organizational pattern would you use? Most important to least important? Least common to most common questions? There's really no right or wrong answer, as long as it has enough logic and clarity so that the audience can easily follow. If I were to create a speech with these items for Montana State University, I would use a "Gimmick" pattern, creating an acronym that reflects our school mascot, the Bobcat. Go **CATS!**

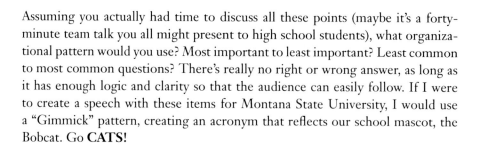

FINAL MAIN POINTS (and sub-points)

*C*AMPUS (Location, Buildings/Dorms, Student Profiles, Services, Costs, History)

*A*CADEMICS (Curriculum/Majors, Reputation/Standards, Graduation Rates/Jobs)

*T*OWN (History, Local Activities, Rental Opportunities/Costs, Weather)

*S*PORTS (Types, Titles, Key Events)

As you can easily see (I hope), I was able to use all twelve brainstormed points, plus a few others that came up as I did intense, hypothetical research and refined the speech. But instead of 12 main points, I simplified it to four, and made it easy for the audience to remember the main points. We listen better in sections, so keep it simple!

Keep It Simple Stupid

The **introduction and conclusion** must also be clear, concise, and effective. Some speakers make them way too long and involved. Please go back and look at page 104 to reinforce your thoughts about starting and stopping a speech. Some **KISS thoughts:**

- *Attention step:* simple and fast, ten to fifteen seconds
- *Purpose Statement:* simple and visual; it is NOT your preview
- *Motivation:* pick ONE reason to listen, not ten
- *Credibility:* Quickly tell research and experience; don't tell a story (until the body)
- *Preview:* LIST main points on a visual aid with one to three words per point; NOT full sentences; do not list your sub-points
- The whole introduction should be sixty to ninety seconds (for a ten-minute speech)

When I was in the Air Force, I was taught to remove **"deadhead words"** from my writing. When you remove deadhead words, you do not lose any meaning. I often see such words on preview visual aids, like the following:

PREVIEW:

1. Today I will discuss how we got to the point where we *need a bailout.*
2. Then I will describe to you exactly *what the bailout is* in terms of money.
3. Finally, I will explain what is in store for all of us in the *future.*

Everything not in italics is a deadhead word. On your preview visual aid, just list:

1. Need for Bailout		1. Need
2. What it is	or better yet . . .	2. Bailout
3. Future Implications		3. Future

Then take that simple, clear, concise preview slide and use it again in the **conclusion:**

- *Restate Purpose:* use the same purpose aid from intro
- *Summary:* Yep, use your preview visual aid here
- *Remotivate:* Just remind us of the one reason you gave in intro
- *Closure:* Simple and fast, maybe ten seconds
- Do NOT talk about credibility again
- The whole conclusion should be done in thirty to sixty seconds

WORDS

Besides the quantity of words, we also want to simplify the quality of words. This does not mean our audience is not smart enough to follow our vocabulary; it means we want to remember the following advice that I learned "somewhere, out there":

SPEAK TO EXPRESS, NOT TO IMPRESS

Story: Once upon a time, there was a speech instructor here at MSU who loved to "pontificate" during her lectures. She would walk back and forth without ever using a visual aid or ever really looking students in the eye, slowly waving her hand in the air to accentuate the beautiful flow (in her mind) of her impressive vocabulary. We were team-teaching lectures at that time, so I watched her to make sure I wouldn't cover the same material. She was flat out amazing . . . in a bad way. I actually had trouble following her lectures because they were so "stuffy" and "pompous" that I would quit listening to her message and just write down lists of her thesaurus words. I questioned her technique at a staff meeting, and she insisted she would not "dumb-down" her lectures for a bunch of "stupid freshmen." Quote, unquote. Well, you can't hide that kind of attitude from students, no matter how impressive your words are. So, one day she was talking about "yadda yadda triggers a synergistic association and yadda yadda therefore must not be truncated because, after all yadda yadda we are not there to dash icons!" One of the brave, confused souls awakened from the dead and dared to interrupt her: "Uh, excuse me, ma'am. I'm lost. What exactly do you mean by *icons?*" She looked at him indignantly, I am not kidding, and replied, "Young man, you can look up that word in your dictionary." Well, I counted, I am not kidding, twenty-eight students who rose from their seats and walked out of the back of the lecture hall. She did not teach the next year. Amen.

> Moral One: If you talk *down* to your audience, it's worse than *dumbing down your words*
>
> Moral Two: If an audience is too bored, insulted, or aghast, they may vote with their feet
>
> Moral Three: If you don't respect your audience, you should never, **ever,** give a speech

This story has been brought to you by the universal association of **KEEP IT SIMPLE, STUPID,** to help foreshadow for Chapter Nine, on Ethics. Okay, maybe I should have said "preview" instead of "foreshadow," but my audience is college students and you probably know that word, right? At least I didn't say "adumbrate."

You have heard my biased, subjective opinion on simple words. Can I pull out my Montana "shotgun" and shoot a bunch of truly expert, objective advice at you?

• Arthur Koch, *Speaking With A Purpose:* Use a conversational style of delivery, which gives it an air of familiarity, **as if the speaker were talking to close friends.** Use your own vocabulary, but eliminate words that might be considered overly casual or inappropriate. If you try to use words with which you are unfamiliar, your style will seem stilted and unnatural.

- Stephen Lucas, *The Art of Public Speaking:* You would be amazed at how many speakers persist in bombarding listeners with complicated words— usually out of the mistaken belief that such words sound impressive. In truth, filling a speech with long, multisyllabic words only marks the speaker as stuffy and pretentious. Worse, it usually destroys understanding.
- Steven and Susan Beebe, *Public Speaking, An Audience-Centered Approach:* Tape record your practice session, and then listen for chances to say what you want with fewer words. Used wisely, simple words and simple phrases communicate with great power and precision. But don't restrict yourself to simple phrases or your speech will be choppy. A few carefully worded complex or compound sentences will add variety to your speech.
- Malcolm Kushner, *Successful Presentations for Dummies:* He reminds us that Abraham Lincoln's Gettysburg Address is mostly made up of words with five letters or less. He also advises us to look through our speeches: "If you find a lot of sentences with more than twenty words, your audience had better be Ph.Ds."
- David McLaughlin, *Talk Like You Talk:* Chapter Three, Content, page 51. Be aware of idioms, jargon, and acronyms that may abuse/confuse your audience. When in doubt, define your words.

This is also a good time to review the advice in Chapter Six, Delivery, page 136, about "Being Too Formal." I want you to remember that oral language does differ from written language. Writing is normally more formal, but it's kinda sorta okay, I think, in a speech book, to also write with slang and sentence fragments to reflect the oral style I hear from students all the time, k? Such spontaneous and interactive styles are important, because they are simple, and the added pauses and vocal variations can clarify and emphasize meaning, ya know? Dude, I know some traditional teachers won't like my style, but I'm gonna do it straight up, cause they ain't the boss of me. But I gotta say somethin' here, from the heart: **Oral style is less formal than written style, but it's also more formal than a drunk dial.**

I honestly never get tired of hearing you young people talk. You're rewriting how we speak about things in this country, and we must allow you that avenue of expression. Just remember that we older folk don't always be understanding your meaning, and try to keep it simple, until we catch up, "aight"? (My daughter, Shannon, had to teach me how to spell *aight*, all right?) One of my students was talking last week and starting to get too complicated, and he caught himself, paused, and then said, "Ok, let me try to put this into *stupid man* words." So funny. So true. Or, as my daughter, Lindsay, loves to say when we are talking over her head:

Well, by Jove, now you've got it. You already had McDreamy and McLovin in your lives, and now you have McSimple. **KISS!** It's such a fine principle, it can only be seen by the eyes of the blind. (Thank you, Billy Joel.) I can sleep easier now, perchance to dream of a simpler place and time, not the hustle of New York City or the bustle of Los Angeles, but rather the tranquility of Bozeman, Montana. And a river runs through it. (Thank you, Norman Maclean) And there, in the river, perhaps, is a yellow submarine, just humming along.

SUMMARY CHECKLIST FOR KEEP IT SIMPLE

(Simple lasts longer than complicated.)

Purpose

Make your purpose statement direct, simple, and visual

Time - "Bikini Length"

- ❏ Most speakers talk too long
- ❏ World needs more short speeches
- ❏ Four-S Strategy: Study Up, Stand Up, Speak Up, Shut Up

Content - "Less is More"

- ❏ Use simple support; short quotes and stories; round off numbers
- ❏ Biggest problem is deciding what NOT to say
- ❏ Stress: "What do I want the audience to really remember?"

Sensory Aids - "Picture is worth a 1,000 words"

- ❏ Avoid too many words and too much clutter
- ❏ Can it be easily seen from the back row?
- ❏ Any sensory aid can save you spoken words

Organization

Two to five main points; quick, simple introduction/conclusion

Words

"Speak to *Ex*press, Not to *Im*press"; conversational; your own vocabulary

P.S. Some people like to shake HANDs (Hugely Annoying, Numbing Details), but most of us know it is better to KISS (Keep It Simple, Stupid!).

I want to keep talking about simplicity, but for some reason, I feel pressure to wrap this up. If I keep rambling, I will lose impact, not pass go, and not collect $200. I know it's not ethical to waste people's time . . . so let's move on to Chapter Nine, Ethics.

Chapter 9

ETHICS

THE GOLDEN RULE RULES!

Note: The Golden Rule, as we all know, basically states that we should treat others as we would like to be treated. It's such a simple guideline that I could have included it in my last chapter. It's so simple and basic that it is universal and timeless. It is the essence of all religion. If I only had five seconds to describe the necessary ethics of public speaking, I would tell you to follow the Golden Rule. Everything else you might now read in this chapter is, therefore, honestly, probably unnecessary, but I swear it will be ethical.

In 1999, I was asked to participate in the Montana State University Residence Life "Last Lecture" series. I was asked to pretend I was dying, reflect on my values, and then talk for an hour on what I thought would be the most important advice I could leave for my students. Many schools have such voluntary programs, made even more popular by the 2008 book, *The Last Lecture*. (The author, Randy Pausch, a professor at Carnegie Mellon, actually *was* dying, so it's an amazing book.) My last lecture topic was "The Golden Rule," and it helped me lay the foundation for this chapter on Ethics.

THE GOLDEN RULE

Every religion I have ever studied promotes the Golden Rule:

- Christianity: As ye would that man should do to you, do ye also to them likewise.
- Islam: Offer to men what thou desirest should be offered to thee.
- Hinduism: Do naught unto others which would cause you pain if done to you.
- Buddhism: Hurt not others in ways that you yourself would find hurtful.
- Confucianism: Do not unto others that which you would not have them do unto you.
- Zoroastrianism: That nature alone is good which refrains from doing unto another whatsoever is not good for itself
- Judaism: Do not unto others as you would not have others do unto you; that is the whole Torah, the rest is commentary.

Yes, if we truly comprehended and followed the Golden Rule, all else "would be just commentary." It fascinates me that religions embrace the Golden Rule, yet some of the worst evil in history rose from a clash of religions (see "Crusades"). No one wants to be robbed or cheated or killed, yet evil persists. Plato said, "To prefer evil to good is not in human nature," and I sincerely believe that most people *are* good. If I did not believe there is *much* more good than evil in this world, I would not get out of bed in the morning. The problem lies in the definition of evil. People have different operational definitions, which allow them to act in ways that do not cause them the same guilt that the majority of people would feel. If we discussed the Golden Rule more often and processed our differences in meaning (semantics), we would have better communication and therefore more world peace and good will. Ta-dum! Let's process some semantics:

How Do YOU Define Evil?

Does it have to be something big, like killing someone just because their skin is a different color, or can it be something small, like spreading a false rumor about a coworker? Let me ask these "Golden Rule" questions:

- Would **you** like to listen to a speech that was total opinion, with no research?
- Do you want to listen to a speech that was total B.S.?
- A speech with no visual aids?
- A speech that someone simply reads to you, copied from the Internet?
- A speech that has nothing "interesting" or "challenging" in it?
- A speech that was laced with profanity and pornography?
- A speech that was waaaaayyyyyy too long?
- A speech that was copied from a roommate or a "friend"?

I know, I know, I know. It's just a speech. It's not a big deal. People cut corners all the time. You have a life, you have other studies, you have a part time job. Jeez, is it that bad if you can't give the perfect speech each time? "Gimmie a break, jerk." Okay, okay, okay. I hear you. Maybe the word *evil* was too strong for your religion. Let's try again:

How Do YOU Define Honesty?

Does it have to be something major, like President Nixon and Watergate, or O.J. Simpson and the death of his wife, or can it be something minor like stealing a candy bar from a grocery store when you're nine years old? Let me ask these "Golden Rule" questions:

- Would **you** like someone to look at **your** answers during a closed-book exam?
- Do you want a lazy friend to copy all your answers on an open-book exam?
- Would you like a group member to lie about being sick for a missed meeting?
- Want a group member to provide bogus bibliographical entries?
- Would you like a classmate to give knowingly wrong information in a speech?
- Want to be moved by an emotional "true" story that was actually made up?
- Would you want students to lie to you about their "printer problems"?
- Want someone to steal your speech outline and use it as if it were her own?

I know, I know, I know. It's just a freshman-level speech course. People "exaggerate" the truth sometimes. "White Lies" and "hyperbole" are okay, right?

No one really gets hurt, do they? It's like white-collar crime; it's against the system, not real people. We gotta fight "the man" before he controls everything, true? Just having a little fun; no real harm meant. I swear I didn't know it was wrong! No one died, man. It was only worth five points. "Gimmie a break," maybe a do-over, like the banks and big car companies got from the federal government in 2008. Okay, okay, okay. I hear you. After all, it seems that everyone is doing what you did. According to Tucker Carlson (co-host of CNN's *Crossfire*), there were studies (circa 2002) by Rutgers University professor Donald McCabe that found that "on most campuses, more than 75 percent of students cheat." I personally don't believe that, but some of my students say it's realistic. As our world moves faster and gets more complicated, I think our definition of honesty gets blurred, moving more from the black and white definitions of legal/illegal actions into the very very gray world of ethics. Let's try that word.

How Do YOU Define Ethics?

Does it have to be something newsworthy, like President Clinton saying, "I did not have sex with that woman!" (oral sex is not real sex, right?), or can it be something rather local and pedestrian like parking in a handicapped parking spot because you're late for class and those stupid spots are never used anyway? Let me ask these "Golden Rule" questions:

- Would **you** want to hear a persuasion speech on America's need to cut down on our use of fossil fuels from someone who drives a Hummer?
- Would you enjoy a dogmatic, one-sided speech on the death penalty from someone who refused to acknowledge any truth whatsoever on the other side?
- If there were a professor who consistently used unethical language and behavior, would you want him/her reported to the Dean before you had to sit in that class?
- Would you want ministers to preach the Golden Rule to you if they cheated on their taxes and their spouses and stole money from the church?

I know, I know, I know. I'm getting too "preachy" myself. This is not a religion or law or philosophy class, although I would argue that effective communication deals with all three of those topics. Want to know how **I** would define evil, honesty, and ethics?

EVIL Is Defined by Your Religion

It is a VERY strong word, and it really is beyond the scope of a basic speech course. According to my 1976 Encyclopedia Americana (I'm not lying), evil disrupts the order of a rational universe and results in "calamity," a powerful word in itself. Evil is basically the opposite of good, but it's much stronger than "bad," and it usually has some universal connotation that is bounced off a higher being. I might argue that "bad" can be skin deep (you can be a good person who happens to do a bad thing), but "evil" is to the bone (an evil person is incapable of good things). We could debate this description for a long time, but suffice it to say that in twenty-five years of teaching public communication, I have never seen an "evil" student or speech, according to my definition. I've had no students named Hitler, and I have not heard the silence of the lambs.

HONESTY Is Defined by the Law

It asks us to tell the truth, the whole truth, and nothing but the truth. It is black and white; you tell the truth or you lie. You do your own academic work, or you cheat. You obtain your own food and materials legally, or you steal. If you lie, cheat, or steal, you may be punished under "the law." My alma mater, the United States Air Force Academy, has the following **honor code:**

> *We will not lie, steal or cheat, nor tolerate*
> *among us anyone who does.*

Some students tell me that I went to an unrealistic military school with tight controls, and that such an honor code would not work at a civilian institution. I like to point out that the MSU student conduct code is very similar to the one I had:

> *Acts of dishonesty include cheating, plagiarism or other breaches of academic*
> *integrity, such as facilitating or aiding academic dishonesty.*

I have had students who turned in other students for stealing and cheating. Many college students feel as strongly about an honor code as I did, and they will not tolerate dishonest behavior. All real-world professional groups have such codes, too. Dr. Albert Schweitzer, the famous philosopher and medical missionary who won the 1952 Nobel Peace Prize, once said:

> Truth has no special time of its own;
> its hour is now—always.

I strongly encourage you to research the honor system at your college or university. When you signed papers to attend school, I guarantee you agreed to follow a code and acknowledged awareness that you could be punished accordingly should you violate its edicts. You MUST understand what you signed. If you are not sure what you signed, go to the Dean of Students' office and find out. ASK. It may be difficult to catch college cheaters, but when the catching is done, the punishment can be harsh. You might have to take the "cheated" course over again, or you might be kicked out of school. At MSU, the Dean of Students can complete a form about the improper actions, and then employers can ask if you have such a record before they hire you. You need to know the potential for ruin. Warren Buffett, the famous (and wealthy!!) American investor, once said:

> **It takes twenty years to build a reputation,**
> **and five minutes to ruin it.**

ETHICS Is Defined by Your Philosophy

Ethics, like philosophy, is not as well defined as honesty or the law. Instead of black and white (you "know" you did wrong), ethics is gray (you "might" have done wrong). Ethics is generally defined as principles of morality, the study of the difference between right and wrong. When I was growing up in the Episcopal church, my ministers used to talk about *situational ethics*. Something that seems evil and illegal in most cases might be ethical under a unique situation. For example, we agree it is evil and illegal to kill someone, but policemen and soldiers can kill "evil people," and it's okay. No one can tell you what is wrong and right under every situation, so you must decide yourself what ethics to follow. One challenge is to be consistent in your actions; ethics is not a toggle switch you turn on and off at your convenience. Another challenge is to base your decisions upon moral principles that serve the greater good. If your decisions are based upon selfish principles that serve only the greater you, they might be unethical. If it is unethical, you don't pay a fine or go to jail like the better-defined crimes of evil and dishonesty, but you might lose friends and family who follow a different code of ethics. You might also lose your reputation, or even worse, your self-respect.

Captain Theodore Harris, U.S. Air Force, was a prisoner of war in Korea who was kept in solitary confinement for fourteen months. You can imagine the ethical decisions he had to make when he was being tortured for military information and slanderous propaganda statements against the United States. His quote, which has inspired me since 1968, was, "If I can't go back with my self-respect, I won't go back at all."

If YOU could use only one word to describe your being, what would that one word be? I ask my students that question, and I get some fun answers, as you might imagine, such as *cool*, *epic*, *awesome*, and *stud*. The answers I like the best, however, are the ones that reflect the point I'm making, such as *honest*, *real*, *integrity*, and *ethical*. To infinity and beyond, I can imagine a character of integrity, like Buzz Lightyear, saying:

Why do I think of Illinois Governor Rod Blagojevich (2008) when I read that advice? In a way, ethics is like your virginity; you either have it, or you don't. It's like being pregnant; can you be "just a little bit pregnant"? Is it okay to be "just a little bit unethical"? You wouldn't cheat on a 200-point exam, but it's okay to cheat on a little five-point quiz? Where do YOU draw the line? I challenge my students to draw the ethical line early in their college careers and to draw it as high as possible. The biggest difference between honesty and ethics is that YOU draw the line for ethics, and the government/police draw the line for honesty. Some judge can say you broke the law, but only your conscience can truly say you broke your code of ethics. If you don't already have an ethics code, begin one now. Such a code cannot wait until you're in the workforce, or you will have developed bad habits that will hurt you and others. (If you lie now about being sick when you miss class, won't you tell the same lie with your employer?) Such a code must be flexible/situational, and it needs a great deal of conscious nurturing and practice. The bottom line is that you must test yourself, daily.

Hopefully, you'll create a personal code of ethics that tends to agree with the majority, in most cases. To help you draw that line, I've listed some guidelines below.

GENERAL ETHICAL GUIDELINES

- The number one best advice for ethics is to follow the Golden Rule. It rules.
- Let your conscience be your guide. (Have you seen *Pinocchio* lately?)
- Follow your heart more than your head. (You know what the right thing is.)
- Use *all* of your resources to shape your ethics (parents, other family, friends, teachers, ministers, coaches, church, books, media, etc.), *not* just friends.
- Always, always consider the consequences of being unethical before you are.
- Choose the difficult right over the easy wrong, and it's easy to cheat.
- Remember, if you lie, you have to remember what you said, remember? You'll tell more lies to cover up the first lie, and it becomes a frustrating game of "Whack-A-Lie," kinda like "Whack-A-Mole." You can't play that game long. If you always tell the truth, you don't have to worry. Best to have less stress, Jess.
- Ethics is small. Honesty is big. Evil is huge. Keep it small, 'fo it grows, Joe.

I'm trying to keep this chapter small, so that's enough thoughts about Ethics in general. With that base, I want to move on to Ethics in public speaking, in particular. Thanks to our First Amendment, I have the freedom to do that.

FREEDOM OF SPEECH

We have freedom of speech in this country, but **it is not an absolute freedom**. We, the people, have agreed to put some constraints upon our freedom of speech to protect our citizens from certain wrongdoings. Therefore, you know the **law prevents:**

- Defamatory falsehoods that destroy a person's reputation
- Threats against the life of the President
- Inciting an audience to illegal actions, such as riots and hangings
- Shouting "Fire" in a theater
- Making bomb threats on an airliner

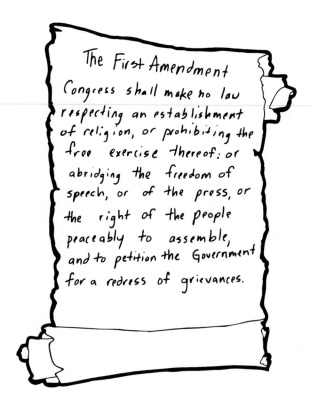

The First Amendment
Congress shall make no law respecting an establishment of religion, or prohibiting the free exercise thereof; or abridging the freedom of speech, or of the press, or the right of the people peaceably to assemble, and to petition the Government for a redress of grievances.

In academic situations, the school or the **instructor may place additional constraints.** I like to lay these out for my students, explain my rationale, and then allow discussion. I like to think you could debate such free speech limitations with your teachers, too.

- We have to put a time limit on the talks or we can't hear everyone's speech.
- Sometimes instructors say no PowerPoint or videos due to equipment availability.
- It's common to not allow speeches outside due to distractions.
- It's also common for schools to say no pets, no alcohol, and no weapons, even if some students argue that such items would make good aids/props for their topics.

- I don't allow certain topics because they have proven to be too huge for short talks, or they typically are not "college level," but I always tell students they can change my mind if they show me a thoughtful, edited outline beforehand.
- Generally, academic speeches have little or no profanity or "provocative" photos.
- I have stopped speeches against a particular religion or group of people.
- Unethical topics are not allowed, like how to make and use a beer bong.
- Illegal topics are not allowed, like how to make fake ID cards.
- Evil topics are not allowed, like how to build a suicide bomber's vest.

If you want to have total freedom of speech, you can go outside, anywhere, and start talking on whatever topic and using whatever language and photos you want, for as long as you want. Just remember, if you exercise this freedom and start getting into "offensive" areas as defined by your audience, they also have freedom of feedback. We used to have a guy named "Preacher Tom" who would come to the MSU campus every year and scream and yell at all of us for being evil sinners. I never saw anyone throw shoes at him (see George W. Bush, Dec 08, Iraq), but I did see people spit on him, knock him over, pour water on his head, and throw snowballs at him. Normally, I don't allow such overt audience feedback in the classroom, but snowballs have been seen.

I grew up with a picture of the Iwo Jima flag raising in my room. My father retired from the Marine Corps; I retired from the Air Force. I was a squadron ethics representative at the Air Force Academy. I have taught accredited courses in military history and the ethics of leadership. I watched *Braveheart* seventeen times (freedom!). I have been in about fifty countries, and I know we are damned lucky to be living in this country, with our freedoms. Please remember that freedom is not free! Many good people gave their lives so that we could guard the First Amendment. Please don't spit on it . . . even though you have that freedom.

FREEDOM OF SPEECH IS NOT FREE!

AUDIENCE BEFORE THY SELF

Just as a patriot would care more about his country than himself, a speaker must ethically consider the audience *needs* before she thinks about her own *wants*. Please note that as a beginning speaker, this is impossible to do. All inexperienced speakers must concentrate on themselves first, especially for a graded academic speech. As you gain experience and confidence, however, your focus will naturally shift to the audience. This would be a good time to review Chapter Two, page 19: Who Is Your Audience?

It is your audience who actually defines the ethics you will follow in a speech. A football coach might yell and scream profanities at his team before a game, if that matched the coach's style and was a proven technique for that particular audience. A kindergarten teacher, on the other hand, would probably not yell (much) or use any profanities with her class. A college audience would generally smile at a light-hearted sexual innuendo; a middle-school audience would run out into the hall with their hair on fire. A joke about drinking might work well with an American audience; it might offend a Muslim audience in Morocco. Remember, *speaking ethics are really situational ethics*, and the most important determinant of that situation is your audience.

To get you started in your ethical audience analysis, here are some universal guidelines:

- According to Isa Engleberg and Ann Raimes, *Pocket Keys for Speakers:* "An ethical speaker has the responsibility to weigh what an audience wants to hear against what is truthful, fair, and beneficial. Have you used the information analyzed about your audience to serve them or to deceive them?"
- According to George Rodman and Ronald B. Adler, *The New Public Speaker:* "There are three guidelines for ethical speechmaking, and these guidelines can also be used to evaluate support: Is it honest, is it accurate, and is it in the audience's best interest?"
- According to Michael and Suzanne Osborn, *Public Speaking:* "The final and most important measure of a speech is its ethical consequences—whether it is good or bad for listeners. If there is a Golden Rule for speaking, it might be: *Do unto listeners as you would have speakers do unto you.* Above all, an ethical speech is one that listeners are the better for having heard."
- And while we're talking about listeners, it's a two-way street, as stated by Douglas M. Fraleigh and Joseph S. Tuman, *Speak Up!* "Be ethical and courteous in your critiques and treat the speaker the same way you hope

and expect to be treated when it's your turn to receive feedback. Avoid prejudging the speaker or topic. Avoid making your comments sound like a personal attack."

These general guidelines all have the same **critical theme: Your audience should benefit somehow from your words;** your audience is *better off* because of your speech. I thought of this great truth as I followed two students in the hallway this term and listened to them discuss an upcoming speech in a business course. One said he was nervous about giving the speech, and the other offered this experienced advice: "Public speaking is easy, man! All you have to do is make a bunch of PowerPoint slides and click through them. Write out all the words you want to say, and just read them. You don't even have to think!" Uh-huh. We like speakers who don't think, don't we? That advice, to me, epitomizes the lazy, selfish speaker who has no regard whatsoever for the audience. Someone who just wants to fill a square. Someone who doesn't care to teach himself or his audience anything. How about you? Do YOU like speakers who just read slides to you? This would be a good time to flip back to that cartoon with robots in Chapter Six, page 124. You WANT to use "extemporaneous" delivery, and that means DoNotReadDoNotReadDoNotRead to your audience.

Most audience members KNOW when the speaker does not care about them.

> *Do not say things. What you <u>are</u> stands over you the while and thunders so that I cannot hear what you say to the contrary.*
>
> **—Ralph Waldo Emerson, *Journals*, 1840**

As I said at the end of Chapter Three: If all you plan to do is read to us, just give us a paper and let us go home early. In other words, **don't waste our time!** If you give the lazy man's speech for ten minutes, you have not just wasted ten minutes of time. No, you have wasted ten minutes for *each* audience member, added together. So, for one of my classes with twenty students, you have wasted 200 minutes, or 3.33 man-hours, or audience-hours. You don't have to be a math major to see that such a conscious waste of time might be unethical. If you sincerely *work for your audience* and do credible research to create interesting CENTS and BECOT for an ethical topic within the prescribed time limit, it will never be a waste.

Let me introduce you to the **11th Commandment**:

- If you pick a topic only because it is "easy," that might be B.S.
- If you tell us you'll talk ten minutes and you know it's closer to twenty, that's B.S.
- If your audience needs "crapons" instead of crampons to climb your mountain of B.S. during your rambling speech on ice climbing, you might be unethical.
- If you tell us your speech on "Invading Canada" was all your critical thinking instead of citing the Internet source you copied, you might be illegal.
- If you brainwash us with false information and eventually persuade 913 of us to drink a cyanide-laced grape drink and die, you might be very, very evil. (Google Jim Jones, People's Temple, Jonestown, Guyana, 1978)

Overall, don't play games with us. We are unique human beings and deserve better.

INTEGRITY IN THY PURPOSE

We, the people, deserve to know *exactly* what you want us to do or think when your speech is over (purpose statement, in introduction, with a visual aid), and we deserve to know how we will benefit (motivation step). Does it reflect an ethical "value" of our society? Under the credibility step, you might also share your personal motive/reasoning for selecting the topic. If your motive (buy my inferior product) does not match the motivation you give us (my product is the best one on the market), then you might be unethical. If your overriding general purpose is to Shock us, offer Hate speech, Intimidate us, or Threaten us, you may have created a new acronym to remind us of unethical intent in a speech.

Please take a few minutes and review my words on *sincerity*. (Chapter Three, page 39 and Chapter Six, page 118.) It would be really sad if you gave a talk about something you did not believe in, such as "recycling" if you never recycle yourself. As you young folks say today, "Ya gotta walk the walk, not just talk the talk." My generation said, "Find yourself, man," and my parents used to quote Shakespeare, "To thine own self be true." I love to quote the great Indian spiritual leader, Mahatma Gandhi, who said:

YOU MUST BE THE CHANGE YOU WANT IN THE WORLD

If you're not sincere about your speech, you are not necessarily unethical, but you are just "filling a square." How sad. I think our lives have enough square filling with mundane routines we follow just to get by. Let me share a personal philosophy I developed that pumps me up and gets me ready to roll:

We have two kinds of days in life, Maintenance Days and Memory Days. Maintenance days are full of those mechanical things we have to do to simply maintain our lives: laundry, shopping, fix cars, pay bills, cut grass, go to school, earn money. Memory days contain something special that we will enjoy and remember: holidays with family, birthdays, graduations, weddings, skiing days, camping/hiking/biking/ fishing days, and most importantly, Carolina/Duke basketball days. The sad truth is that we have far more maintenance than memory days, so we have to consciously work hard to even the score, to win the game. Now, here's the gimmick: **find something each day that makes a memory for you**.

Whether you admit it or not, **most of you will remember your speech days!** I regularly talk with prior students, sometimes five or ten years later, and they can *always* tell me what their speeches were about. You may not think it's a great memory, but it is usually exciting. Your adrenalin is pumping, and adrenalin means memory. You are SO happy when the speech is over that at the end of the day, there is more gain than pain. I mean, how many days in your life actually include a speech?! Why not take advantage of this rare opportunity and help yourself and others GROW?! Put integrity of purpose and effort into your speech, and **make a memory for your audience!** (See Chapter Four, page 64, about memories.) Why would you take the maintenance option if you don't have to? Here are some reasons/excuses for poor talks from students I have counseled after a minimal-effort, "fill-the-square" speech:

- I honestly do not see any value whatsoever in giving a speech.
- I cannot think of a topic that excites me; nothing excites me.
- I do not like the other members of my speech group.
- I am bored with the class and school in general.
- My memory days are defined by drugs, alcohol, or video games.
- I don't know how to do credible research, so I just "go for it."
- It was too tempting to just use the speech my roommate did last year.
- It's just not cool to care too much. (This could be called the *Bart Simpson Phenomenon.*)

I just described one of the real problems I occasionally see: apathy. Apathy is not unethical, per se, but it can sometimes lead to unethical actions if you "cut corners." Be careful. The best way to fight apathy in a speech is to **pick a topic you sincerely care about,** one that you *want* to research and share, in order to help others. With some counseling, anyone can find such a topic. ASK your speech instructor for some help.

Ethics is not determined by the topic itself, but rather by the *intent* behind the topic. If you give a speech about building a bomb so that your audience can kill innocent people, it's unethical. If your intent, however, is to educate your audience on homemade bombs so they can identify them in the airport and save people's lives, it is ethical. A good acid test is this thought:

> Would you give the same speech with the same support and visual aids and word choice . . . if your grandmother were sitting in the front row?

INTEGRITY IN THY CONTENT

Here are some of the more common ethical concerns for speech content:

- **Quotes out of Context:** As the Osborns say in *Public Speaking*, "You must be particularly careful that a quotation you select reflects the overall meaning and intent of its author. Never twist the meaning of testimony to make it fit your purposes." Surely you've been in an argument with a friend who threw your own words back in your face, and you said, "Hey, you *know* that's not what I meant!" Well, if you know what the author meant, but shape his words to create a new meaning, you are unethical.
- **Omitting Information:** If you say you were a policeman to show credibility for a speech about gun control, but omit the fact that you were kicked off the police force for buying black market handguns, you are unethical.
- **Half-Truths:** I suppose you could also call this Half-Lies, if your glass were half-empty. You know your audience is not getting the "full story," and you know if they did, they would react differently. If you give a speech on losing weight and tell how you did it with exercise and diet, but do not mention that you also had tummy-tuck surgery (abdominoplasty), you are unethical.
- **Stretching Statistics:** I like to call it this because I *a*lways *a*ppreciate *a*ctive *a*lliteration, but mostly because you can make numbers "sing" if you *streeetch* the truth. As comedian Steven Wright said, "42.7 percent of statistics are made up on the spot." Somewhere along the line, I learned the following axiom:

FIGURES LIE, AND LIARS FIGURE

I could argue that Juan is a better football runner than Brian because he averages ten yards a carry, and Brian only averages six yards. Those numbers are accurate and true. What if you knew, however, that Juan is the Spanish soccer-style place-kicker who only ran the ball one time this season, after a failed kick, and he was lucky to get ten yards, but Brian is the stud star tailback who has carried the ball 140 times this season and had his story told in *Sporting News?* Who is really the better runner?

- **The Boldfaced Lie:** (I had to put that one in bold print.) Let's face it. You know what a boldfaced lie is. Your audience knows. I know. If you lie to me, Dog, you're dead to me. If kids lie, we say, "Liar, liar, pants on fire." If adults lie, we say, "You're fired." (Thank you, Donald Trump.) You're only as good as your word. Word.
- **Faulty Logic:** You have studied some of these "logic loopholes;" some are new:
    - *Faulty Dilemma;* no middle ground exists. "If you have sex with multiple partners, you have only two choices: wear a condom or die of AIDS." Ben gave a speech that told us "Love steak, or hate America!"
    - *Faulty Analogy;* comparing two things that are actually different. "We can successfully reintroduce wolves into Yellowstone because it worked in Minnesota."
    - *Hasty Generalization;* jumping to conclusions from limited examples. "You should not wear a seatbelt because I know two people who would have died in their car accidents if they had been wearing a seatbelt."
    - *False Authority;* quoting an expert who really isn't an expert. "Meredith and Will live in Canada, so they know all about socialized medicine, and they say America should adopt that system, too!"

- *Causal Fallacy*, or *Post Hoc*; just because one event follows another, the second event is said to have been caused by the first event. "David gave me a bad grade on my speech today just because I dyed my hair purple yesterday, and I wore a dog collar."
- *Non Sequitur Fallacy*, Latin for "It does not follow": "Terrell Owens, the extremely gifted wide receiver for the National Football League, will make a great future coach because he was such a talented player."
- *Primacy of Print Fallacy*, or I like to call it "Idiocy of Internet" fallacy; something must be true because we saw it in a book or magazine, or by gosh, it was on the Internet! "We did not land on the moon; I found this Internet site that proves it was a hoax."
- *Bandwagon Appeal*; something is correct or good just because it's popular. Hasn't every mother in the history of the world grabbed her kid at some time and screamed, "If Andrew jumped off a cliff, would YOU jump off a cliff?" Did you vote for Obama only because you were told the majority of college students would vote for him? Would it be okay to cheat on an exam because everyone else was cheating?
- *Glittering Generalities*; using emotional words/phrases to make a weak idea sound better, and "*professional studies* indicate all *real Americans* should avoid such words."
- *Name Calling*, also Ad Hominem, or "Attacking the Person"; using negative labels for an opponent to distract an audience who might like the opponent's ideas. "Don't listen to Brianna and Aidan's complaints; they're just being *babies!*"
- *Red Herring*, or "Changing the Subject"; purposely shifting the discussion to another point because you are losing your argument. "I don't know why you're talking so much about ethics among college students; politicians are the real problem!"
- *Slippery Slope*; Once a chain of events is set in action, no one will be able to stop it. "You better not smoke marijuana, because it's a proven gateway drug and you will end up doing meth, coke, and heroin, and die." Chris Farley of *Saturday Night Live* fame made a fortune sliding down slippery slopes. He would have said something like this: "You better not cheat on a five-point quiz, or it will be too easy to cheat on a fifty-point test and then a 200-point final, and then you'll plagiarize papers and motivational speeches and break into the school's computer to change all your grades, and then you'll get caught, and they'll kick you out of school, and your family will disown you and you won't be able to get a good job, and you'll lose all your self-respect, and you'll be depressed and start doing drugs, and you'll end up . . . living in a van . . . down by the river!"

Now that you're familiar with these faulty logic terms, listen for them on the news, especially the political talk shows. Analysts love to mention the logic loopholes of their fellow debaters. In the academic world, however, such faulty logic usually happens on a very innocent level. As with topic selection, the **ethics of content must be judged by the intent.** Let's pretend I once heard a speech by a freshman who argued that "we cannot tighten the laws on hand guns because that will lead to tighter laws on hunting rifles in Montana, and the deer would take over our yards, and where will the madness end? Will we lose our hunting knives, too, and eventually all knives and all silverware and have to eat cereal with our hands?" Now, that is a true story, and it's funny and innocent. Most freshmen don't know about Slippery Slope logic. The intent was to get us excited, not to lie to us or even mislead us. But if you DO know that your logic is poor and misleading and you DO use it anyway, you ARE using unethical support.

INTEGRITY IN THY WORDS AND AIDS

It's a wise person who knows the difference between free speech and cheap talk.

I heard that powerful quote in a student speech; it was attributed to Doug Larson, United Feature Syndicate. I think most students know the difference between what words are acceptable in a speech and what words aren't. Again, you really have to consider your audience, which does include your instructor and may include a wide diversity of age, ethnicity, and nationality. In general, you want to avoid "offensive" speech.

> *By swallowing evil words unsaid, no one has ever harmed his stomach.*
>
> **—Sir Winston Churchill**

HATE SPEECH is extremely offensive. *A Pocket Guide to Public Speaking* by O'Hair, Rubenstein, and Stewart contains this advice: "As an ethical speaker, it is vital that you avoid expressions of ethnocentrism, stereotypes, or outright prejudice. Hate speech is any offensive communication—verbal or nonverbal—that is directed against people's racial, ethnic, religious, gender, or other characteristics. This kind of speech is never acceptable." I'm guessing that speeches at KKK rallies might be unethical.

PROFANITY can be offensive, too. You want to "Talk Like You Talk," but if your normal talk is laced with inflammatory words, you know you'll have to do some !!#&*%!* editing. You can't use the "N" word or the "F" word, for sure. Or . . . is it for sure? Hmmmmm? What is the *intent* of your words? Do you want to intimidate or threaten us (both unethical in speeches), or do you want to *educate* us on the use of profanity in the media? Let's say you want to persuade us to fight for tougher censorship laws, so you show us the lyrics, verbatim, from the DMX song, "Bring Your Whole Crew." (If you decide to google those lyrics, be prepared to hear the ghost of Dana-Carvey-past muttering in his best Church Lady voice, "Now, isn't that special?!") I allowed that DMX example in my class because I know there *are* times when offensive words might be ethical in a speech, such as an informative speech on George Carlin's *Seven Dirty Words.* But, be careful. You should clear those moments with your instructor, and you should warn your classmates, "I'm about to show/tell you something a bit shocking." If your intent is honorable and your disclaimer is clear, you can maybe get away with some profanity and provocative visual aids.

Profanity is a fascinating speech issue with me. We hear it all the time on television and in movies, and I hear it often just walking behind students on campus. I certainly heard a lot of profanity from my coaches and military leaders during "motivational" talks. And yet we, as teachers, basically outlaw it completely from the academic classroom. Can the classroom not reflect the real world *at all* in this regard? I understand there shalt be absolutely NO profanity in secondary education classrooms, and most senior citizens really don't like questionable language, but isn't "some" profanity okay in college? I just now took ten minutes and scanned the indices of fifteen different speech texts. Only one of them included the word "obscenity" in the index; none listed "profanity."

I think there is a basic reason for this: profanity is not "needed" in a speech, and even the most mild form might offend someone in the audience. You might "want" to use profanity, but please ask yourself first if you really "need" to use it. Most audiences, I think, expect a public speech to be a bit "classier" than your average *Super Bad* movie script. I personally can see some value in profanity for pathos (emphatic emphasis, surprise, anger, humor, all to "make a memory". . .), but that's a style choice, and I would not push my style on other speakers or an unwilling audience. Some people can get away with profanity; most cannot. If you "slip up" during an emotional part of your speech and happen to utter some profane word, you can usually recover by just saying, "Sorry. Pardon my French." (Just hope you don't have any French people in your class.) Bottom line: If YOU think some profanity would be okay in your academic speeches, ask your instructor and classmates to discuss it. They are your audience, so THEY will dictate the ethics to follow in your situation. Overall, keep the following edict in mind:

PROVOCATIVE SENSORY AIDS must also be chosen ethically. If you want to show an example of profane lyrics, it is usually better to let your audience read the words silently than to have you say them out loud. If you want to play the music, twenty or thirty seconds will make your point; do not play the whole song. If you want to show "sexy" photos, and we all like sexy photos, show them to a few friends first and get their reactions. I tell my students they'll get extra credit for pictures of Faith Hill, but the ceiling will fall in if they show photos from *Hustler* magazine. I often see gross photos from car wrecks during speeches against drinking and driving, but I think you should warn your audience first. Personally, I don't need to see another 8 x 10 color photo of a swollen penis during the famous STD speech; warn me so I can turn my head. When I see videos of bodies without helmets flying off motorcycles or being swept away by an avalanche, I want to know if the body lived. Tell us. Now, imagine how the family of a dead relative would feel if they suddenly saw that loved one crushed under a truck during your speech. Wow. You can find anything you want today on You Tube videos, but that doesn't mean every scene would be ethical in a speech. Finally, don't forget that YOU are the first visual aid the audience will see. If you are too "suggestive" in your dress, it will be distracting, if not unethical. Overall, don't let your sensory aids make your audience uncomfortable.

PLAGIARISM VS CITATION

Plagiarism is the *un*attributed use of another's ideas, words, or pattern of organization. Citation, the opposite of plagiarism in my mind, must then be the *attributed* use of those same ideas, words, or patterns of organization. In other words (my words) you do your research, and then decide how to present it. If you decide to make it sound like your own thoughts, you plagiarize. If you decide to give credit to the authors of the facts and ideas you present, you cite. As long as you cite, you can use as many "borrowed" ideas as you want, which adds truth and therefore impact to comedian Steven Wright's funny line: "To steal ideas from one person is plagiarism; to steal from many is research." Here are more **differences between plagiarism and citation:**

Plagiarism is bad; citation is good.

Plagiarism is easy; citation is harder.

Plagiarism is illegal; citation is legal.

Plagiarism is unethical; citation is ethical.

Plagiarism is common; citation is more common.

Plagiarism is lying to your audience; citation is telling the truth.

Plagiarism will eventually hurt you; citation will give you more credibility.

Plagiarism takes no brain, no heart, and no courage; Dorothy won't like you.

Just as each line above got longer, each act of plagiarism can become a lame analogy to Pinocchio's nose. It's simply a bad practice that cuts corners and leads to poor work habits, which will, someday, catch up with you. I'm sure you've had some education on plagiarism in writing; those same guidelines apply to speeches. You know you can find whole papers online to copy and claim as your own; such papers can be turned into speeches. It's easy. According to Gay Jervey, author of the article "Cheating; But everybody's doing it," found in the March 2006 *Reader's Digest*, "60% of high school students say they've plagiarized papers." Sadly, we all know that most of those cheaters will never be caught.

Technology has made it easier to cheat, but it has also made it easier to catch plagiarism. There are several software programs available now that allow an instructor to just type in a few lines and quickly compare with thousands of published works on similar topics. Plagiarized speeches are also more stilted/mechanical than original speeches; they have no heart or soul. Cheaters tend to read speeches. (See Chapter Six, page 118, about sincerity.) I have personally been involved with seven plagiarism cases in my teaching career; it is not a fun process for anyone. (Two were kicked out of school; the others met with the Dean of Students and had letters of reprimand placed in their files.) That does not include the students I counsel each year on actions that "could" be construed as plagiarism. Some people make honest mistakes. Some do not know the guidelines. Some panic at 4 A.M. when they have an 8 A.M. deadline. You can counsel/correct those problems. Some students, however, are just stupid, and as Ron White, the Blue Collar comedian says, "You can't fix stupid."

I quoted Ron White directly, so I need to attribute that quote to him. I also quoted him verbatim, so I need to put those words in quotations. If I had changed his words some, and said "Stupid people can't be helped," that would be a paraphrase. I could remove the quotations, BUT I still have to cite it because I got the *idea* from Ron White. Some students honestly believe they can change one word in a whole paragraph, and it's now considered to be "in their own words." All of you freshman, seriously, should do some extra research on plagiarism vs paraphrasing.

Here are some other basic **guidelines to avoid plagiarism:**

- Do NOT download twenty pages of text and take them back to your room; you'll be too tempted to copy verbatim. It's best to take notes with as few words as possible, so that when you write/speak, it will be in your own words.
- Before you take notes, write down all the information you need to put the source into your bibliography. Then staple all those notes from that one source together. That way, you won't "forget" where you got the information and therefore just not cite it.
- You can procrastinate on organization of a speech and sensory aids, but *do research* for data gathering and idea generation *early* in the speech-making

process, when you're not rushed. Rushed ideas are too often copied ideas, and rushed data could be made-up data.

And here are some **guidelines for citation,** from my personal beliefs:

- Every research source you used must be listed in your speech bibliography. (Ask your instructor if you need to list sources you read but did not directly use in the speech.)
- Each source in your bibliography should be cited at least once, out loud, in your speech.
- Each main point should contain at least one verbal citation.
- Any visual aid with numbers/quotes/graphs should have a citation on the bottom.
- Verbal cites should be short; we'll get details after the speech if we care.
- Do not verbally cite the whole URL (http://www...); just say "Red Cross web page."
- For a professional touch, prepare a full bibliography to hand out after the speech.
- Do not say your source is the "Internet" or the "Library." Be specific.
- Avoid vague terms like "reliable source" or "recent study." Be specific.
- When you quote people, explain why they are experts.
- There is no need to cite "common knowledge" that most people know.
- If you can't remember a source, just call it a Chinese Proverb. (That's a joke.)

> *To do good is like ascending a mountain;*
> *To do evil is as easy as following an avalanche.*
>
> **—Chinese Proverb**

I want y'all to do good. Remember, you *want* to cite, because that's how you let the audience see all the ghostwriters on your team, and a "team" is normally more credible and therefore more persuasive than you, by yourself. (Whoa, Déjà vu. Chapter Seven?)

SUMMARY CHECKLIST FOR ETHICS

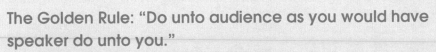

*The measure of man's real character is what he
would do if he would never be found out.*

—Thomas Macaulay, British Essayist, 1800s

The Golden Rule: "Do unto audience as you would have speaker do unto you."

❑ Honesty is defined by the law; black and white; concerns cheating
and plagiarism
❑ Ethics is defined by your philosophy; gray, situational areas; what is "right"
❑ If you have ethics, nothing else matters; if you don't, nothing else matters

General Ethical Guidelines: "Be Pinocchio"

❑ Follow your heart more than your head; you *know* what is right
❑ Choose the difficult right over the easy wrong

Freedom of Speech: "Freedom of Speech is not Free"

❑ First Amendment does not guarantee absolute freedom of speech
❑ Instructors and students might add more restrictions on academic speech

Audience Before Thy Self: "Do not B.S. Thy Audience"

❑ Consider audience *needs* before speaker *wants*; don't waste audience time
❑ The audience decides the ethics you must follow, so benefit the audience

Integrity in Thy Purpose: "You must be the change you want in the world"

❑ We have maintenance and memory days; let your speech be a memory
❑ Ethics is ultimately judged by the *intent* of your purpose

Integrity in Thy Content: "Figures lie, and liars figure"

❑   Avoid quotes out of context, omitted info, half-truths, stretched stats and lies
❑   Many types of faulty logic; can be unethical if done intentionally

Integrity in Thy Words and Aids: "Is it free speech or cheap talk?"

❑   Limited profanity "might" be okay, but it's never wrong to avoid all profanity
❑   Provocative sensory aids "might" be okay, but warn audience first

Plagiarism vs Citation: Plagiarism is bad; citation is good. Be good.

Ethics is a critical topic in life and in speeches. I hope you have been listening . . .

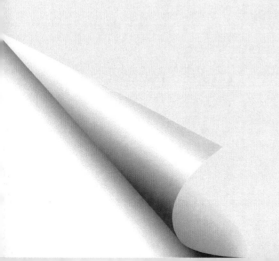

Chapter 10

LISTENING

ARE YOU LISTENING TO ME?!

Note: All of us have had someone else ask us that question: "Are you listening to me?!" As a public speaker, you will surely be tempted to ask your audience that question at some point. As an audience member, you don't want to be asked that question. Hopefully, this chapter can help you comprehend listening so that you can become both a better listener and speaker, and friend, and spouse . . . if you listen to the written words.

In my last chapter, I wrote about ethical speaking and dropped a few hints about ethical listening. If the speaker were unethical, I hope you would "vote with your feet" and leave the scene. In *Beauty and the Beast*, would you have listened to Gaston as he rallied the mob to "Kill the Beast!," or would you have run to warn Belle? (In real life, would you hang around a White Supremacy gathering very long?) In this chapter, I'll assume your speech class will contain valuable talks and that you'll want to be a good listener. You do want to give an ethical speaker a chance to speak and not provide any audience distractions, but more importantly, you want to *listen critically* and try to learn something. Therefore, I'll also assume you want to learn something about listening so you can get more out of those boring lectures and survive college. And maybe get a date.

As the wonderful American writer Oliver Wendell Holmes said, "It is the province of knowledge to speak, and it is the privilege of wisdom to listen." Listening is not the passive, "follower" activity you might think. Indeed, it is more important than speaking. Jonathan Swift, the Anglo-Irish author of *Gulliver's Travels*, acknowledged this great truth when he said:

> Nature, which gave us two eyes to see and two ears to hear,
> has given us but one tongue to speak.

Many teachers use this quote to stress that we should talk less and listen more, especially in the fifth grade. So, forget public speaking for now. Welcome to Public Listening 101!

LISTENING BASICS

Most speech texts say that most people are mostly poor listeners, for the most part. Most marriage counseling involves better communication skills, with a strong emphasis on listening, so I've heard. Hear (sic) are some basics you might not have heard:

LISTENING IS NOT HEARING: There is a BIG difference between hearing and listening:

- Hearing is continuous; listening is intermittent (like windshield wipers that are sometimes on, sometimes off)
- Hearing is passive; listening is active (you have to *want* to listen)
- Hearing is natural; listening is something you must learn

When you're in a fifty-minute lecture, you will *hear,* something, for fifty minutes. You will only *listen* for part of that time; it's flat out impossible to listen 100 percent of the time. It takes too much energy. So, the next time you're in a conversation with your girlfriend, and she says, "Steve, you're not listening to me," you should say, "I'm sorry, Kathy, I'm trying, but my speech instructor said it's actually impossible to listen to you *all* the time." And then play the Paul Simon and Art Garfunkel song, *Sounds of Silence,* to reinforce the lesson of "people hearing without listening." Women listen better to men who use sensory aids.

ATTENTION SPANS DIFFER: Women listen better than men. I have no proof of that, but I thought it would make some good points with my wife and daughters. I do know that, in general, attention spans improve with age, and decline again with senior citizens. Most adults can focus on listening for three to five minutes without having a brain fart. Most eighth-grade boys will only listen about fifteen seconds without having an off-topic, random sexual thought. Again, I'm sorry, I have no proof for my statistics . . . but you know I'm right. This human failing has always been known, but public speakers were slow to acknowledge it. In the nineteenth century, church sermons regularly lasted three hours; today a twenty-minute sermon is too long. In the '60s, political commercials lasted five minutes; today the average is thirty seconds. So, be aware of attention spans when you give a speech. Understand we listen better in sections, and give us time for our mental breaks, or in some cases, breakdowns. *Section* your speech into main points, three to five minutes per main point, and wake us up again as you transition between sections with a change of sound or scenery. "Mix up the air" often.

LISTENING RATE IS HIGHER THAN TALKING RATE: Part of the attention span problem comes from the fact that we can basically listen at a rate four times faster than any person can speak. Apparently we can *speak* about 150 words a minute, *listen* and process about 400 words a minute, and *think* at the rate of 500 to 800 words a minute. At any rate, every speech text I've read says this rate difference leaves the listeners time for their minds to wander. Such wandering will lessen if the speaker and listener can reach an unspoken agreement. . . .

IF YOU PROMISE TO WORK HARDER FOR ME (RESEARCH, CENTS, BECOT), I'LL PROMISE TO LISTEN HARDER TO YOUR SPEECH. MEET ME IN THE MIDDLE.

LISTENING RETENTION IS POOR: According to Sherry Devereaux Ferguson in *Public Speaking, Building Competency in Stages:* "As a society, we suffer from attention deficit disorder (ADD). When tested immediately after a ten-minute presentation, the average listener hears, comprehends, and remembers only about 50 percent of the information. After forty-eight hours, the amount retained has diminished to 25 percent. In classroom situations, 10 percent is a common retention rate." (Thanks, Sherry, for reminding me I'm a teacher.)

LISTENING TAKES TIME: There are four major components to communication, at least among humans; Reading, Writing, NOT Arithmetic, Speaking, and Listening. Listening takes up more of our time than all the other three combined! It's interesting to note, however, that big brother makes us all take full school courses in reading, writing, YES arithmetic, and speaking—but NOT listening. No wonder most of us are poor listeners; we simply aren't trained. I've never even seen a whole semester course offered in listening. I hope one exists, somewhere over the rainbow. I hope someone is listening.

LISTENING CAN BE LEARNED: Listening may not be taught much in our schools (just in bits and pieces, like this one chapter as part of a bigger course), but the good news is that it can be learned. In fact, if you have read this whole book up to this point, you have already become a better listener. You're more aware now of what it takes to be a good speaker, so you will probably be more patient and listen more consciously to the next speaker you hear. Then when you give your own speeches, you become acutely aware of good and bad listeners in your audience, so you can improve your own listening ability. Just as a writer can improve by reading, a listener can improve by speaking. (And vice versa, of course.) There are self-help books, infinite online sources, and counselors you might also use to learn listening skills, or just watch Dr. Drew.

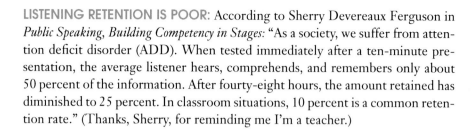

Fun
Information
Therapy
Evaluation

MOST PEOPLE FITE TO BECOME BETTER LISTENERS: You may not realize it, but there are four basic types of listening, which I call FITE, and they all represent things you and Joe Sixpack want:

- **Fun** listening: We all want to laugh, smile, and be entertained or relaxed
- **Information** listening: We need information like we need food, to live
- **Therapy** listening: We listen to give support to others, or to get it
- **Evaluation** listening: We must make judgments and then decisions

Persuade
Inform
Entertain

Remember the three general purposes of speaking, easy as PIE? (Chapter Two, page 26) A persuasive speech requires evaluation listening; an informative speech requires information listening; and an entertainment speech would be fun listening. Therapy listening is mostly those heart-to-heart interpersonal talks with family/friends or maybe professional counselors. If you watch Dr. Phil, you probably have all four types. Overall, just think about what's important to you, and you'll FITE to become a better listener.

BETTER LISTENING = HAPPIER PERSON: I doubt that I learned that formula in math class since I wasn't such a great listener in math, or chemistry, or physics. I was not a happy camper in those classes, and my grades reflected it. If I knew then what I know now about listening, I know I would have gotten more out of all of my classes and gotten better grades and had better dates and bought a Corvette instead of a Vega and invested in an IRA sooner and smiled more. Listening skills really do apply to *every* facet of your happy life: school, job, recreation, family, and friends. Try to learn those skills now, so YOU don't have to look back later, with a pathetic sigh, and mumble that trite, old-person thing, "If I had only known then what I know now . . ." Really. A Vega.

LISTENING IS A LEADERSHIP SKILL: Some people think that leaders only talk and followers only listen. Take a leadership course, however, and you'll see that listening is critical for everyone in the group, *especially* the boss. Major General Perry M. Smith, in *Taking Charge, A Practical Guide for Leaders*, said: "If a good listener, the leader can accept ideas, criticism, and other feedback that can improve the organization and create an atmosphere of excellence and caring . . . Listening is an acquired art. It requires self-discipline and well-developed skills. Leaders should listen and listen and listen. Only through listening can they really find out what's going on." The last part of that quote is especially applicable to the leaders we call teachers and parents.

> *Research shows that you have a greater impact on people by how you listen than by what you say.*
>
> **—Steven W. Vannoy, *The 10 Greatest Gifts I Give My Children***

REAL LISTENING IS REAL HARD: If listening were easy, we would all do it better. Since we know it's hard, we really value the people who do it well. Those people fully comprehend the numerous barriers to good listening and consciously work to tear them down. I'm reminded of a famous speech about a famous concrete barrier to listening, understanding, and peace. President Ronald Reagan, on

June 12, 1987, was at the Brandenburg Gate in West Berlin, talking about the need to destroy the Berlin Wall, which was dividing a city, and indeed, a world. He demanded, "Mr. Gorbachev, tear down this wall!"

BARRIERS TO LISTENING

Speaker
Environmental
Audience
Mental

As a speaker, it behooves you to comprehend the barriers that might separate you from your audience. As a listener, you want to be the explorer who crosses barriers to get the pot of gold, the message that might help you. Anything that hurts the communication process can be called "noise," and **everything you've learned in this book is designed to cut through that noise**, so that your audience has a better chance to listen to your message. This would "SEAM" like a good time to review the four main types of noise, from Chapter Six, page 125: *S*peaker, *E*nvironmental, *A*udience, and *M*ental. I highlighted the speaker viewpoint then; I'll expound upon the audience viewpoint now. **Note: To better determine the type of noise, ask yourself where it originated.**

SPEAKER NOISE: As a listener, you must fight your urge to prejudge the speaker or topic. Speakers can be too short, fat, or old; their clothing can be too sloppy, formal, or tacky; their voice can be too quiet or high-pitched or have too much of an accent. Is no one perfect? The trick is to **listen to the message; don't shoot the messenger.** I have seen many "silly nerds" and "dumb blondes" and "macho jocks" give truly inspirational speeches. If you hate the speaker's topic, you can at least politely pretend to listen, or follow the advice from George Rodman and Ronald B. Adler in *The New Public Speaker*:

> The key is to ask "What is of interest in this topic?" rather than "Is this topic interesting?" The difference between those two questions is crucial, because the first one presupposes that there will be *something* of interest if you listen closely enough. It might be the human side of the story, it might be something that relates to your own life . . . and it might not emerge until later in the talk.

It might be something testable, and that can be reason enough to override speaker noise. For student speeches, remember that there is value in the experience for the speakers, and their talks are usually short, anyway. For longer, real-world speeches, you might take action to lessen noise. If Shawn is too quiet, perhaps you could ask her to speak up or use a microphone. If Heather's words confuse you, you might ask for clarification. If the left tackle blocks the righteous visual aid, you could ask him to move. If you're not free to give verbal feedback, try nonverbals. (e.g., cup your ear to speak louder, move your hand to request movement). If a professor is creating barriers to your listening, a group of you students might gently offer some feedback for improvement after class. It's tough, but it's possible. If an instructor is habitually awful, rude, or unethical, you can talk to the department head, or at least write evaluations on end-of-course critiques or some Web site, like ratemyprofessor.com. In the meantime, focus on the message.

ENVIRONMENTAL NOISE: This is any "noise" coming from the physical environment, auditory or not. You might not have any control over it, but you can try. If the room is too cold, ask the instructor if the heat can be adjusted, or wear a sweater. Too hot? Open a window, or take off the sweater. Uncomfortable seat? Maybe you can move, or bring a pillow next class, or sit on your sweater. Weird smell? Maybe it's in the trash can, and you can set the can out in the hallway. Maybe you need to put the sweater out in the hallway. I hope you get my point; **if something bothers you, try to take some action.** Most environmental noise bothers the whole group, so you can take a group vote: "Should we close/open the door/window, turn on/off the light/fan, move/adjust the screen/podium, turn the volume on the TV/laptop up/down?" I had a student one time who just couldn't take it anymore and blurted out, "Can't we do anything about Lori's squeaky chair?" I laughed, and said, "Okay. We could send Lori to Florida, or I could try to find some oil." I actually had learned a long time ago to keep some WD-40 in our supply room, and two minutes later the chair did not squeak. Moral: The squeaky chair gets the oil. ASK!

AUDIENCE NOISE: Don't you hate it when you're trying to listen, and the people behind you keep talking? The guy next to you is playing his iPod so loudly you can hear it from his ear buds? You're forty-five years old, trying to finally finish your degree and paying for it all yourself, and the girl in front of you is texting her BFF the whole time and totally ignoring the instructor? (This noise would not have happened without the texting girl... so it is "audience" noise.) We all expect *some* noise from any audience, but **try hard not to be the problem yourself.** Why are you in the lecture if you're not trying to listen and learn *something*? If you're only there for attendance purposes, fine; don't listen. But don't create noise for others, either. My pet peeve is to look out during a lecture and see a student with her eyes glued to her laptop. When I nudge such students back into reality, they usually say, "Oh, I listen better that way." Uh-huh. I usually ask, "When you're giving your speech, do you want everyone to be looking at *their* laptops?" **Remember the Golden Rule.** Be polite listeners. Give the speaker some eye contact and positive nonverbal feedback. Nod your head some; smile. If you look angry or bored or distracted, it creates noise for the speaker, if not others. It's hard enough for students to give their speeches without looking out and seeing people whispering to friends, playing with cell phones, hiding under hats, or doing homework for their next class. If you're sitting near people who forget that they are no longer in high school, you can quietly remind them, and the noise usually stops. If not, you can mention the problem to the instructor, or maybe just sit somewhere else next time. If the noise happens to be coming *from you*, here are some quick **hints to get ready to listen:**

- Get a good night's sleep, so you don't put your head on the desk or pop your neck
- Eat something before class, so your stomach does not rumble, but avoid beans . . .
- Take a shower; B.O. can also distract the person next to you
- Got a cold? Take some medicine; be prepared with Kleenex
- Sit up straight; you'll daydream less, listen better, and help the speaker
- Sit in the front third of the lecture hall; less audience noise and better grades, really
- Also, you might need to get a hearing aid, or at least clean out your ears

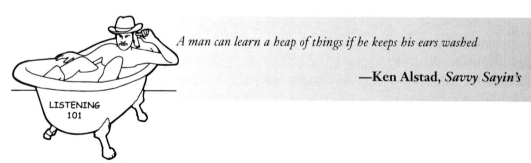

A man can learn a heap of things if he keeps his ears washed

—Ken Alstad, *Savvy Sayin's*

LISTENING
101

MENTAL NOISE: ("Daydreaming"): I suppose all noise ultimately becomes "mental" since we must decide if we are bothered by the distraction, but re-member: did the noise start in your brain or from the speaker, environment, or audience? I think mental noise is the most common noise and the **hardest to combat,** because it's really hard to ignore your own brain and totally concentrate on the message at hand. "I'm trying to listen, but my mind keeps interrupting me!" Here are some **hints** that may work for you:

- Read the lesson *before* the class/lecture; you'll react quicker to the data
- Take notes; you'll focus on the message better, but don't write down everything
- Don't get hung up on words you don't understand; you can research them later
- Leave your "baggage" outside (Review Chapter Seven, page 160); consciously put your social/monetary/school concerns aside, and *concern yourself with listening*

Bottom Line: The best way to fight mental noise is to become a critical listener and thinker.

CRITICAL LISTENING/THINKING

Listening is an *active* exercise. You make a choice to listen, and that's half the battle. *Critical* listening, then, must be *really active!* If the definition of communication is the "sharing of meaning," I would assume that critical listening is a really active process of attaching meaning to what you hear. You have to concentrate, to *think*, and try to relate your listening to your life. You have to care. Let's listen to what some experts say:

- From George Rodman and Ronald B. Adler, *The New Public Speaker:* When listening to a speech, you should jot down questions you want to ask. Questions are particularly important to critical listening, because critical thinking is a process of asking questions: Does this make sense? Is this backed up with evidence? Is the evidence valid?
- From Stephen E. Lucas, *The Art of Public Speaking:* Critical listening is listening to evaluate a message for purposes of accepting or rejecting it, as when we listen to the sales pitch of a used-car dealer, the campaign speech of a political candidate, or the closing arguments of an attorney in a jury trial. You must use your mind as well as your ears. When your mind is not actively involved, you may be hearing, but you are not *listening*. In fact, listening and critical thinking are so closely allied that training in listening is also training in how to think.

Critical listening is directly tied to *critical thinking*, which is quite the buzzword in college lesson planning today. We instructors need to show that we are challenging the critical thinking of our students. I've read numerous definitions; here's my favorite:

- From *Rereading America*, 1998: Critical thinking is when someone probes for motives and causes instead of relying on facts. A critical thinker looks for underlying assumptions and ideas and cultivates the ability to imagine and value points of view different than his or her own—then strengthens, refines, enlarges, or reshapes ideas in light of other perspectives.

I refined and reshaped that idea into a statement I use in my lectures:

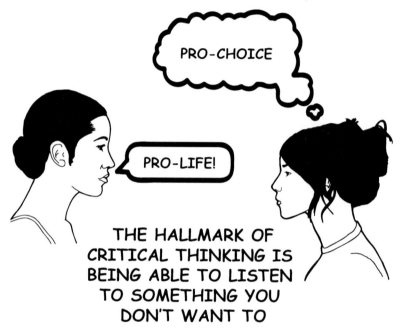

TEACH YOURSELF

You are mostly in college not to learn facts, but to "learn how to learn." In other woods (sic), your acorn brain won't grow into a strong oak, with probing branches seeking truth, unless you learn to *teach yourself.* As Sir Walter Scott said, "All men who have turned out worth anything have had the chief hand in their own education." Ultimately, you will not teach yourself how to adapt to new situations unless you learn to really listen, critically. (It also helps to *read* and *think* critically.) We instructors cannot make you listen anymore than ranchers can make a horse drink water, but we can *guide* you to the fountain of wisdom . . . allowing you to drink, once you decide you want to. Are y'all thirsty? Here are some **guidelines for becoming a more critical listener:**

Consider the SPEAKER:
- Do not stereotype the speaker for gender/age/size/shape/race/accent.
- Simply respect the difficulty and stress of giving any speech; be patient.
- Adapt to the speaker's style; don't expect her to adapt to your listening.
- Focus *more* on speaker's content than style/delivery, but *do* consider speaker nonverbals that reinforce or contradict the message.
- Focus *more* on speaker's ideas than your own, but *do* consider your values.
- Ask yourself if the speaker is unbiased, credible, and passionate.
- Consider what the speaker is doing to keep or lose your attention.
- Try to empathize with the speaker overall, to "walk a mile in his/her shoes."

Consider the TOPIC:
- Do not stereotype the topic: "Don't judge a book by looking at its cover."
- Consider that every topic has *some* value, at least to the speaker, and appreciate that.
- Try hard to find *some* value for yourself (be selfish); "How might I use this topic?"

Consider the ORGANIZATION:
- Listen consciously for steps of the introduction (Chapter Five, page 104).
- Is it a speech to persuade, inform, or entertain? Persuasion takes the most effort.
- Listen to topic *sections* (main points) rather than trying to listen to the whole topic.
- Consider the pattern of organization (Chapter Five, page 100) and try to follow the flow.

Consider the CONTENT:
- Is it ethical (Chapter Nine, page 197); do you feel uncomfortable?
- Is it logical (Chapter Nine, page 202); does it pass the "common sense" test?
- Is it relevant and representative, current and credible? (fabulous and fun . . . ?)
- Is it well researched? (SMILE, Chapter Three) Good citation?
- Does it have a variety of support? (CENTS, Chapter Three)
- Does it seem like more fact or more opinion?
- If a persuasive speech, are you hearing both sides of the argument?
- Does it create questions for you? If so, track them; ask when able.

Surveys
Media
Internet
Library
Experts

Consider the MEANING:
- Stress the meaning more than the words; "Concepts" more than facts.
- Stress main ideas more than details; "Big Picture" more than snapshots.

Comparisons
Examples
Numbers
Testimony
Stories

- Don't listen "too hard"; you're not a tape recorder, so do NOT write down every word in your notes; just use key words, like your outlines (Chapter Five).
- Do not get hung up on "word problems" (Chapter Six, page 136) or sensitive "trigger words" that anger you; focus on the meaning, and "listen through" such distractions.
- Can you draw your own conclusions? Maybe discuss them with friends?
- Think you'll actually use any of this information/advice? Why?
- Don't assume anything; *listen to the whole speech* before thou passeth judgment.

Consider HOW YOU LISTEN:
- Be active, not passive; concentrate (like you're doing now . . .), don't daydream.
- Be positive, not negative; listen more to agree than to argue, don't you agree?
- Be polite, not rude; listen to ask questions later, not to interrupt now with your story.
- Listen to understand, not to "win"; communication is not a competition.
- Listen more with the brain than the heart; be objective and control your emotions.
- Listen with your whole body (feet on floor, lean forward, eye contact, smile).
- Most importantly, *listen with an open mind*, not closed.

> *Most listening is done through heavy filters or screens of judgment, evaluation, and condemnation. Most of what we hear, we immediately weigh on personal scales of right or wrong, good and bad. We rarely hear what someone has to say. We're much more likely to evaluate whether or not we happen to like the speaker's voice, appearance, and mannerisms. We're often very trite and superficial in our listening habits. The first step to listening effectively is to listen with an open mind.*
>
> **—Randy Fujishin, *The Natural Speaker***

I'm not as pessimistic about listening as Mr. Fujishin seems to be, but I certainly agree with the *meaning* of his words. People *do* need to work on their listening skills, and by people, I mean everyone except you and me, because we are just fine. As I learned from Dr. John Kline, educational advisor to Air University in 1985, "We always think listening is a problem with others." (Dr. Kline, by the way, was my role model for teaching communications.) In truth, we *all* need to work on more critical listening. The first step, as Mr. Fujishin said, is to have an open mind, so that's why the first guideline I listed was "Do not stereotype the speaker." All the guidelines provided apply to *public listening*, but most of them can also apply to *interpersonal listening* between two people. (Except you probably shouldn't take notes.) That's why I stress to my students: Pay attention to this course, and it might help you get a date for Friday night. Guys, **women *love* good listeners!**

Interpersonal Hint: Next time you're over at Angie's place and she starts to talk with you, say, "Uh, excuse me a second. I hate to interrupt, but would it be okay if we turned off the TV so I could listen to you better?" This statement is even more powerful (and hypothetical) during the Super Bowl.

Personal Note: If I didn't sincerely believe in the guidelines listed, I could not listen to 1,200 speeches a year. I never get bored, because each speech has a lesson for me. I learn a lot. As I critically listen to others, I also critically critique myself.

CRITIQUE YOURSELF

> *Criticism may not be agreeable, but it is necessary.*
> *It fulfills the same function as pain in the human body.*
> *It calls attention to an unhealthy state of things.*
>
> **—Winston Churchill**

Criticism/critiques in academic public speaking are more positive than negative (Chapter One, page 9), and in team situations such criticism is essential to break up groupthink (Chapter Seven, page 159). In the real world, however, Mr. Sad Truth says it's very difficult to get any kind of criticism at all (see Chapter One, page 11). So, take advantage of the nice critiques you do get in your college courses, and then concentrate on critiquing yourself once you graduate. In order to critique your own listening/speaking skills, you have to answer some questions:

Are you a **good listener?** Only you can really answer that question. Follow the *general* listening guidelines provided and engage in some *major* reflection, without *Captain* Morgan. I hope that pun wasn't too *rank* for your *private* use, soldier, because you simply have to be honest with yourself:

- Do I come across as a good listener? (Look at the team talk guidelines on page 163)
- Am I really trying as hard as I could, or am I pretending to listen?

- Am I helping the speaker, or am I a distraction?
- Did I prepare to listen, or am I just a body in the audience?
- Am I consciously practicing to become a better listener?
- Am I good enough, smart enough, and doggone it, do people like me? (Sorry, Al Franken won his senate race, and I had an *SNL* flashback of Stuart Smalley.)

Another great question to ask yourself is, "Am I making use of my spare listening time?" Back on page 215, I explained that we listen faster than anyone can speak, and a critical listener makes use of that extra time, so the mind don't wander wherever with whomever:

- Am I thinking ahead of the speaker some, guessing what he might say?
- How would I paraphrase what the speaker just said?
- How would I summarize the main points and main lessons?
- Am I reviewing my notes occasionally, thinking "How can I use this stuff?"

Such questions are similar to those asked by speakers, silently, during their own talks. (Yes, speakers also think faster than they talk and can't listen 100 percent to themselves.) The umbrella question might be, "Am I *listening* to my audience's nonverbal feedback?"

- Did my words make sense, or did I just confuse them?
- Did I already say that?
- Why is that guy in the fourth row looking at me like that?
- Is that girl over there listening? Hey, isn't she in my Stats class?
- Am I loud enough, moving enough, and doggone it, looking at people enough?
- Am I throwing out too much information, going into too much detail?

Note: information overload is real: You students today have many more choices in life than I had. There are more careers, more styles of cars and clothes, *much* more media, and endless types of pizza. It's stressful to make decisions. To separate all those choices, you need more information, and somewhere along the information highway your engine simply overheats and explodes. Your brain shuts down and cannot (will not) absorb any more information. If speeches only add to the barrage of facts and advice without adding personality and sincerity and making a memory, audiences will quit listening. **Information overload is a HUGE barrier to listening.** ("TMI, baby, TMI!") Go back and read Chapter Eight of my book for the eighth time and, doggone it, keep your speeches simple.

Are you a **good speaker?** Others can help you with this question. Your instructor will be your first line of defense (don't forget you can also ask for extra instruction), but your classmates will also be filling out critiques on you. Look for trends that reinforce your good points and indicate areas that can be improved. If one person says you need to add that motivation step, he could be wrong (maybe he wasn't listening); if five people tell you the same thing, work on it. Friends and family are also a great source of feedback; do practice sessions with them, and invite them to hear the "real thing" if possible. (I encourage such invitations in my classes.) There are many checklists in this book that you might use to ask yourself, "Am I a good speaker?"

Don't forget the power of **videotaping your speech.** (Chapter Six, page 117) Your self-critique means more if you get to watch your own speech as if you were watching a fellow student. Use the same critique forms as you use in class. You'll be harder on yourself, and you'll learn more.

The best way to learn to critique yourself (listening and speaking) for the real world is to "practice critique" others in the classroom. The next time you complain that you have to critique another stupid speech, remember that you *are* helping someone else, but mostly, you're helping yourself.

CRITIQUE OTHERS

Every speech instructor has a unique method of running the class and evaluating the speeches. Most people use some verbal feedback for immediate reinforcement after the speech, and add some type of written feedback, which might come later. Both types might employ peer feedback as well. I personally use the *Peer Evaluating Questions* you'll find at *Appendix D*, which match the *Peer Evaluation Form* at *Appendix E*. I hope they help you get in the "ballpark" for playing the critiquing game.

KNOW WHAT TO CRITIQUE: Appendix D shows you what to critique. First, think about the speech in sections: How good was the intro/body/conclusion and delivery? Then look at the sub-points under each section and you can get more specific. If you consciously listen for such specifics (credibility step? citations?), then your critique can be more specific. It took me ten years to create the list of Peer Evaluating Questions. It's an "almost" perfect listing of *everything . . . you'll ever . . . need to know.* It's such a thorough summary of all speech lessons that I told my students they could throw away the text and just use Appendix D. Of course, that was before I wrote my own text.

NO CRITIQUE IS PERFECT: Keep in mind that critiques, like speeches, are never perfect. There is not enough time in an academic class to critique a speech 100 percent, and no one could digest that much information at one time, anyway. Try to write one comment for each major block on the critique form, and try to offer one short verbal comment after the talk. If you want to offer more feedback, talk to the speaker after class. The most meaningful comments come from peers later, unprompted, outside class, when they're not "on stage" being judged by everyone. (Note: As the speaker, if you don't hear a critique you want of a specific item, ASK. "Hey, guys, what did you think of my story? Was it too long?" Remember, in the real world, you must **fight for feedback.**) I designed my Peer Evaluation Form to reflect a *bottom line*, which is cleverly placed at the bottom of the form: What's the best part, and what part needs the most improvement? Sometimes, you don't have the time to discuss much except the bottom line. Do the best you can.

BE POSITIVE: Please review what I said about critiques in Chapter One, page 9. I believe strongly that criticism should be **mostly positive.** I found several authors who talked about a "Good-Bad-Good" or "Plus-Minus-Plus" technique, or the "Criticism Sandwich" image that I prefer. I try to avoid the terms *bad* or *minus* and, instead, discuss "things to work on." We all have something about public speaking we could improve, and students want to know those areas, but accentuate the good stuff. I try to remember my mother Rosemary's sage advice from the universal mothering handbook: "If you can't say something nice about someone, don't say anything at all." Even with weak speeches, I can usually say something nice about the delivery, visual aids, or topic choice. Then I ask them to critique themselves, and *they* will bring out the negative items, trust me. Speech is very confessional by its nature, so the critic doesn't have to play the priest so much. Be the cheerleader!

BE PERSONAL: That personal, individual, spontaneous critique can be very meaningful: "Barbara, I *loved* the dog painting you did! I have a schnauzer myself, and it really touched me." Speakers love to hear such *personalized* comments. One way to do this is to explain "why" you liked something: "I loved your story about how your name, Martha, got turned into your nickname, *Mop*, because I did the same thing with my twin's name. Instead of Stevie, I called him *TV*." We all like to know that we touched at least one audience member, in the heart, with our message. So, **put your heart on your sleeve.** Personalized comments

also draw the class together better as a team (dare I say *family?*), which creates a friendlier atmosphere and therefore better critiques.

BE POLITE: Don't be so personal and spontaneous that you blurt out something rude, crude, or socially unattractive. Remember the power of the pause, and pause before you offer a critique that comes from anger. (Were you ever taught to count to ten first?) The Golden Rule really rules when it comes to critiques (Chapter Nine, page 197). You want the speaker to benefit somehow from your words. You want to be truthful, but also **be tactful.** If I'm upset by a speech, I'll talk to the student, alone, after class. I learned a long time ago in leadership training to *praise in public, admonish in private.*

CRITIQUE THE SPEECH, NOT THE PERSON: One way to be polite is to focus on the speech rather than the speaker. Instead of saying, "You're lazy; you didn't do any research," try "I would be even more convinced if I had heard some citations." Instead of "You're not very creative," try "If you use some music or video clips, it might clarify your ideas." Try to critique specific actions from Appendix D instead of perceived character flaws.

CRITIQUE WHAT CAN BE IMPROVED: It does no good to tell people they are too short. Instead, suggest they step to the side of the podium so you can see them better. Instead of saying, "Your stuttering is very hard to listen to," try something like, "If you put more of your good ideas on visual aids, we could follow them better." Such comments "problem-solve" the negative instead of just mentioning the problem.

BE SPECIFIC: When people first start critiquing speeches, this seems to be the hardest guideline to follow. You might want to scan again what I said in Chapter Three, page 55, about specific support. Consider the following common critiques and how to improve:

- "Your speech was good." Well, *why* was it good? *What* was good? *When?*
- "You had great visual aids." Okay, but pick one and say *why* it was great.
- "You seemed to really know your topic." What made you feel that way?
- "I learned a lot." So, tell us one thing, specifically, that you learned.
- "You really kept my attention." But *How?* Voice, gestures, sensory aids?
- "Your support was credible." *How so?* Give an example. Mention cites.
- "You motivated me to find out more." How? What touched you the most?
- "I could really relate to what you said." Why? What's your background?

The above common critiques are good. SPECIFICS can make them great. Be great.

SUMMARY CHECKLIST FOR LISTENING

Listening Basics

- ❏ Listening is not hearing; it's intermittent, active, and can be learned
- ❏ Most attention spans are only three to five minutes; retention is poor, 50 percent at best
- ❏ We can listen at a much faster rate than you can talk, so our minds wander
- ❏ We spend more time listening than we do reading, writing, and speaking combined
- ❏ Four basic types of listening: Fun, Informative, Therapy, and Evaluation (FITE)
- ❏ Listening is not easy; it's a leadership skill, for sure

Barriers to Listening (Types of Noise)

- ❏ Speaker: Annoying looks, voice, acts; focus on message content instead
- ❏ Environmental: Auditory, temp, smells, comfort; if possible, take action
- ❏ Audience: Talking, sleeping, movement; don't be the problem yourself
- ❏ Mental: Daydreaming, worries, confusion; study critical listening skills

Critical Listening/Thinking

- ❏ Listen to evaluate, to accept or reject the idea
- ❏ Listen for motives and causes, not just facts
- ❏ Learn to value points of view different from your own

Teach Yourself

- ❏ Speaker: Don't stereotype or prejudge; empathize with his/her situation
- ❏ Topic: Don't stereotype; find some value for yourself
- ❏ Organization: Listen in sections
- ❏ Content: Is it ethical, logical, objective, relevant, and researched?
- ❏ Meaning: Think "big picture" vs details; draw your own conclusions
- ❏ How You Listen: Active, positive, polite, with an open mind

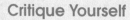

Critique Yourself

If you want to improve, you have to learn to critique yourself

Critique Others

Great practice for critiquing yourself! (See Appendix D)

At the end of Chapter Five, I asked you to pretend you were a pilot taking your audience on a trip. Now, pretend you are that audience who wants to go on the trip (lecture). Study those airport requirements (homework) *before* flight day. Sleep and eat well. Arrive early, check your "baggage" (mental distractions), and get comfortable in your seat. Be ready for takeoff (ready to take notes). Buckle your seatbelt in case of turbulence (noise), but trust your pilot and look for good things (message). Don't be annoying to the pilot or your fellow passengers. Thanks for flying Listen Airlines!

Chapter 11

ONE TO
WATCH

BE THE ONE!

You will stand out in the crowd, in a good way, if you employ some of the "extra credit" ideas in this chapter.

Image © iQoncept, 2012. Used under license from Shutterstock, Inc.

I think I have already covered more than enough material in this book for a 100-level public speaking course, but I know some people want more. My students regularly ask me about *extra credit*, things they might do to earn a few extra points. Rather than give them extra assignments, I like to see people add extra thought/effort to their speeches, using some of the ideas in this chapter. I am biased, of course, but I think these extra items can help you **"separate yourself from the pack."** They are ideas that you might add to your private as well as public communication bag. I also suggest students take more communication courses, if possible, and certainly look for more opportunities to give speeches and practice the basic lessons in this text. For now, just be willing to add some extra spice to your cooking and be a little *different*, in order to be a little *better*. Be willing to explore your own very unique style.

YOU HAVE STYLE!

You cannot not communicate (Chapter Six, page 125), you cannot not have influence (Chapter Seven, page 146), and **you cannot not have style!** You might stand in one place with your hands in your pockets and stare at the floor and mumble, but that is still "style," and no one can take that away from you. It might also work better than you think. Your style is largely a reflection of your personality, and you can't really fake or force your personality. You can *stretch it* and *test it*, however, depending on how much you want to experiment and grow. The trick is to use a style that is effective for your audience, and since audiences are varied, you might want to vary your style some. You can improve style variety without selling your soul to the Devil, especially in these three basic speech areas:

Surveys
Media
Internet
Library
Experts

- **Content** (Chapter Three): You can have a variety of research (SMILE) and content (CENTS) if you want to. Don't just use the Internet; try an interview. Don't just give us a bunch of numbers; mix in a story and a quote. Even the most boring personality can show some style with content variety. Try to use some sort of support that you have never used before. Variety is the spice of life, remember . . . so spice it up some.

Comparisons
Examples
Numbers
Testimony
Stories

- **Sensory Aids** (Chapter Four): Use a variety of sensory aids (BECOT) to show your style. I had a quiet, shy student last term who was a good artist, so he made cartoon drawings for all his main points, and people laughed, including him! Some people use more music

Blackboard
Electronics
Costuming
Objects
Transparencies

or posters; some make their own videos. Try to use an aid you have not yet seen in your class. You surely have *some* sort of unique talent and personality when it comes to sensory aids. Unleash that beast!

- **Delivery** (Chapter Six): If you use a mix of sensory aids, it will lead to more natural movement and voice inflection. You can make yourself get out from behind the podium and "mix up the air" more if you consciously plan ahead with your aids. I often see nervous people enhance their style with this one, single piece of advice. Try to do something that makes *you* smile. Audiences love the smile style.

I think delivery is overrated. I like to ask people if they have style, and they usually say no. They'll tell me they just aren't good speakers, meaning they don't have some vibrant, animated delivery style. Well, *style* involves MUCH more than delivery. If that statement weren't true, Bob Dylan and Willy Nelson would have never sold one recording. Awful voices! You can't even understand Dylan, and my family thinks Nelson's voice is worse than scratches on a blackboard. I love them both, for their words. For energy, my eyes water when I hear the unbelievably powerful voice of Sugarland's Jennifer Nettles, but some losers complain she is too *twangy*. I've heard rumors that some people can't stand Snoop Dog, either, but hey, guess what? **No one style works for everybody,** in music or speeches, so you can do no more than allow yourself . . . to be . . . yourself. These artists all know themselves and have *style*, in spades, and they are very effective in their own worlds. They even make a little money, but their success is due to more than just delivery. You have so many other style points you can make with your audience, especially if you have a good attitude.

> *The only disability in life is a bad attitude.*
>
> **—Scott Hamilton, Olympic ice skater and cancer survivor**

Style is really all about your 'tude, man. We don't always know what to call it, and we don't always know why it grabs us so, but we know what we like. It has much to do with Confidence and Positive Energy. Sincerity is embracing, and Creativity is inspirational. Dress and Posture and Beauty are captivating. Dependability is comforting, and Consistency is refreshing. Calmness makes us secure. Humor makes us laugh, inside and out. Volume allows us to hear; Pauses allow us to think. Music and Videos get us excited, and Stories give us hope. Giving is so caring . . . and Caring is so . . . giving. Knowledge is a powerful tool, and Effort is damned sexy. Timing can be emphatic, and Word Choice can be memorable.

Overall, then, we might all want to follow advice from Big and Rich, some other stylish singers, and "add a little zing to our zang zang."

WORD CHOICE

In Chapter Six (page 137), I wrote about word choice that could be distracting to your audience, such as poor grammar and pronunciation. In Chapter Eight (page 181), I stressed to keep your words simple and speak to express, not to impress. In Chapter Nine (page 205), I advised you to be careful with the integrity of your word choice, especially profanity and hate speech. Now, I want to encourage you to use some words with style . . . some utterly unique utterances.

- **Active vs Passive:** We react better to active vs passive wording. Instead of saying, "Bock's trial summary was given with simple eloquence," say, "Bock used simple, powerful words in his trial summary." Not "This chapter was read by Lorraine," but "Lorraine read this chapter and loved it and used it to make her speeches extra special . . . but she's still very glad it's the last chapter."

- **Figures of Speech:** I learned that a figure of speech was basically any way of saying something other than the ordinary way, or maybe saying one thing but meaning another. Under any definition, figures of speech spark imagination, and audiences like that. There are more figures of speech than any English major can digest, but some are worth mentioning here. I explained **similes** and **metaphors** earlier (Chapter Three, page 48), two ways to compare items with a more stylistic flair. I'm sure the explanation was *like* a breath of fresh air; it *was* a veritable *oasis* in a barren *desert* of dry verbiage. **Personification** gives human qualities to inanimate things or abstract ideas. In other words, if your *speech has a heart attack*, personification can *give CPR*. **Apostrophe** is similar, addressing something not alive as if it were around and could reply: "Oh, sweet *justice*, will David give me an *A+* on my speech?" **Metonymy** is the use of something closely related for the thing actually meant. Instead of saying, "President Obama says we must stop using so much oil," you could say, "The *White House* said that our *vampire guilt* dictates we use less of the *world's blood*." (I suppose that's also personification and metaphor.) An **oxymoron** is a compact paradox in which two words seem to contradict each other: "Your *deafening silence* tells me I'm about to lose my audience. So, even though I want to mention a *gazillion more* figures of speech, I shall stop here." That last statement was **hyperbole,** or exaggeration for the purpose of truth,

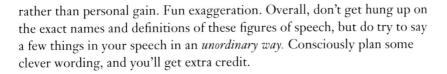

rather than personal gain. Fun exaggeration. Overall, don't get hung up on the exact names and definitions of these figures of speech, but do try to say a few things in your speech in an *unordinary way.* Consciously plan some clever wording, and you'll get extra credit.

- **Sensory Imagery:** If you can use words *alone* to make our senses tingle, you have used great sensory imagery, and you have made a vivid memory for your audience—even without visual aids. In Chapter Three (page 52), I said that *description* makes a conscious effort to appeal to the five human senses of sight, hearing, touch, taste, and smell. Think about how poets and songwriters touch your senses, and try to use a touch of that style. Allow me to describe a snow skiing experience, which always brings out my inner poet:

  - **Sight:** I stood at the top of the ski-run for a moment, staring at least twenty miles to the next mountain range, which looked like a stegosaurus arching its back.
  - **Hearing:** I studied the skier below me as he crunched through the icy run at a steep angle, grinding his edges so he wouldn't slip, slamming his poles into the hill, grunting through each turn.
  - **Touch:** I decided to tighten my boots, and I had to remove my gloves to get more pressure on the clips. My sweaty hands started stinging in the frigid air, so I worked fast. I needed my feet in a vice grip for this run, pinching off blood flow.
  - **Taste:** The sharpness of my peppermint gum was a perfect match for the hill.
  - **Smell:** As I launched off the edge, the pine trees blew a woodsy reminder at me that mountain air is better than city smog, every day, and I held my breath.

There is really no such thing as a bad day of skiing, and there really is no such thing as a bad speech. Some ski days, and some speech days, just happen to be better. Work in some extra sensory imagery for both memory days, and you will smile more.

- **Poetry:** I cannot stress enough that a **little** bit of poetry **goes a long way.** Do NOT read a three-minute poem to your audience. If it's more than two short lines, you should have a visual aid so we can follow along. Audiences also prefer some words that actually rhyme. If you wrote the poem or have some personal connection with it, let us know and we will listen harder.

For example, like most people, I wrote some rather earth-shaking poetry in college, back when I knew everything:

As time leaps and creeps and weeps,
she only has strength to carry
for length the pointed
message of a
smile.

Most poetry I enjoy in speeches is short and to the point, like the sign I saw in Wintzell's Oyster House in Mobile, Alabama, in 1987:

> *The hand that lifts the cup of cheer should not be the one to shift the gear.*

That would be a great line in a speech about drinking and driving. You could probably make up a line like that yourself, just for fun. I had a student who gave a persuasion speech on the benefits of breastfeeding vs bottle-feeding babies, and she simply said, "Breast is Best!" Try to rhyme a time or two, Sue. Don't you agree, Bri?

- **Play Words:** Sometimes words exist for no other reason than to have fun. Don't ever forget that audiences love to have fun. Watch some comics and pay attention to their word choice. Our high school class clown, Sam Taylor, had a line he used when people would ask him how he was feeling: "Oh, I'm beginning to feel more like I do now than I did before I got here." It got mixed reactions, but it always got a reaction. My 1985 Air Force communications book, *Tongue And Quill*, has this playful quote on the back cover:

> *I know that you believe you understand what you think*
> *I said, but I am not sure you realize that what*
> *you heard is not what I meant.*

I'm not sure such wording has a formal name label, but some phun-words do:

- **Neologism:** Made-up or coined word. I probably should look up *neologism* to make sure I didn't make it up. In Chapter Two, I made up *mixographics*, *professographics*, and *bossographics*—all pretty vivid, *graphic* word use, yes?

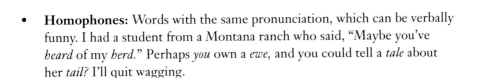

- **Homophones:** Words with the same pronunciation, which can be verbally funny. I had a student from a Montana ranch who said, "Maybe you've *heard* of my *herd*." Perhaps *you* own a *ewe*, and you could tell a *tale* about her *tail*? I'll quit wagging.

- **Paronomasia:** Most of us call this a *pun*, a corny/cheesy play on words. I think people like a little **pun**ishment, but don't overdo it. On my thirty-first wedding anniversary in July 2008, we had a huge hail storm here, and predictably, the newspaper headline read: "All Hail Breaks Loose." (The headline referred to the weather, not my anniversry.) I *love* puns, but my daughters, the education and English majors, actually got me to remove some of my puns in this book. It just *bugged* them too much, but I thought it was the lesser of two *weevils;* I could have used more double entendre.

- **Double Entendre:** Terms with an extra, often *racy* meaning. For example, I would not give a speech on nudist camps because I couldn't find enough good support. Women, however, might disagree, so I would be open to airing our differences.

People don't laugh or snicker or even necessarily smile with play words, especially puns. I would call it more of a *slow groan*, with half-turned heads, clinched teeth, and closed eyes. Such reactions provide variety, though, and variety is the spice of life.

- **Repetition (or *Good* Redundancy):** I used to keep a sign on my desk that said, "Department of Redundancy Department," mostly just for the fun play on words, but also because I believe strongly in the power of redundancy in speeches. Technically, redundancy is bad because it is the "unnecessary repetition" of words, but if such excess reinforces the audience's memory of a lesson, I think it's good. The best lessons in a speech should probably be mentioned more than once, so that we poor listeners have a better chance of comprehending.

I have said "variety is the spice of life" more than once in this book. I have also repeated advice such as *do not read* to us, *keep it simple*, it makes *CENTS* to have good support, don't *BECOT* without sensory aids, follow the *Golden Rule*, and *ASK* questions! (This was *planned* redundancy, for good effect, not the annoying, unconscious repeat words and phrases explained in Chapter Six, page 139.) I suggest you take *your* best lessons or lines from your speech, and consider saying them several times. You would be in good company. Dr. Martin Luther King made great use of repetition, especially in his famous 1963 "I Have A Dream" speech. He did not need to repeat words so often, so you might argue he was redundant. I would agree it was unnecessary, but argue it was an extremely effective style, and therefore good redundancy. I studied his speech and tracked the following phrases he repeated:

2 times: We refuse to believe . . .
3 times: Free at last!
4 times: One hundred years later . . . ; Now is the time . . .
6 times: We can never be satisfied . . . ; Go back to . . . ; Let freedom ring . . .
7 times: I have a dream!

I think the speech could be named "Let Freedom Ring," because he stressed that phrase at the end of his speech, with a more powerful voice, but I guess "I Have a Dream" won because it was said the most often, seven times. I couldn't help but notice that when Barack Obama gave his 2008 Presidential Acceptance speech, he repeated the phrase, "Yes, We Can," seven times. (As a side note, both speeches were also sixteen minutes long.)

For you college-age students, especially sports lovers, a more relevant example of good redundancy came in 2008 from the University of Florida's Heisman-winning quarterback, Tim Tebow. Here are his words to the media, after the Gators were upset by the University of Mississippi for their only loss of the season:

> *"A lot of good will come out of this. You have never seen any player in the entire country play as hard as I will play the rest of the season. And you'll never see someone push the rest of the team as hard as I will push everybody the rest of the season. And you'll never see a team play harder than we will the rest of the season. God bless."*

Tebow's words came true, and we might *never see* a team effort like that again. The Gators did *play hard* and did NOT lose another game *the rest of the season*, on their way to a national championship. It's a script made for Disney, inspired by a young speaker who knew the power of good redundancy. (P.S. I think his credibility, sincerity, integrity, passion, and simplicity also helped the speech some.) All speakers should occasionally visit the Department of Redundancy Department.

- **Structures of Speech:** Repetition is technically a structure of speech. Here are some of the other common structures, or word organizations, you might use:

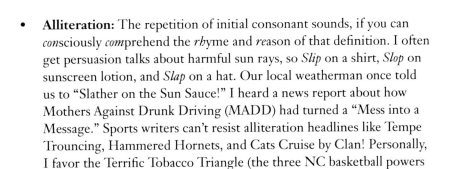

- **Alliteration:** The repetition of initial consonant sounds, if you can *con*sciously *com*prehend the *rh*yme and *rea*son of that definition. I often get persuasion talks about harmful sun rays, so *Slip* on a shirt, *Slop* on sunscreen lotion, and *Slap* on a hat. Our local weatherman once told us to "Slather on the Sun Sauce!" I heard a news report about how Mothers Against Drunk Driving (MADD) had turned a "Mess into a Message." Sports writers can't resist alliteration headlines like Tempe Trouncing, Hammered Hornets, and Cats Cruise by Clan! Personally, I favor the Terrific Tobacco Triangle (the three NC basketball powers of North Carolina, Duke, and NC State).

- **Antithesis:** A contrast or opposition of words or feelings, next to each other. During a speech on blood donations, I heard this anonymous quote: "To the world, you might be one person, but to one person, you might be the world." Bruce Pearl, when he was the Tennessee basketball coach, was quoted in *Sporting News* (October 27, 2008): "My players don't care how much I know until they know how much I care." Politicians love antithesis. In August 2008 at the Democratic Convention, President Bill Clinton said, "People the world over have always been more impressed by the power of our example than by the example of our power." Of course, the most famous antithesis in our culture is from President John F. Kennedy: "Ask not what your country can do for you, ask what you can do for your country."

- **Parody:** Take the structure of serious speaking and imitate it for humor. In other words, "Ask not what your audience can do for you, ask what you can do for your audience." One thing you can do is try a bit harder to use some clever wording.

- **Parallelism:** The similar structure of a series of words or phrases. Besides repetition, the Tim Tebow speech also has great parallelism, as does Dr. King's dream speech: "Let freedom ring from the prodigious hilltops of New Hampshire. . . . Let freedom ring from the snowcapped Rockies of Colorado. . . . Let freedom ring from every hill and molehill of Mississippi." One of my students gave a speech on the awfulness of divorce, and said, "We must protect marriage, protect children, and prohibit divorce." When I talk about teamwork, I encourage people to fall into the group TRAP (Chapter Seven): Be there, be ready, be attentive, and be polite. If you do, you'll have unparalleled success.

WORD CAUTIONS

- **Cliché:** A once colorful expression that has lost impact through overuse. Be aware of clichés, and don't use too many. Such talk is cheap, because supply exceeds demand. I'm not talking apples and oranges here, and I'm not pulling your leg; I really want you to be the breadwinner and bring home the bacon. So get back up on your speech-writing horse, think outside the box, quit fighting city hall, and avoid clichés like the plague. As you might guess, many clichés are also metaphors and *idioms* (Chapter Two, page 23), so besides being boring to your American audience, they can be very confusing to your international friends. Just in case you think this is not a real-world problem, I want to quote the famous baseball slugger Barry Bonds from an April 3, 2002, Associated Press newspaper release, after his San Francisco Giants team won its first game of the season: "It's not how you start, it's how you finish. We want to be in the race until it's over. It's early, one game doesn't make a season." Barry, baby, those lame expressions could stand to be pumped up with a few steroids . . . if you want to create better bonds with your audience.

- **Euphemism:** Substituting agreeable words for offensive words, or as we say it today—being *politically correct*, or "PC." Another term for euphemisms is *doublespeak*. Sometimes PC terms really help ease the pain. Instead of saying someone died, we say he *passed away*—and it wasn't because his own troops accidentally shot him during their mass confusion, it was due to *friendly fire* during the *fog and friction of war*. Your friend Jill wasn't fired; her company was *downsized*. Sometimes, however, euphemisms irritate folks because they want you to just be honest and tell it "like it is." Did you know that police never kill anyone anymore? No, instead, they *neutralize the opposition*. If a student is a little clumsy, do we have to say, "Paul is *athletically challenged?*" Can we say someone cheated, instead of *she seems to need help in following rules of fair play?* I got a peer critique in 2005 from a student who was not happy with his team-talk members. He actually wrote that one of the girls was "an element of boundless creativity who habitually digressed from matters at hand." It really would have had more impact and been okay to say "immature and got side-tracked easily." I understand teachers have to be very careful in school reports and bosses very PC in performance reports. In most speaking situations, however, I think your audience will appreciate it if you are a little bit more straightforward. Just be ethical and avoid being too *economical with the truth*. Uh, don't lie to us.

- **Word Meaning:** I'm sure it's some trite cliché and antithesis to "mean what you say and say what you mean," but I mean it—if you don't know the exact meaning of some word you plan to use, **look it up in a dictionary!** (Or, use a different word.) I usually see this problem when a student uses a quote and likes the overall purpose of the words, but may not know the meaning of an individual word or phrase somewhere in the middle. It might be mispronounced, or someone might ask, "What's that mean?" The speaker is embarrassed either way, and loses some credibility. **When in doubt, rout it out!** (Wait a second, did I use the correct word there? Rout? Route? Root? Let me check.)

- **Spelling Test:** If you are not 100 percent sure that you have the correct spelling for a word on a visual aid or in your outline, **look it up in a dictionary!** Today, you can use your computer to check single words very quickly, even if you're off by several letters. You can also use the spell check function to screen your entire text, but of course, spell check does not catch the most common spelling errors that I see. I want to show you a spelling test I give my students. I won't list the definitions or uses. Do you know the differences?

— It's or its	— Which or witch
— Where, wear, or were	— Except or accept
— Elude or allude	— Cite, site, or sight
— Two, to, or too	— There, they're, or their
— Your or you're	— Definitely or defiantly
— Effect or affect	— Aid or aide

If you have some personal favorites you don't see here, please have your people call my people. If you will take the time to carefully study this list of words, you can avoid 90 percent of the spelling errors I see on a regular basis. As a professional in the real world, you might hurt your reputation and your business if you can't keep these common words *straight*, which some of my students spell *strait*. (Montanans do like

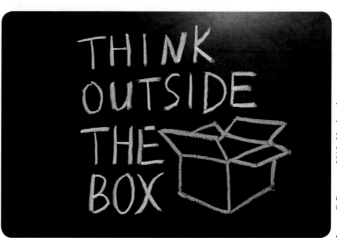

Image © Raywoo, 2012. Used under license from Shutterstock, Inc.

George Strait's music.) I guess that TV show knows what it's talking about when it asks, "Are you smarter than a fifth grader?" We should have learned these words a long time ago, but a lot (NOT *allot*) of us need to refocus on them. These are *easy* words, really. If you'll just teach yourself, they will be in your brain, and you will be all right. (Note: *alright* can be alright, but *all right* is really more right.) Aight?

HUMOR

I sure hope most of you smiled when I ended that last sentence with "aight." I was just trying to add a little humor. As you can see from the section on word choice, there are numerous, subtle ways you can add humor to a speech. You do not have to be a stand-up comic, where the audience expects a lot a humor. Be a stand-up speaker, where the audience really, really appreciates a little bit of humor. (See Chapter Two, page 20, where I answer the question, "What is an audience?") Every human bean got some gas; you just gotta find a PC way to let it out. Don't try to get a laugh as much as you just try to get a smile. Don't try to *be funny* so much as you try to *use humor*. Mostly, adapt to the audience and the situation, and be yourself. Use *your* style. You *cannot* force humor.

- **Need Humor?** I might argue that no speaker *needs* humor, but every audience *wants* humor . . . even at a funeral. (Maybe, especially, at a funeral.) I don't think anyone would argue that it is healthy to laugh, good for our body and soul. Try to be a soul doctor.

- **Types of Humor:** Humor has been like a hobby for me. We may not always know what it is or how to define it, just like "style," but we know what we like. I like to think of humor in three categories:

  - **Superiority Humor:** We laugh at someone's expense, including ourselves. We laugh at misfortune or stupidity; we laugh at the odd, absurd, or sick. We laugh out of relief that we are "superior" and do not have those problems, which can extend beyond individuals to groups, organizations, or even ideas. Satire, sarcasm, and slapstick comedy can all represent superiority humor. I've seen numerous talks where speakers used a cartoon which poked fun at some political leader, sports icon, Hollywood idol, or better yet, themselves.
  - **Surprise Humor:** We all enjoy a *twist* or *shock* that we did not see coming. It disrupts our orderly lives, in a good way. It's the right brain

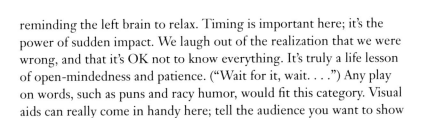

reminding the left brain to relax. Timing is important here; it's the power of sudden impact. We laugh out of the realization that we were wrong, and that it's OK not to know everything. It's truly a life lesson of open-mindedness and patience. ("Wait for it, wait. . . .") Any play on words, such as puns and racy humor, would fit this category. Visual aids can really come in handy here; tell the audience you want to show them a photo of one thing, but show a "funny" thing instead.

- **Simple Humor:** This is humor that releases tension, the classic "sigh of relief." It often goes from complex to simple, using analogies, in order to explain or illustrate a point better and therefore decrease confusion or worry. It touches our childhood euphoria, giving us a chance to throw away adult burdens for a moment and truly embrace our inner child. Jokes and stories represent simple humor, as do photos, videos, music, and objects. They remind us of sitting on grandma's lap and hearing fairy tales, or laughing with our brothers as we watched Saturday morning cartoons. So, share some cartoons; wear a funny hat; hold up your teddy bear. TELL A STORY in your speech, one with a touch of humor, and we will love you.

- **Make Yourself Smile:** You also want to love yourself, so do something *early* in your speech that makes YOU smile, or laugh. Your audience will then smile, and the chain reaction will relax everyone in the communication process. Malcolm Kushner, author of *Successful Presentations for Dummies*, emphasizes that audiences will maintain a "conservative demeanor" and "won't let their guard down until they know it's safe." The speaker cannot just tell the audience it's safe; he or she must SHOW them. Try hard to incorporate some humor during the introduction of your speech. During my first lecture each semester, I challenge students to think of the two most important words in the English language, implying words like "Speech Communication." Then I play some emotive music and reveal the real answer: David McLaughlin. We chortle and hug.

- **Humor Hints:** Here are some helpful humor hints for Hugh.
  - Jokes are much, much better if they are short short
  - Stories are much funnier if short, true, and personal
  - If you have to explain the humor in a joke or story, don't use it
  - Old photos of people (especially you) with old clothes and hair = funny
  - College-age people LOVE Simpsons, Family Guy, and South Park
  - Any tin man with a heartbeat can use funny visual aids
  - Any scarecrow with a brain can research a funny quote

- Any lion with courage can make a funny voice or accent
- Any poet can make funny use of word choice/structure
- Any artist can add funny flair to lettering and drawings
- Any computer genius can create photo-shopped humor
- Any photographer can take a funny photo
- Any obnoxious dad with a video camera can make a funny video
- Any poor student can rent or borrow a funny DVD
- Any singer can sing silly in a rock-and-funny-role band
- Any actor can act out a funny skit
- Any comic can make up a funny acronym or definition
- Any clown with a mirror can see if "costuming" is funny
- Any reader can find humor in any newspaper or magazine
- Any listener can learn what humor works in other speeches
- Any speaker with ethics can test out PC humor with friends first

Bottom Line: **If you want to add humor to your speech, you will.** You know, I think it's kinda funny how many people tell me they can't be humorous. It's about the same number of people who tell me they can't give a good speech. Both numbers, in reality, are zero. I've yet to have a student who could not give an acceptable speech, and I will never know a human who does not have some sense of humor. If you have a "sense" of something, you can explore it and enhance it . . . if you want to. We want you to.

QUESTIONS AND ANSWERS (Q&A)

At the end of every speech, *after* your finite "closure" (Chapter Five, page 110), you should thank the audience for listening and then ask if there are any questions. It's even more professional if you ask for "any questions or comments." If you really don't want to answer questions, don't open yourself up to a Q&A period. You must be sincere. If you really want to answer questions, the audience will know; if you don't, they'll know.

In the academic world, there might not be enough time for Q&A, or your instructor might prefer to use the time to get you more oral peer critiques. When I have shy students who give a short speech, I like to keep them up in front of the class a bit longer to answer questions, to give them more experience with talking. It always seems more natural for them than giving the graded speech. In the real world, the Q&A can be the most important part of your presentation. Answers

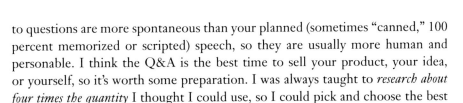

to questions are more spontaneous than your planned (sometimes "canned," 100 percent memorized or scripted) speech, so they are usually more human and personable. I think the Q&A is the best time to sell your product, your idea, or yourself, so it's worth some preparation. I was always taught to *research about four times the quantity* I thought I could use, so I could pick and choose the best information. Such "extra research" also helps preparation for questions.

You might also get questions *during* the speech, if you are open to it (and if your instructor allows it, for time control). I advise real-world speakers to mention this possibility during their introduction. Either encourage folks to ask questions during your presentation, or ask them to hold questions until the Q&A period afterward. I think you should encourage questions for a long talk because you don't want someone sitting there confused or lost for very long. Besides, it makes you feel good to get questions ("Hey, someone is listening!"), and it loosens up the atmosphere for everyone. I think you should discourage questions during a short talk unless they are quick, clarification questions, like, "Can you repeat that number again, please?"

I want to really really stress the **number one rule** about any answers you give, during or after your speech: **SHORT answers!** You will get many more questions if you give short answers. That's just a fact, Jack. Let me tell you a story . . .

During my four years at the Air Command and Staff College, we had regular lectures (for 400 students) from high-ranking political and military guests, followed by one hour of Q&A. An aide moderated the Q&A, and he or she would start off by asking, "Who has a question for our guest?" Forty hands would go up! Forty students eager to ask questions! The speaker would take the first question . . . and proceed to . . . beat the topic . . . to death . . . for twenty minutes. The moderator would then, finally, get to ask, "Who has the next question?" NO hands would go up. None. Nada. Zip. Thirty-nine people had magically forgotten what questions they wanted to ask. The moderator could prod and plea and beg and whine all day, but no one would ask that second question. I saw this phenomenon every week, and eventually the audience would be excused early. In case you think the motivation to avoid questions was to leave early, please understand that speakers who gave SHORT answers would always, easily, take up the whole Q&A hour. *Please* remember a simple rule:

If I ask you the time, don't build me a watch.

P.S. That rule also works great in interpersonal relationships. You know, on a date.

Here are some other important **guidelines for Q&A periods**:

- Make it "safe" for your audience to ask questions
    - There really are no stupid questions; they're *brave* questions
    - Do NOT say, "I already answered that, stupid." Answer it again.
    - Do NOT say, "Please repeat that louder so everyone can hear." If you understood the question, it's better if YOU repeat it for the people in the back.
    - Let them finish the question before you answer; it's rude to interrupt
    - Sometimes compliment the question and thank the person for asking it, but don't overdo it, or you might come across as "insincere"
- If it's a long question, paraphrase it before you answer
- If it's a confusing question, ask for some clarification before you answer
- If you don't know the answer, admit it, and add, "But I'll find out for you." Then make sure you track the question, DO find out, and get back to the person with the answer. I like to ask if anyone in the audience might know the answer and get them involved.
- Don't let one person dominate the Q&A period; be polite and say something like, "I like your enthusiasm, but I really want to give some other people a chance, okay?"
- After answers, if you have doubts, ask, "Did I answer the question?"
- Overall, **be positive and be brief!**

There are many techniques for answering questions. If you want to get the audience involved, you might try to **deflect** the question onto them: "Hey, this is a key point, so I want to know what some of *you* feel about this. Who's got an opinion?" You might also **reverse** the question right back to the questioner: "Good question. What do *you* think the answer is?" Afterward, be sure to give your answer as well.

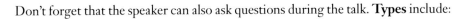

Don't forget that the speaker can also ask questions during the talk. **Types** include:

- **Rhetorical:** You don't expect (or want) an answer; you just throw the question out for the audience to ponder. "What would you do if you were King or Queen for a day?"
- **Overhead:** Throw the question out "over all the heads" and wait for someone to pull it down and answer. "Does anyone know the capital of Montana?"
- **Direct:** You direct your question at one individual only (which you might do if no one answers the overhead question). "Tammy, what is glossophobia?"
- **Closed:** The answer will be quick, often one or two words. "What is your name? Did you ski last weekend? Do you believe in the death penalty?"
- **Open:** Longer answers; the question begs discussion. "How did your folks choose your name? What all did you do last weekend? Why do you favor the death penalty?"
- **Show of Hands:** Creates some movement in the audience, helps wake them up. "So, how many of you are married? Raise your hands. Hold up your marriage license."

A good question-and-answer session is just one of many ways that public communication can seem like teaching . . . or preaching.

TEACHING AND PREACHING VS SPEAKING

There is much overlap of teaching, preaching, and speaking. They are, basically, all forms of public communication, where one person is generally talking to the masses. Every term, I see advanced students who begin to slip into the teaching and preaching modes, very effectively. Play with that thought if you want, especially if you coordinate such experiments with your instructor, but keep the following distinctions in mind:

- **Teaching** and **Preaching** are professions with serious commitments. They take MUCH special training. We expect certain skills and demand certain ethics from teachers and preachers. They are role models for good public speaking skills, and we look up to them as moral guides. We learn from them. It's a long-term, slow process, which requires trust between speaker and audience. This trust says, "You are here for me. I can ask for help. I can grow as a person." Even though teachers and preachers speak to the masses, the individual audience member can (should) feel an *inter*personal

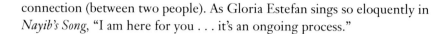

connection (between two people). As Gloria Estefan sings so eloquently in *Nayib's Song*, "I am here for you . . . it's an ongoing process."

- **Speaking** is just an activity, with no commitment, that anyone of any profession or walk-of-life can try, and we hope you do. It requires NO special training. We *hope* for certain skills and ethics from public speakers, but we can't demand them—especially from young, student speakers who are just learning the game. Most speakers are not moral guides; they are conduits to move information and meaning between people. We may or may not learn from them. Speaking is an extremely short, fast activity that requires little or no trust, for the moment. It's an unwritten agreement that says, "You will give me information and maybe opinion. I can ask for clarification and maybe give my opinion. I might grow as a person, if I'm extremely lucky, but either way, I probably will never see you again." Individuals will feel an *intra*personal spark (within themselves) rather than an interpersonal connection. Speeches can be routine. As Kenny Chesney sings so eloquently in *Shiftwork*, it might just be "a big ol' pile of shiiiiift work."

Okay, I don't want to be too flippant about your academic speeches. Mostly, I want you to just relax your expectations. Your speech can certainly "make us a memory" (See page 201), but one speech will not change the world. Please review the three main types of speeches (Chapter Two, page 26): persuasion, informative, or entertainment. Note that "teaching" is not one of those types. We do not *need* to know everything you know, or even spit back the most basic information you give us. There will be no exam after your speech. The name of this course is Public Speaking; this course is not about your speech topic. Your topic is just a tool to show us you comprehend some basic guidelines about speech structure and delivery. As for "Preaching," you may have to give a persuasive speech, to show your understanding of persuasion theory, but no one is going to ask for a show of hands to see if you really persuaded us to accept your side of an argument. Most of you won't do serious preaching until you become a parent. Amen.

Since it's my job, I obviously think public speaking is VERY important, but it really doesn't have to be so important to most of you. These academic speeches might honestly be the only formal talks you ever give, forever and ever. However, if you want to become a teacher or preacher (or politician, or lawyer, or leader of any kind), you should strive to become the best speaker possible. For you people, you would want to seek out extra opportunities for public speaking.

EXTRA CREDIT SPEAKING

Practice does not make perfect, but it does make *better*. Seek out speaking opportunities whenever possible. If your political science instructor gives you the option of a paper or a speech, give a speech. If any instructor gives extra credit for any "activity of choice," choose a speech. You could perhaps join a speech and debate club on campus, or become an officer in any club that gives you the chance to talk in front of a group. You might join **Toastmasters,** an international organization that provides a speaking forum for anyone, usually once a week after a meal. (Just look online, or ask your local chamber of commerce.) I've known shy students who gained speaking confidence by working with the campus radio station, or they participated in some way with a local theatrical group. Many churches allow student sermons. The list of opportunities is really endless.

In particular, you may consider what is commonly called **Special Occasion Speeches:**

- **Introduce a Guest Speaker:** Volunteer to introduce a guest speaker who visits your class, your campus organization, or your formal evening function, maybe with dinner. Talk with the guest to see what she or he wants emphasized, keep the focus on the speaker's credibility for the topic, do NOT talk about yourself, and keep it BRIEF! If you're really good, your introduction can match the tone of the speech, whether it is serious or lighthearted. One final, important caution: Do NOT build the speaker up so much that you create unrealistic expectations. "This person is so awesomely fantastic that you'll be literally rolling on the floor laughing in about two minutes!! Now, Heeeeeeeeere's Johnny!"

- **Present an Award:** Volunteer to present an award at your awards ceremony. If the winner is not known yet, talk about the award first, its purpose and criteria. Then call the winner's name. If people already know the winner, have that person come up to you, and then you can describe the award and the winner's qualifications. Let the winner thank the organization that supports and funds the award, and let the winner compliment the competition if need be. Try hard to keep such a presentation talk to one or two minutes.

- **Wedding Toasts/Talks:** Anyone can give a SHORT wedding toast, but usually only family and close friends would actually give a "talk" of more than two minutes. People in the wedding party are traditionally expected to make a toast, just a minute or two. It's common to tell a brief story about your personal association with the bride or groom or give a quick example of one or two of their better-known attributes. Quotes, slogans, and lines from songs or poems can work really well. Actually plan what you'll say. It flat out amazes me how many people talk at a wedding and start with this comment: "Well, I don't really know what to say," or "I don't have anything planned, but here goes." Come on, people! You've known about this moment for months. Try just a little bit to make a memory for your friends and family. Crosscheck your thoughts with friends, to be PC. You don't want to embarrass anyone, including yourself, so don't drink too much before your wedding talk. We probably all have stories of the drunken uncle or the bridesmaid who fell down. And make sure you are LOUD! The vast majority of wedding toasts I've heard, well, I actually could not hear. There are usually microphones at weddings. Use them. Overall, keep the focus on the wedding couple, not on you. P.S. If you're the father, and you had to pay for the whole glorious event, talk as long as you want, about whatever you want, until your wife stops you. Smile a lot.

- **Eulogies:** Technically, a eulogy is a written or spoken tribute to someone living or dead, praising good qualities. For most of us, it means talking at a funeral. It is usually family who will talk, and I wouldn't dare tell other people what they should or should not say at an emotional funeral. It must come from the heart, at the moment, so it is situational ethics at its finest hour. If you must talk at a funeral, and you have no idea what to say or how to say it, ask for help, and people will help you. Trust that. You cannot be wrong. It is common to relive good moments, perhaps sharing a story that everyone knows . . . or no one knows. Poems and songs might help, or passages from old letters or the Bible. Some people cling to an object that has special meaning, and they talk about that. Let the family do its thing. Then, some funeral directors "open the floor" for any comments. If you take that opportunity as a non-family guest, just keep your remarks genuine and brief, focusing on your relationship with the loved one. A key concern at funerals is memory, so talk about what you'll "always remember." Remember that your audience is the family of the deceased, so try to match their mood. Some funerals are really a "celebration of life," and humor could be very appropriate. Watch the family, and you'll know what to do. **When in doubt at a funeral, don't talk.**

INSTRUCTOR COMMUNICATION

- **Office Visits:** Some people never want to communicate directly with an instructor. *If you want extra credit, however, you'll have to talk with your professor eventually.* I suggest you do it early in the semester, with an office visit. (Unless it's Steve Carell's office.) You can tell a lot about someone by looking around at pictures and plaques, or books and bulletin boards. Are they neat and organized? (Better do your work on time!) See a lot of art? (You might want to show more creativity in your work.) If you talk to your instructor one-on-one in the office, it can be much different, and friendlier, than around other students in the classroom. Is that a picture of a family? (This guy is married?!) As with any other person, more insight into values and personality can enhance communication. It is not "sucking up" or "brown nosing" as much as it is "credible research" for survival. I bet it will surprise you, in a good way.

- **Ask Questions:** If you are ever lost or confused or abused, ASK for help! **The average students don't ask questions, ever. The above-average students ask questions, often.** (Hey, inquiring minds want to know.) One question you can always ask an instructor is whether or not extra credit is available. Another question is, "What do you expect from me in order to get an *A* in this course?" You can also request to see sample outlines, sample papers, or even sample speeches. (I have many videotapes of student speeches that I can loan to students.) You should also be able to request more feedback on speeches outside of what could be covered in class. Around mid-term time, you could cross-check grades with your instructor to see if you're on the right track. Whatever. I'm always challenging my students to be more aggressive in terms of managing their own progress and grades, in every course. Don't be afraid to talk to your instructors occasionally to get help in such analysis. ASK!

> *To question a wise man is the beginning of wisdom.*
>
> **—German proverb**

> *Better ask twice than lose your way once.*
>
> **—Danish proverb**

Know it all and make enemies; ask questions and make friends.

—McLaughlin proverb

- **E-Mail Protocol:** E-mail serves a purpose, but it sometimes confuses the communication process. To borrow a thought from Jerry Seinfeld, e-mail basically means you want to communicate, but you don't want to talk with the people, or even see them. First of all, there is no guarantee that your e-mail will be read; there are MANY reasons that people would miss your message, such as they deleted it from junk mail before they noticed it wasn't junk. Some people go days without checking e-mail, so it can be a very slow communication exchange. The sender, who checks e-mail thirty times a day, simply can't understand why the stupid instructor didn't reply and gets angry. Some students really don't want a reply; they send messages like this: "I can't make it to class today. If that's a problem, please let me know." I find this message *after* the missed class, and it *is* a problem. People also send me attached outlines to review, but I can't open the attachment, due to program incompatibility. I could go on and on. Let me offer some strong advice for e-mail protocol with instructors (or really anyone):

  - If you must send an important e-mail, one that concerns your grade or needs a fast response, follow it up with a phone call to make sure the receiver received.
  - Always be sure your FULL name is listed; your instructor might have four Andys.
  - Be sure to list your exact class/section; don't just say, "I'm one of your students."
  - Always list your phone numbers; we old people might prefer to call you back.
  - In the subject block, clearly list a course name so it stands out from junk mail.

- **Phone Protocol:** I stress for my students to CALL ME or text me whenever possible, rather than sending an e-mail. They will a get a much faster, more personal response. I check e-mail once or twice a day; I check my cell phone 20 times a day. Besides, it is a *communications class*, so it's nice to actually communicate in person. Some instructors, for a very mixed bag-o-reasons, really don't want you to call them, even in their offices. If so, you'll have to use e-mail or hand-signals, I don't know. If you can use the phone, here are some protocol items, which again, really apply to any phone call.

- **When you make the call,** ALWAYS identify yourself immediately when someone answers the phone. "Hi, my name is David McLaughlin. Is this Diane?" I think it's rude when I answer the phone, and some no-name demands, "Let me speak with David." I usually hang up. Be Polite, which means use "Please" and "Thank You," like your mother taught you. "Hi, this is David McLaughlin. I'm one of Cara's instructors at MSU. May I speak with her, please?"
- **When you answer the phone** and you don't know who it is, identify yourself. Think of business phone calls: "Salutations! Sparky's Spas. Sparky speaking." At home, I usually say, "Hello. McLaughlins." At work, I say, "Howdy. This is David McLaughlin." I never answer the phone, "Yeah?" or "What!?"
- If you leave a voice mail, I recommend you list your phone number immediately after your name, and then leave your message. How many times have you had to listen to the whole message again to get the phone number? (Many home and office phones don't capture a phone number, as cell phones do.) Speak slowly and enunciate clearly; we all get voice mails we just can't understand. And voice mail is a great time to remember the KISS lesson. The world needs more short messages.

Image © YuryImaging, 2012. Used under license from Shutterstock, Inc.

Bottom Line: In academic or real-world situations, business or social, a phone call may well be your first impression with someone important to you. Make it a good one.

ONE, LAST, EXTRA THOUGHT

I don't believe in extra credit so much as I believe in *extra effort*. The items in this chapter will definitely show extra effort if you decide to use them, because most student speeches (and real-world speeches) do NOT use them. You can also do "more than the minimum" with other recommendations throughout this whole book. Instead of just "going for it" on another speech, consciously start your research early, use a variety of research and support and sensory aids, show up early on speech day, dress for success, show some energy and humanness, employ some clever words and even some humor, and end on time. People might be able to cheat on exams and papers, but great speeches don't happen without true effort. Like great lives. So, **instead of aiming at an A+,** which can be limited by your instructor, **try going for an E+,** which has no limits, except yourself. Make yourself smile.

SUMMARY CHECKLIST FOR EXTRA CREDIT

YOU HAVE STYLE! "You cannot not have style"

- ❑ You can show style by using a variety of research, content, sensory aids, and delivery
- ❑ No one style works for everybody, every time; adapt to your audience
- ❑ The only real disability in a speech (or life) is a bad attitude

WORD CHOICE: I have a dream you'll remember this section

- ❑ Use active vs passive voice; a touch of poetry; some repetition, again.
- ❑ Figures of speech are fun: simile, metaphor, personification, oxymoron, hyperbole
- ❑ Try words that appeal to our five primary senses and/or our sense of play
- ❑ Consider structures of speech: alliteration, antithesis, parody, parallelism

WORD CAUTIONS: Trite clichés, overly-PC euphemisms, misused/misspelled words

HUMOR: Not necessarily *needed* by speaker, but always *wanted* by audience

- ❑ Types: superiority, surprise, and simple
- ❑ Don't try to be *funny* so much as you try to *use humor*
- ❑ Make yourself smile and make it safe for your audience to relax
- ❑ Any speaker can use humor if it's treated like a type of support or aid

QUESTIONS AND ANSWERS (Q&A): This part can be more important than the speech

- ❑ Make it *safe* for the audience to ask questions; be polite, positive, and brief with your answers... especially brief.
- ❑ Speaker may use questions, too: rhetorical, overhead, direct, closed, open

TEACHING AND PREACHING VS SPEAKING: We won't take an exam after your speech

- ❏ Teaching and Preaching are professions with special training and skills; long term
- ❏ Speaking is an activity without special training or skills demanded; short term

EXTRA CREDIT SPEAKING: Practice doesn't make perfect, but it does make better

- ❏ Try Toastmasters, or join a campus club/activity that requires speaking
- ❏ Special Occasion Speeches: introduce guests, present awards, weddings and funerals

INSTRUCTOR COMMUNICATION: Ask twice instead of losing your way once

- ❏ Try an office visit with your instructor early each term; see his/her human side
- ❏ Average students never ask questions; above-average students often ask questions
- ❏ Be polite, clear, and brief with e-mails and phone calls; follow up if necessary

CONCLUSION

(See page 104)

RESTATE PURPOSE: (Overhead slide) The purpose of this book was to inform you about public speaking, in particular, and communication, in general.

SUMMARY: (Refer audience back to handout on Table of Contents.)

- Scan the Table of Contents to see the main points of this book again.
- Pages 12–14 in Chapter One highlights some key lessons.
- Appendix A, Summary Checklist for Summaries, is, indeed, a good summary.
- Have a variety of research (SMILE), support (CENTS), and sensory aids (BECOT). Interview is the best research; story the best support; video the best sensory aid.
- Have a variety of delivery skills, but stress the extemporaneous style. *Talk Like You Talk.* We must hear you; you must look us in the eye; you must move some.
- Tell us what you'll tell us, then tell us, then tell us what you told us.
- Public speaking is not a competition or an exercise just to get a grade; it's an exercise in critical thinking, to share meaning and to grow as a person. Amen.

> I think public speaking is as easy as 1, 2, 3 (go to blackboard):
>
> 1. Golden Rule
> 2. CENTS and BECOT
> 3. Ethos, Logos, and Pathos

REMOTIVATION: (PowerPoint slides, "Reasons to Remember Book"; hold up book)

- Craig White did an amazing job with his cartoons in this book. High five!
- Speaking can be sorta fun, kinda, so you might want to do it again.
- Remember, **public speaking is never perfect, but it does get better.**
- Appendix D, Peer Evaluating Questions, really is a perfect storm of advice.
- Communication skills (speaking, writing, teamwork) will help your career.
- I hope this book gave hints to survive not just as a speaker, but also as a student, and maybe as a teacher. You never know.
- This book might help you get a date for Friday night.
- If you're actually reading this line, there is great hope for you as a speaker.

- If you would like to give me feedback on this book, please use the contact information in the Introduction. I would love to hear your ideas about public speaking (examples, gimmicks of your own, whatever), and if I use them in my next edition, I will give you credit. Probably no money, but good credit.

CLOSURE: (Video, teacher Ben Stein in *Ferris Bueller's Day Off*; then show quote.)

> *Everything you ever need to know about public speaking can be learned by watching bad teachers.*
>
> **—David McLaughlin**

GOOD LUCK WITH YOUR NEXT SPEECH!

APPENDIX A

Summary Checklist for Summaries

(Brought to you by the Department of Redundancy Department)

Chapter One, Nerves: Their is no such thing as a purfect speech.
- ❑ It's mostly *eustress* (good stress), which keeps you focused
- ❑ You never look as nervous as you feel
- ❑ It's good to be nervous; it shows you care
- ❑ Don't take yourself too seriously

Chapter Two, Getting Started: Any good speech should mix Ethos, Logos, and Pathos.
- ❑ Why give the speech? Crystal-clear purpose; "Hit me with a board!"
- ❑ Who is my audience? Must consider demographics and psychographics
- ❑ What type of speech? Easy as PIE: Persuasion, Informative, or Entertainment
- ❑ Where and When will it be? Consider location, equipment, preparation time

Chapter Three, Content: If you work harder for the audience, they'll work harder for you.
- ❑ Pick a topic that aligns with your interests/talents and audience needs
- ❑ Research Variety (SMILE): Surveys, Media, Internet, Library, Expert Interviews
- ❑ Content Variety (CENTS): Comparisons, Examples, Numbers, Testimony, Stories
- ❑ Stories are the most memorable; every speech should have a story

Chapter Four, Sensory Aids: Sensory aids are the *cure-all* for all public speaking ills.
- ❑ Variety is the spice of life, so don't BECOT without a good mix of aids
- ❑ Blackboards, Electronic, Costuming, Objects, and Transparencies
- ❑ Sensory aids, especially videos, are best to "Make Me a Memory!"
- ❑ Prepare, Proofread, Practice, and Position

Chapter Five, Organization: Plan the Flight, Fly the Plan.
- ❑ You must outline; check plan for logic, flow, balance, and time control
- ❑ Outline is more for planning than execution; it is a *cane*, not a *crutch*

- ❑ Hardest task is deciding what *not* to say; must edit and practice
- ❑ Need Introduction, Body, Conclusion; follow a logical pattern in body
- ❑ Use any format that works for you, as long as it's a *speaker outline*

Chapter Six, Delivery: *Talk Like You Talk!* We don't like robots.
- ❑ Be conversational and human, with your own vocabulary; be sincere; smile
- ❑ Be extemporaneous; do not read do not read do not read do not read do not read
- ❑ Key elements: Volume, Eyes, Face, Inflection, Movement, Gestures, and Posture
- ❑ Cut through the noise; avoid filler/repeat words, wrong articulation/pronunciation
- ❑ You cannot not communicate, and you don't want to be Chairman of the Bored

Chapter Seven, Team Talks: You cannot not have influence on other people, so make it good.
- ❑ If you want something done fast, do it yourself; want it done better, use a team
- ❑ Each team needs a single leader, but everyone will "lead" at certain times
- ❑ Fall into the Team TRAP: Be There, Be Ready, Be Attentive, Be Polite
- ❑ Groups must compromise and have *rigid flexibility*, but avoid *groupthink*

Chapter Eight, Keep It Simple: Simple lasts longer than complicated.
- ❑ Remember the Four-S Strategy: Study up, stand up, speak up, and shut up
- ❑ Remember that *Less is More*, and keep your speeches *Bikini Length*
- ❑ Introductions and Conclusions, especially purpose statements, must be simple
- ❑ Speak to express, not to impress; simple words and simple sensory aids

Chapter Nine, Ethics: The Golden Rule rules! Be the change you want in the world.
- ❑ Freedom of speech is not free, and it is not absolute; we need some restraints
- ❑ Speaking ethics is *situational ethics;* your audience dictates what is proper
- ❑ You must benefit the audience; consider their needs and don't waste their time
- ❑ Plan integrity in content, words, aids, and citations; Don't B.S. thy audience

Chapter Ten, Listening: Listening is truly a leadership skill . . . and it's sexy.
- ❑ Unlike hearing, which is constant, listening is intermittent, but it can be learned
- ❑ FITE to learn the four types of listening: Fun, Informative, Therapy, Evaluation
- ❑ Listening barriers SEAM to create noise: Speaker, Environmental, Audience, Mental
- ❑ Become a critical listener/thinker by teaching yourself to listen and critique better

Chapter Eleven, Extra Credit: You cannot not have style. Embrace that thought.
- ❑ Figures and structures of speech can add extra spice to any speech
- ❑ Humor may not be *needed* by a speaker, but it's always *wanted* by the audience
- ❑ The Question and Answer period can be more important than the speech
- ❑ Seek out speech opportunities; practice doesn't make perfect, but does make better

APPENDIX B

It Makes Good CENTS to Use a Variety of Support

COMPARISONS & CONTRASTS

- Literal and Figurative
- Similes and Metaphors

EXAMPLES & EXPLANATIONS

- Actual and Hypothetical
- Each main point should have an example
- Explanations include Definitions

NUMBERS

- Round off your numbers
- Do not group numbers all in one place
- Each speech should have a few numbers

TESTIMONIES (QUOTATIONS)

- Personal, Layperson, or Professional
- Each speech should have an expert quote!

STORIES

- Personal or Third Person (personal is best)
- Stories = the most memorable support
- Each speech should have a story!

Key Support Guidelines

- Use Surveys, Media, Internet, Library, Expert Interviews
- Comparisons are vivid, especially when using numbers
- In Doubt? Define your words, and explain acronyms
- Personal examples/stories are best
- Real is better than fiction (try to use local examples)
- Short is better than long: KISS!
- The more current, the better
- Use Sensory aids
- Key numbers (pie charts and bar graphs are great)
- Short quotes
- Picture is worth 1000 words
- Tell your sources (Must Cite!)
- Variety is the "Spice of Life"

APPENDIX C

Don't BECOT Without Sensory Aids

BLACKBOARD

- Topic/Preview
- Clarify names
- Quick statistics

ELECTRONICS

- PowerPoint
- VCR/DVD
- CD/Cassette
- Digital camera
- Various lights/objects
- Computer video/music

COSTUMING

- Anything on your body that relates to topic
- T-shirts, hats, ties, buttons, pins, buckles
- Sports/exercise/hunting clothing
- Or just dress "nice" (Dress to impress)

OBJECTS

- Objects bring out our inner child
- Anything 3-D you can hold up, like models
- Also posters, maps, handouts, books, food

TRANSPARENCIES

- With the overhead projector
- Handwritten or made with computer

BECOT = Movement = "Mix up the air!"

Guidelines for Using Sensory Aids

1. Consider audience's educational level

2. Consider your own skill and experience

3. Consider the location and equipment

4. Practice with your sensory aids

5. Keep your aids SIMPLE (KISS!)

6. Make aids EASY TO SEE

7. Don't let your aids talk for you

8. Talk to your audience, not your aids

9. Do NOT just read aids to us

10. Done with an aid? Remove it

11. Don't pass around "busy" handouts until after the talk

12. No dangerous/illegal aids

13. Normally, no animals/kids

14. Remember "Murphy's Law" and have a backup plan

15. Variety is the "Spice of Life"

APPENDIX D

PEER EVALUATING QUESTIONS

Introduction

- What got your attention? Think it was effective?
- Was the specific purpose clear? Know *exactly* what the speaker wants you to do/think?
- Were you motivated to listen? Speaker relate topic to you?
- Did the speaker mention his/her connection with topic? Hear some "expert" research?
- Were the main points clear? Visual aid used? Simple words used?

Body

- Did the main points follow in the same order as the preview?
- What type of organizational pattern do you think was used? Was it effective?
- Did each point have adequate/effective support? Any suggestions for improvement?
    - Did you hear a variety of support? Did it make "**CENTS**"? (Comparisons, Examples, Numbers, Testimonies, Stories) Were there too many numbers or quotes?
    - Which support item will you remember the best? Why?
- Did you hear citations? Seem credible? Any references/experts shown on the vis aids?
- Balance OK? "Roughly" same amount of time/support for each main point?
- Did you notice some transitions or signposts? Smooth?
- If this were a persuasion speech, did the speaker acknowledge the opposition?

Conclusion

- Did you hear the specific purpose again? Visual aid used?
- Main points (summary) and key "lessons learned" covered well enough? Visual aid used?
- Were you told WHY you should remember the speech? Will you think/act differently?
- Did you know the speaker was done? What technique was used for "closure"? Was it good?

Delivery

- Did the speaker look left and right, include the whole class? Ever look at you? Did he/she try to hold eye-to-eye contact with individuals for a second? Too much use of notes?
- Was the voice loud, clear, energetic? Or too soft, too fast, too monotone?
- How were the movements/gestures? Natural? Speaker move left/right of podium?
- No speaker should **"BECOT"** without sensory aids, so did you see a good variety? (Blackboard, Electronics, Costuming, Objects, Transparencies) Used well? Advice to give?
- Look professional? Standing straight, squared to the audience?
- Was the overall style extemporaneous (not memorized, not reading)?
- Did he/she "talk like you talk," in a conversational tone? Or too formal/preachy?

Overall

- Was this a good topic/speech for you and the audience? Why? What held your attention?
- Did the speaker seem "genuine"? What personal examples/stories were shared?
- Were you distracted by the speaker? Got any advice to prevent that distraction next time?
- Do you think the speech met the assignment criteria? Seem well timed and practiced?
- Did you see a good mix of ethos (credibility), logos (logical support) and pathos (emotion)?

Created 2009 by David C. Mclaughlin, Speech Instructor, Montana State Unviersity

APPENDIX E

Peer Evaluation Form

Speaker Name: _____ Topic: _____ Date: _____

Evaluator Name, if required: _____

SPEAKING ELEMENT	A	B	C	D	O	REMARKS
INTRODUCTION						(Note: "O" means Omitted)
-Attention Step						
-Specific Purpose (or Proposition)						
-Audience Motivation						
-Speaker Credibility						
-Preview						
BODY						
-Logical Organizational Pattern						
-Points Well Supported						
-Cited Credible Sources						
-Balance between Main Points						
-Smooth Transitions						
-Addressed Opposition (Persuasion)						
CONCLUSION						
-Restate Purpose (or Proposition)						
-Summary						
-Remotivate Audience						
-Closure						
DELIVERY						
-Strong Eye Contact						
-Clear, Loud Voice						
-Movement/Gestures						
-Presentational Aids						
-Appearance/Posture						
-Overall Extemporaneous Style						
OVERALL ASSESSMENT						
-Beneficial Topic (Make a Memory?)						
-Confident/Sincere Demeanor						
-Adapt to Audience; Held Attention						
-Met Time Limit						
-Met Assignment						

Best part of this speech:

Part that needs the most improvement:

APPENDIX F

Outline Template

(Review Chapter Five, pages 104–110, and Chapter Eight, pages 180–181)

Use the following "Speaker" outline format (template) if it fits your assignment and your style. Remember to use single words and/or short phrases; avoid full sentences. **Your outline should be typed,** so that the content gets into your head better. I strongly suggest you use "prompts" to indicate where you will use visual aids and where you will mention (cite) each source from your research, as you use that source in the body of the speech. Appendix G shows sample outlines with such prompts.

Full Name:
Course/Section:
Date:

I. **INTRODUCTION** (sixty–ninety seconds total; don't start with a three-minute story/video)

    A. **Attention Step:** See text pages 105–106 for some good strategies. This step should be quick, ten to fifteen seconds. "Grab" our attention. That's all.

    B. **Purpose Statement:** To inform or persuade what audience on what topic? (Use a visual aid) Keep it simple. See page 107.

    C. **Audience Motivation:** Why should we listen to your topic? Try to touch the needs and values of your audience, especially for persuasion. See pages 107.

    D. **Speaker Credibility:** Why should we listen to YOU? Tell us your research and any unique connection/experience with the topic. See page 108.

    E. **Preview:** What are your main points? (List your points on a vis aid.) Try hard to use just one to three words per main point. See page 108–109.

II. **BODY** (The number of main points and sub-points will vary greatly; your call)

    A. First Main Point (prompt: cite first source)

        1. Sub-point (map/photo)
        2. Sub-point (overhead slide)

B. Second Main Point (blackboard)

1. Sub-point (quote expert)
2. Sub-point (prompt to move)

   a.   sub-sub point (video)
   b.   sub-sub point (object held up)

C. Third Main Point (PPt slides with statistics, showing the source)

1. Sub-point (cite second source)
2. Sub-point (handout; tell story)

PROMPTS can be typed with **bold** font, or <u>underlined</u>, or often highlighted with colors. They can be within the text, or off to the left/right side. Very often, they are handwritten in colors. It's your outline, so it's *your* style/technique.

(Note: Some people also like to plan transitions between main points.)

III. **CONCLUSION** (Thirty to sixty seconds. Much like introduction, minus credibility)

A. **Restate Purpose Statement:** Use visual aid from introduction again.
B. **Summary:** Like the preview: use same visual aid. Stronger summaries also stress a key "lesson" or two to remember. See page 109.
C. **Remotivation:** Like motivation. Why should we remember your talk? See page 109.
D. **Closure:** Most ideas that work for an attention step also work well for a closure. It's the final appeal; the "clincher," so the audience knows you're done. See page 110.

TIME CONTROL HINT: Break your speech into pieces, as if you're giving a two-minute talk for each of three main points. Add a ninety-second introduction and a thirty-second conclusion, and you have an eight-minute speech.

After typing your outline, skip a few lines and list your **WORKS CITED.** (Use MLA or APA format, depending on your instructor's guidance.) Alphabetical order.

APPENDIX G

Sample Informative Speech Outline

(Composite outline from two student speeches and odd dreams)

Note: It will be *your* outline, so use whatever style/symbols/prompts you like.

SET-UP: Wear fishing vest and hat to start. Set book and fishing rods on table. Tape Alaska map on wall. Play Olympic theme music as slowly unveil photo of me with fish.

❖ INTRODUCTION

■ Attention: (Overhead photo of me) Who knows what this is? (music off)
■ Purpose: (OH aid) To inform my class about salmon (hold up toy fish)
■ Motivation: Amazing fish! Salt and fresh water; unique; healthy
■ Credentials: Book, interview, my Alaska catch (show book; remove hat)
■ Preview: Navigation, Spawning, Socioeconomics (blackboard)

❖ NAVIGATION (cite EnchantedLearning.com)

■ Ocean navigation (overhead of salmon area)
  ❒ Map and compass method
  ❒ Like always knowing where you are, which way home
■ Inland navigation (rivers/lakes; PPt map and photos)
  ❒ Spawn in stream in which they grew up
  ❒ Imprint smell of stream; find among tribs, even if blind (cite King)

❖ SPAWNING (cite Bond)

■ Single-Minded Purpose (PPt quote and Life Cycle poster, Bond)
■ Will reach their objective or die in attempt (OH with stats)
■ Barriers to spawning (list on board) Re: My Alaska trip, wall map
  ❒ Human intervention: dams (map), fishing, destroy habitat
  ❒ Animals: bears (show video) and seals
  ❒ Natural barriers (waterfalls, PPt photos)

❖ SOCIOECONOMICS

- ■ Economic (cite Reisler)
  - ❏ Sport fishing in PNW, Alaska
  - ❏ Commercial fishing jobs
  - ❏ Salmon farms (pie chart compared with other fish)
- ■ Social (PPt photos of me in river; touch of Olympic theme music again)
  - ❏ Sport; so powerful, difficult to catch (my story; trout comparison)
  - ❏ Just viewing them in rivers, leaping falls (video again, if time)
  - ❏ Food! So healthy (quote King), delicious (Show salmon bites . . . coming soon)

❖ CONCLUSION

- ■ Restate Purpose: (aid) To inform you about salmon
- ■ Summary: (Touch blackboard list) Main points again; stress fresh and ocean water, one-minded spawning need (like humans . . . ?), and so fun for us
- ■ Remotivation: (life-cycle poster) We can learn from their determination
- ■ Closure: . . . but in meantime, let's eat them! (pass out smoked salmon bites)

Works Cited

Bond, Carl E. *Biology of Fishes.* Orlando: Saunders College Publishing, 1979.

Montgomery, David R. *King of Fish: The Thousand-Year Run of Salmon.* Jackson, TN: Westview Press, 2003.

Reisler, Mark R. Alaskan Fishing Guide. Personal interview, by phone; 25 minutes. 8434 Sourdough Trail, Sitka, AK. Phone: 907-361-8224. *Mreisler@gmail.com.* 16 Mar 2009. (Note: This is a format we created at MSU for interviews, since the MLA format does not tell why the interviewee is an expert, how long you talked in what medium, or even how to contact the person.)

Salmon. 2009. <EnchantedLearning.http://www.EnchantedLearning.com> (18 Mar 09)

Sample Persuasion Speech Outline

(Actual outline by speech student Geoff Blatter, 26 Apr 2007)

Note: These sample outlines are not perfect. They are guides to help the speaker remember "most" of what he or she wants to say. These are speaker outlines, done for the speaker, not the audience. This was a great speech, graded 77/80 for a strong "A." It had ethos, logos, and pathos, which someone else might not see in this outline.

I. Introduction
   A. Attention Step. Mike's Story (Mike & Ali)
   B. Purpose: Propose Alternative Medicine can be good (Proposition aid)
   C. Motivation: Everyone gets sick, answers not always there
   D. Credentials: Vicki, Books, Dr. Irish, Dr. Lemley
   E. Preview: Poster

II. Dispel Myths
   A. Not a bunch of pot smokin' hippies (George Bush photo)
      1. Bad image (Seinfeld 14:19–15:15)
      2. Most simply have a different philosophy of health

   B. Remedies
      1. Medicines are designed after naturally occurring compounds
      2. FDA—not approved, still effective, not always "safe"

   C. MD's are still necessary
      1. Emergency care
      2. Surgery can't always be replaced

III. Types
   A. Homeopathy
      1. What it is—"Like cures Like"—Sidney Skinner (Book)
      2. What is it good for—As many as 40% now seek A.M.

   B. Applied Kinesiology
      1. What it is—Alternative Medicine does not heal (Vicki quote)
      2. What is it good for (Units aid)

IV. Benefits
   A. Cost
      1. Not covered by health insurance
      2. Very cheap comparatively (500 vs. ~45,000)

   B. Less Harsh Treatments
      1. Some medications require other medications to counteract side effects
      2. Always try alternatives to surgery

   C. Finish Mike's story

V. Conclusion
   A. Restate Purpose (Proposition Overhead)
   B. Summary (Poster)
   C. Remotivation: Everyone gets sick. Remember Mike
   D. Closure (Mike & Ali)

Works Cited

Russell, Vicki. Kinesiologist. Personal Interview, in person; 90 minutes. 1381 Guest Place, Langhor, MT. 59712. Phone: 406-745-5387. 5 Apr 2007

Seinfeld Season 2 Episode 11. Prod. Jerry Seinfeld and Sony Pictures. DVD. Castle Rock Entertainment, All Rights Reserved, 1991.

Skinner, Sidney E. *An Introduction to Homoeopathic Medicine in Primary Care.* Gaithersburg, Maryland: Aspen Publishers, Inc., 2001

Smith, Laura K. et. Al. *Brunnstrom's Clinical Kinesiology.* 5th ed. Philadelphia: F.A. Davis Company, 1996.

Wikipedia. "Alternative Medicine." 24 Apr 2007. *http://en.wikipedia.org/wiki/alternativemedicine* (18 Apr 2007)

APPENDIX H

Sample Topics for Informative Speeches

Note: Informative speeches do NOT get "preachy" and opinionated. They stress the facts: Who, What, Where, When, and How. If you start stressing a "Need" to do something and telling us "Why," you are likely slipping into the persuasion area.

The following topics were all actual academic speeches heard at Montana State University. They may or may not apply to your class; ask your instructor.

ANIMALS:	Dog training; Ferrets; Elk; Greyhounds; Falcons; Dog shows
ART:	Ansel Adams; Batik; Tattoos; Tap dance; Hair Styles; Photography
DRUGS:	Meth; Marijuana; Alcohol; Prescription drugs; Caffeine; Prozac
ECONOMICS:	Types of life insurance; Credit ratings; Budget techniques
EDUCATION:	Sign language; Rural schools; Mentoring programs; Head Start
ENVIRONMENT:	Fire management; Noxious weeds; Hurricane planning; Smog
FOOD:	Sushi; Bubble gum; Organic food; Food allergies; Cannibalism
GAMES:	Pool; Bowling; Chess; Frisbee golf; Ping Pong; Paintball; Dating . . .
GROUPS:	Various campus clubs; bands; sports teams; charities; KKK
JOBS:	Maine lobster fishing; Saudi Arabian farms; Bullriding; Piloting
HEALTH:	Hearing loss; Weight management; E-coli; Diabetes; Nutrition
HISTORY:	MT Vigilantes; Holocaust; St. Patrick's Day; Iwo Jima; Halloween
HUNTING:	Ducks, elk, bear, cougars, gophers; bows; rifles; training
LITERATURE:	Shakespeare; Mark Twain; *Lord of the Rings* trilogy; Jane Austen
MILITARY:	Snipers; F-15; Tank evolution; 82nd Airborne; Hurricane Hunters
MEDIA:	Spielberg; Simpsons; Bollywood; Forrest Gump; Film editing
MEDICAL:	Alzheimer's disease; Viagra; FAS babies; Midwives; ACL surgery
MUSIC:	Bob Marley; Jazz greats; Flutes; Dave Matthews band; Drum use
MYTHS:	Curse of the Bambino; Vampires; Crop circles; Haunted houses
NATURE:	Tsunamis; Hurricanes; Avalanches; Whirling disease; Redwoods

OBJECTS:	Old glass bottles; Mountain bikes; Toy chest chair; Glue; Swords
PEOPLE:	Garth Brooks; Drew Barrymore; Howard Hughes; Sarah Palin
PLACES:	Glacier Park; Moon; Mt Everest; Any city, state, or country
POLITICS:	Misc. famous politicians; Voting trends; Hitler's power growth
PROGRAMS:	National Student Exchange; Alcoholics Anonymous; Food banks
RELIGION:	Gandhi; Crusades; Wicca; Hutterites; Muslims; Religious persecution
SAFETY:	Pepper spray; Self-defense options; Float devices; Bowhunting rules
SCIENCE:	Einstein; Lucid dreaming; Jane Goodhall; Palmistry; GPS; Beer
SOCIAL ISSUES:	Dating etiquette; Wedding planning; Alcoholism; Agoraphobia
SPORTS:	Tour de France; Ted Williams; Rugby; Ice climbing places; Doping
TECHNOLOGY:	Rotary engines; Farm tools; computer animation; Digital cameras
TOYS:	Barbie dolls; Teddy bears; Puzzles; Comic book history; Yo-Yos
WHATEVER:	Cattle mutilations; Psychopharmacology; Mullet evolution

Sample Topics for Persuasion Speeches

Persuasion topics should be controversial. If there is no controversy, you probably have an informative speech. Someone should disagree with you as soon as you state your proposition. Other good questions to ask yourself would be: "Is my topic of important social concern?" (organ donation), and "Does it create apprehension?" (airport security). So, do some "College Level" research, acknowledge both sides, and then TAKE A STAND!

CAUTION: Topics where you tell us to buy something, try something, or go visit some place are sometimes just glorified informative speeches about that given thing or place. If you "compare" two items and truly stress "why" we should choose one over the other, it would be more persuasive. Try to show a "NEED" to do what you are persuading people to do; appeal to value systems. Show the audience how they or others, or the world, will be better off if they accept your proposition.

ANIMALS:	Save whales/seals; Boycott fur business; No animal experiments; Ban exotic pets; Pit Bulls are not killers; Spay/Neuter pets
CAMPUS:	Improve parking; Eliminate core curriculum; Decrease student fees
ECONOMICS:	Buy a house; Move off campus; Don't get credit cards; Start an IRA; Avoid Big Box stores; Outsourcing jobs; Job loss in America
EDUCATION:	Learn a 2nd language; Study abroad; Work before college; Internships; Sex Education; Music/arts vs sports; Home schooling; Teacher Pay
ENERGY:	Alternative fuels; Build Green; Ban SUVs; Hybrid cars
ENVIRONMENT:	Save rain forest; Recycle; Pesticide damage; Global warming
FAMILY:	Adoption; Single parents; Divorce issues; Gay marriages; Day care
FOOD:	Avoid caffeine; Drink red wine; Eat organic; Drink more water; Genetically modified foods; Breast feeding; Buy local food
HEALTH:	Exercise more; Stop smoking; Annual pap smears; Wash your hands; Obesity; Avoid fast food; No tanning beds; Health care reform
LAWS:	Lower drinking age; legalize hemp; raise speed limits; Simpler tax laws; Abolish death penalty; Legalize euthanasia; Affirmative action
MEDIA:	Censorship laws; Pirating music; Effects on children
MEDICAL:	Learn CPR; Give blood; Use condoms; Recognize depression; Medical marijuana; Organ donation; Stem cell research
MILITARY:	War in Iraq/Afghanistan; nuclear disarmament; Defense budget needs

POLITICS: Electoral college; Vote; Limit campaign spending; Term limits

RELIGION: Danger of cults; school prayer; Creation vs. Evolution

SAFETY: Drinking and driving; Helmet laws; Avalanche beepers; Bear spray; Cell phones and driving; Learn to swim; Guns vs kids; Learn Judo.

SECURITY: Airport security reform; Gun control issues; Patriot Act; National ID

SOCIAL: Homeless people; STDs; Poverty; Unwanted pregnancy; Drug abuse

SPORTS: Wood vs metal bats; Steroid abuse; Title IX; Rodeo stock welfare

VOLUNTEER: Join Peace Corps; Tutor/coach children; Habitat for Humanity

BIBLIOGRAPHY

Alstad, Ken. *Savvy Sayin's.* Tucson, AZ: Ken Alstad Company, 1986.

Beebe, Steven A., and Susan J. Beebe. *Public Speaking, An Audience-Centered Approach,* Second Edition. Englewood Cliffs, NJ: Prentice Hall, 1994.

Cragan, John F., David W. Wright, and Chris R. Kasch. *Communication in Small Groups; Theory, Process, Skills,* Sixth Edition. Belmont, CA: Thompson Wadsworth, 2004.

Department Of The Air Force. *The Tongue And Quill.* AF Pamphlet 13-2. Washington, DC: U.S. Government Printing Office, 1985.

Engleberg, Isa, and Ann Raimes. *Pocket Keys for Speakers.* Boston, MA: Houghton Mifflin Company, 2004.

Ferguson, Sherry Devereaux. *Public Speaking, Building Competency in Stages.* New York: Oxford University Press, 2008.

Fraleigh, Douglas M., and Joseph S. Tuman. *Speak Up! An Illustrated Guide to Public Speaking.* Boston, MA: Bedford/St. Martin's, 2009.

Fujishin, Randy. *The Natural Speaker,* Second Edition. Needham Heights, MA: Allyn and Bacon, 1997.

Grice, George L., and John F. Skinner. *Mastering Public Speaking,* Sixth Edition. Boston, MA: Allyn and Bacon, 2007.

Hindle, Tim. *Making Presentations.* New York: DK Publishing, 1998.

Koch, Arthur. *Speaking With A Purpose,* Fourth Edition. Needham Heights, MA: Allyn and Bacon, 1998.

Kushner, Malcolm. *Successful Presentations For Dummies.* Foster City, CA: IDG Books Worldwide, 1997.

Lucas, Stephen E. *The Art of Public Speaking,* Seventh Edition. New York: McGraw-Hill Companies, 2001.

O'Hair, Dan, Hannah Rubenstein, and Rob Stewart. *A Pocket Guide to Public Speaking.* Boston, MA: Bedford/St. Martins, 2004.

Osborn, Michael, and Suzanne Osborn. *Public Speaking,* Third Edition. Boston, MA: Houghton Mifflin Company, 1994.

Peoples, David. *Presentations Plus, Second Edition.* New York: John Wiley & Sons, 1992.

Perrine, Laurence. *Sound and Sense, An Introduction to Poetry,* Third Edition. New York: Harcourt Brace & World, 1969.

Rodman, George, and Ronald B. Adler. *The New Public Speaker.* Fort Worth, TX: Harcourt Brace & Company, 1997.

Smith, Perry M. *Taking Charge, A Practical Guide for Leaders.* Washington, DC: National Defense University Press, 1986.

Sprague, Jo, and Douglas Stuart. *The Speaker's Handbook*, Eighth Edition. Belmont, CA: Thompson Wadsworth, 2008.

Trump, Donald J., with Meredith McIver. *Trump: How To Get Rich.* New York: Random House, 2004.

Wintzell, J. O. *Bits of Wit and Wisdom, The Signs at Wintzell's Oyster House.* Mobile, AL: America Printing Company, 1973.

Yeager, Chuck, and Leo Janos. *Yeager, An Autobiography.* New York: Bantam Books, 1985.

Index

A

academic speeches
  nerves and, 6–10
  topic choice for, 36–37
active words, 236
administration, for team speeches, 147–150
adrenaline, 4
agenda, 158–159
agoraphobia, 2
alliteration, 241
American Psychological Association (APA), 97, 272
analogies, 48–49
analysis, 52
animals, 78, 79
antithesis, 241
apostrophe, 236
articulation, 137–138
attention span, 215, 216
attention step, introduction as, 105–106
audience, 19–25
  analysis of, 20–21, 25
  audience noise, 219–220
  audience outline, 93, 95
  defined, 20
  demographics, 21–24
  ethics and, 197–199
  fears of, 63 (*see also* sensory aids)
  "mixographics," 25
  "professographics," 25
  psychographics, 24
  questions and answers (Q&A) during
        speeches, 246–249
award presentations, 251

B

balance, 91
"BECOT," defined, 61, 265. *see also* sensory aids
bibliographies, 98–99
blackboards, 67–68
books, for research, 44
brainstorming
  brainstorm outline, 93
  explained, 38–40

C

cassette players, 70
CD players, 70
"CENTS," defined, 35, 263. *see also* support
citation
  American Psychological Association (APA),
        97, 272
  Modern Language Association (MLA), 97,
        99, 272, 274
  plagiarism *versus*, 208–210
closure, 110
communication. *see also* listening
  group communication, 11
  with instructors, 253–256
  interpersonal communication, 11
  noise in, 125
  open, 159–160
  public speaking as unique medium of, 17
  "share meaning" and, 7–8
  with style, 234–236
comparison, 39, 48–49, 174
compromise, for team speeches, 161–162
computers, as sensory aids, 70